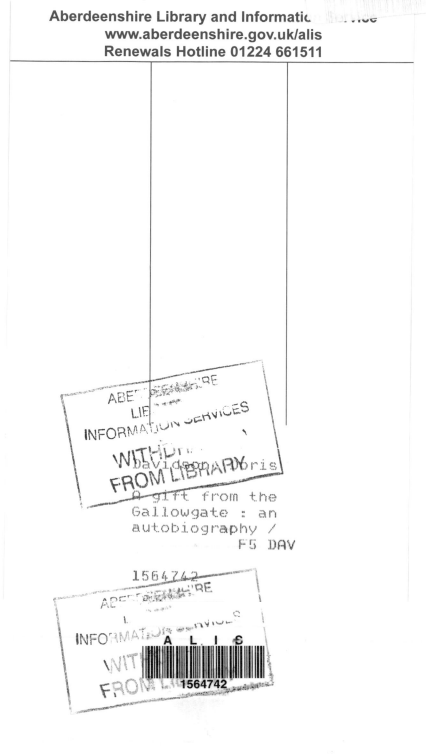

A Gift from the Gallowgate

A Gift from the Gallowgate

An Autobiography

Doris Davidson

Birlinn

First published in 2004 by
Birlinn Limited
West Newington House
10 Newington Road
Edinburgh EH9 1QS

www.birlinn.co.uk

ISBN 1 84158 301 4

British Library Cataloguing-in-Publication Data
A catalogue record for this book is available from the British Library

Typeset by Initial Typesetting Services, Edinburgh
Printed and bound by Creative Print and Design, Wales

Contents

INTRODUCTION

Introduction

I was born on the last day of June 1922, and my parents, Robert and May Forsyth, chose my name very carefully. Doris, according to the book of names they studied, meant the Gift of God. What could be nicer than that? When I was old enough to think for myself, I was secretly pleased that they hadn't called me after somebody. Not that any of our relatives had outlandish names, but it was good to have a name all to myself. It has had its ups and downs, of course.

When I started my second job – in a tiny office in the Coast Lines sheds on Jamieson's Quay – I'd to walk along South Market Street, the part of the harbour where the coalboats unloaded their cargoes. It was safer to go along the edge of the quay rather than the other side of the street, bustling, even in 1938, with horse-drawn carts as well as smelly fish lorries and whisky drays rattling over the cassies (the Aberdeen version of causeways, our granite cobblestones). Newly sixteen, I enjoyed the appreciative whistles and wolf calls of the seamen, black-faced with coal, the stevedores on shore and any other males who happened to be around.

Then I bought myself a handbag with my initials on the flap. 'DF' they proclaimed, in large metal letters that no one could miss, and everything changed. The whistles and wolf calls were suddenly replaced by sniggers, even loud splutters of laughter.

'Oh, would you look at that!' one black-faced minstrel sang out, looking round to make sure that his mates were listening. 'She's got her initials on her bag.' He turned to me again, grinning. 'What's the DF stand for, darlin'?'

Pretending not to hear, I walked on. I wasn't going to tell them anything about myself. Alas, another wag picked up the teasing, but he went a step further.

'You shouldna need to ask that, Billy Boy. It's simple enough – stands oot a mile. DF. Damn Fool.'

This was taken up by all, completely deflating my ego, and although I knew they meant it as a joke, I clung on to that bag, with its initials, to prove that I didn't care. I couldn't afford to buy another one then, anyway, and there was no way to remove the offending metal letters that had been sewn right through the lining as well as the suede outer covering. I never told anyone about this incident, getting so used to the teasing that I would call back, 'Wouldn't you like to know?' when anybody asked the fateful question.

Many years later, my young sister bought a bag with her initials on. She was working in the office of Hall Russell and Company, Shipbuilders, and fared even worse than I had. 'BF'? Poor Bertha!

In the early forties, I was astonished to read that Doris Day, a young American singer, had taken the film world by storm. I was well aware that she hadn't been named after me, but I enjoyed the reflected glory that came my way because of it. In company, somebody always announced, 'And now we'll have a song from Doris Day . . . (long pause) . . . vidson.' The only thing was – I couldn't sing for peanuts! But I went to see all her pictures, bought her records, fell in love with all her leading men. Oh, that Rock Hudson! What a heart-throb! Why did some wicked journalist have to spill the beans on him when he was dying of Aids?

The girlish dreams I had cherished through thick and thin, through war and peace, through marriage and motherhood, were swept away as if by a raging torrent. Oh, well, at least Doris Day, herself, is still hanging in there.

My maternal granny also took an occasional dig at my name, though never in a nasty way. She could never be nasty. I used to spend a lot of time with her at the weekends when I was young (the word teenager hadn't then been spawned), and I always told her what I'd been doing at school during the week, or at work when I started to earn my living.

'Maybe your Mum and Dad thought Doris meant the Gift of God,' she would say, giving a mock sigh, after I'd been speaking non-stop for ages, 'but nae in your case, lassie. The Gift o' the Gab would be mair like it.'

I wasn't offended, or hurt in any way. I knew my Granny loved me . . . and she loved to know what had been happening to me.

Of course, admitting also to my middle name (after my mother) gave rise to more teasing. Doris May? As soon as one of the opposite sex learned that, he came up with a load of suggestions, innocently humorous or indecently lewd – depending on the type of person he was.

For instance . . . 'Doris May? And will you, if I ask you?'

That perhaps doesn't strike you as having a *double entendre*, but accompanied by a leer and a sly wink, you can bet your bottom dollar it had.

*

I've long passed all those stages. Any comments on my name these days come from other women. 'So you're a Doris, too? There's not many of us left now.'

I usually laugh and say, 'No, there's not,' but it makes me feel like I should be thrown on the scrap heap.

Just the same, it still gives me a real thrill to see novels I've written on display in bookshops. My first name lets readers know I'm not a young thing writing in today's style, about today's problems. Mind you, the emotions underlying today's problems are not so unlike those of fifty or even a hundred years ago; only the underlying causes of the problems are different. But I don't intend to lecture on something as controversial as this. I'm too old to argue . . . though I still have my off moments.

I'm inclined to agree, however, with my Granny's assessment of me all those years ago, and my family will no doubt endorse it. The Gift of the Gab never really leaves a person, does it?

THE FORSYTH SAGA

(or My Saga as a Forsyth)

1

My father, Robert Robb Forsyth, served his time (or part of his time) as a cabinet maker – we had a beautifully carved oak wardrobe in the house for as long as I can remember – but, for some reason, he then took up butchery, learning his trade from his namesake father. He was one of the sons mentioned in the sign above the shop at the top of the Gallowgate. 'R. Forsyth and Sons', it proclaimed, proudly, but before they joined him, it had proclaimed, just as proudly, 'R. Forsyth, Flesher and Poulterer'.

When anyone asked him why it didn't just say 'Butcher', he always replied, 'Anybody can be a butcher, but it takes skill to be a flesher.'

The other son of the sign was my Uncle Jack, but more about him later. A third son, Billy, was foreman in Murray's Meat Market, the killing-house, or abbatoir, to give it its Sunday name. We'll come to him later, too.

There were seven girls in the Forsyth family, the butcher's daughters as my mother was told when she wondered who the three strapping damsels were who marched regally down the hill past the veggie shop where she worked. They were the three eldest, all well built even then. They gradually bloomed until they averaged around seventeen or eighteen stones, though it didn't seem to bother them . . . or their husbands, for that matter.

They sometimes went to Blackpool on holiday, without their menfolk for some reason, and signed their postcards, 'From the Three Fairies'. This always convulsed me. I could picture them dancing around in a circle (they were quite light on their feet considering their size . . . like Oliver Hardy, in fact), waving a wand in one hand and hoisting up wings and bosoms with the other. Awesome bosoms! I can recall Auntie Jeannie boasting that she could rest a cup and saucer on hers. She could, too.

The middle one in age, Jeannie, was a great swimmer earning several life saving certificates, and my cousins and I were made to go to the Beach Baths every week when I was about six or seven, to learn to swim. I was never very happy in the water, but Bella, the aunt assigned to me, was determined that I would not shame the Forsyth clan and battled bravely on. She used the method of holding me up at the back by the straps of my bathing costume, and I was making some progress across the water one day when I happened to look behind to make sure she was still there. She wasn't, and with no confidence in my own ability (well founded, I may say) down I went, swallowing gallons of water mixed with large amounts of chlorine and small amounts of urine . . . or vice versa?

I never mastered that fear. The most I ever managed was about half a breadth before my toes took cramp. Jeannie, of course, took every opportunity to show off her skills. She dived from the very top platform and darted this way and that like a seal . . . an elephant seal? She made me feel ashamed of myself, but not enough to make any difference.

My mother and Auntie Ina, Uncle Billy's wife, used to come along with us, and sat in the spectators' gallery to keep tabs on our progress, but they were absolutely mortified one day when an oldish man, possibly there watching his grandchild, said to them, 'I'm getting my kill at that fat woman. She's making a right exhibition of herself, but you can't help admiring her, can you? Not many her size would dive off the top board, and she hits the water with that much force, I'm aye expecting her to empty the pool.'

(Auntie Jeannie's own description of hitting the water was, 'If I don't go in at the right angle, I land in a belly flop, and it feels like I've split myself in two.')

Needless to say, Mum and Auntie Ina didn't admit that they were in any way related to the 'fat woman', who had to give up swimming eventually because she couldn't get a costume large enough to fit her. She had, as a last resort, actually knitted one, but you can imagine what happened. The weight of the water pulled it so far down that her hands weren't big enough to cover what shouldn't be on display as she came out of the pool . . . for the very last time! I hope the elderly gentleman wasn't there on that occasion; the excitement might have been too much for him.

Robert Forsyth Senior also had four younger daughters, making up his total of ten children, three boys and seven girls, but none was so prolific as he. Between them, they only gave him seventeen grandchildren. One, Annie, emigrated to Canada in 1920, not long after her mother died, and didn't marry until she was past childbearing age. She never came home, so I never met her, but she kept in regular touch with Jeannie, who seemed to take on the mother role for all her siblings.

Mum once confessed to me that, even after she married into the Forsyth family, her in-laws made her feel like a country mouse . . . which indeed she was, having only come to the city when she was about sixteen. My aunts and uncles could never have realized that she felt like this. They were extroverts with a tremendous sense of humour, and all very musical, Billy playing the violin and ukulele, Jack the mandolin, Bob (my father) the Japanese fiddle (one-stringed, with a horn at the side). He could also coax hauntingly beautiful tunes from an ordinary household saw using the same bow – his rendition of 'Danny Boy' and 'Ae Fond Kiss' brought tears to the eyes. They could all play the piano, and the girls had beautiful singing voices. I can't recall hearing the men singing; we children were packed off up to the attics while the adults had their musical evenings.

I suspect that Mum felt lacking in some way when she was with them. She was oldest in a family of four, her father, James Paul, being a farm servant who, like all of that ilk, shifted his place of employment, if not every six months, fairly frequently. She had one sister, Nell and, eventually two brothers, James and Douglas. It must have been quite a cultural shock to her when her father got a job at Rubislaw Quarry and they flitted to Aberdeen. I'm not too clear about his job there, I think he was on the crusher, but Maisie was still a shy, naïve country lass, so naïve, in fact, that at twenty-one, she had an even greater shock when she went home from work one day and found a pram in the kitchen. 'Whose bairn is it?' she asked, and couldn't believe what she was told. The infant was a new brother and she'd had no idea that her mother had been 'in the family way'.

My mother was a very clever child even though she'd had to change schools so many times, but there had been no money to allow her to carry on her education, and it ended at Peterhead Academy when she was fourteen. Her first job was as a kind of maid/nanny to the owners of a 'Johnnie-a'thing' shop at Stockbridge, not far from her grand-parents' croft at Toddlehills, near Longside, which is only a few miles from Peterhead, if you want the exact location. She liked Mrs Duncan, the shopkeeper's wife, and would have been quite content to stay there until she met a young man she'd be happy to marry, but her father had found a new job and insisted that she accompany them to the big city. I'm quite sure, however, that she never had any regrets about being uprooted.

In 1918, when she first saw the 'butcher's daughters', their brother Bob would still have been with the Welsh Fusiliers in France. In the photos we have of him, he had three different cap badges during his army service, because of the vast numbers killed in the various battles. The remnants of each regiment were amalgamated into one, taking the badge of whichever had most survivors. Reading a photo/postcard he sent to his sister Jeannie, listing the various places he had been, it is obvious that he was lucky to come through the conflict alive, yet it was only after my mother's death that I discovered the Military Medal he'd been awarded for bravery in 1917. I made enquiries about it and was sent a copy of the commanding officer's report for the three days in November when the Allies were trying to recapture a wood near Ypres. This certainly explained why the men under him were from so many different regiments, but only mentioned that Corporal Robert Forsyth had been commended for outstanding bravery in the field, and gave no details.

Mum and Dad must have met after he was discharged from the army – sadly, I heard nothing about their courtship, but I wish now that I had asked – and they were married in 1920. This was an eventful year for the Forsyth family. Jane, their mother (a most imposing figure of a woman from her photographs, always wearing huge hats with feathers or some sort of decoration) died having her gall-bladder removed in a private nursing home, and Annie emigrated to Canada. Billy, Jack, Bob (my Dad) and Jeannie all got married, although their father told Bob Mackay, 'You can't take my housekeeper away from me.' Fortunately, Jeannie's husband was quite pleased to move into the house above the butcher's shop, where they lived until the property was condemned early in 1939. They were given a council house in the Middlefield area, where hundreds of new square blocks were springing up. With the intervention of a war, all of the condemned buildings in the Gallowgate would be left standing until well into the fifties.

My parents rented a two-roomed furnished flat in Rosemount Viaduct, an impressive street of granite-built tenements with shops at ground level, that sweeps down to the Central Library, the South Church (now called St Mark's) and His Majesty's Theatre. Aberdonians once knew this trio as Education, Salvation and Damnation, but that's by the by. Dad paid £50 for the key to the flat, as was usual in those days, and he built a garage he named Erskine Villa (the make of his car) in a lane off Raeburn Place at the rear of our tenement. We could see it from our kitchen window. Our parlour looked up the hill towards S. Mount Street, with a big mill-like building as a focal point. This was a canning factory, where, for instance, the Co-op sent their oatmeal to be tinned for exporting. It later became a secondhand (junk) store run by a man nicknamed 'Cocky Hunter', why, I don't know. After the last war, this eyesore of a building was pulled down and replaced by a circular block of flats, which won the architect some special award. We ordinary mortals, though, look on this, too, as a monstrosity, and there have been whispers that it will be demolished soon.

Before he acquired the Erskine, Dad had a motorcycle/combination, and early snaps show me as a tightly wrapped bundle in my

mother's arms in the sidecar. Most of the men in the family, Dad's
brothers and brothers-in-law, owned a vehicle of some kind, from
humble one-stroke motorbikes to the impressive Lagonda that was
Uncle Billy's pride and joy. Every Sunday, there was a mass exodus of
Forsyths from the city – it's strange that they all thought of themselves
as Forsyths, even those who had just married into the family – looking
for interesting places to have our picnics. I can't remember bad
summers in the late twenties and early thirties; it always seemed to be
sunny, cold perhaps even in June, but still sunny. Ah, the rose-coloured
memories of youth.

No buying sandwiches and ready-made pies or quiches from Marks
and Sparks in those days, though. This was a time when wives were
expected to cook everything themselves, long before Aberdeen at least
had ever heard of Mr Marks and Mr Spencer. It was a case of each
family carting potatoes, a basin to peel them in (water to come from
the burns and rivers we parked alongside), salt, sausages and bacon,
an ordinary pan, a frying pan, two Primus stoves, cutlery and dishes,
not forgetting matches, because not one of the brood smoked. None
of the men drank or swore, either, so although they were a somewhat
raucous crew, there was no harm in them and they certainly knew how
to enjoy life . . . which was just as well. Most of them died quite
young.

Uncle Bob was the exception, surviving Jeannie, all her brothers and
sisters and their spouses, and living until he was almost ninety. Before
he died, he told me that Granda Forsyth had been a bit of a drunkard
when he was young, which is probably why his three sons were
teetotal. On another visit, Bob surprised me by sighing, 'I'm the only
Forsyth left.' He was absolutely serious, and I didn't have the heart
to remind him that he never *was* a Forsyth. I suppose, in a way, it was
a compliment to his in-laws that he considered himself born as one of
them.

2

My earliest memory is of being taken through to Granny's 'room' (the parlour) to see my great-grandfather's coffin – James Paul, Senior. When his wife died, he had given up his croft at Toddlehills near Longside – not far from Peterhead on the north-east Scottish coast – which was in a sad state of repair and eventually accidentally burned down. This was the house pictured on the cover of my second novel as Rowanbrae, over sixty years later. The fire and the building of a bungalow on the site in the thirties were as near to the truth as the story came; the rest was pure fiction.

Well over eighty, Great-grandfather Paul had been living with his elder son in Aberdeen's Ord Street for some months before his death. This became Quarry Street when I wrote *Time Shall Reap,* because Rubislaw Quarry was in close proximity. I was only about four at the time of his departure from this world, but I can still remember looking at the fearsome wooden object with its silent occupant, the bushy white beard resting on the satin lining, and saying, 'Why's Grampa sleeping in that big black box?'

*

While I was still a babe-in-arms, we went to Toddlehills in the motorcycle and sidecar on occasional Wednesday afternoons – Dad's half day. Obviously, I can't remember anything about those times or the place itself, but snapshots show that the house had a thatched roof and a big stack of peats built against the gable end.

Other photos show the old couple themselves, Great-grandma in a long black bombazine dress, with her hair dragged severely back off her face . . . but it's a kindly face. Her husband, on the other hand, looks quite stern, in a tweed jacket and trousers – I can't tell if it's an actual suit, probably not – and a snouted cap covering his white locks. They made a perfect Darby and Joan.

Once, when my mother was clearing out, she asked if I'd like to have her grandmother's hatbox. She had kept it well hidden, but intrigued, I accepted with delight. There was nothing unusual about its slightly oval shape, but it was made of tin and painted black. The lid was hinged at the back and lifted upwards to reveal two mutches, much softer than bonnets, though similar in style. One was plain black, with wide strips of the same cotton material to tie under her chin. The other, also black, was beautifully adorned with loops of black satin ribbon, the extensions at each side becoming the tiers. This was her Sunday-go-to-kirk mutch, and according to my mother, was hardly ever worn on any other occasion.

I treasured that tin for many years, proudly showing the contents at every chance I got, but sadly, it was in a crate that went missing when we moved to our present home. Also lost was a waistcoat belonging to my husband's great-grandfather – a truly magnificent creation of royal blue satin quilted and embroidered with gold. Willie Davidson must have been a real masher when he put it on, though I can't for the life of me think of an occasion when he would have been likely to wear it. But he doesn't belong here.

The visits to Toddlehills ended when the old lady died, of course.

It must have been in the mid 1920s that my Uncle Jim, my mother's brother, was accepted for the Metropolitan Police and moved to London. As a bachelor, he lived in the Section House with the other unmarried young men, several other Scots amongst them, but soon began courting. Gwen Schaper, his lady friend, was the eldest daughter of an ex-sergeant/cook in the Royal Artillery, I think, who had taken over a hotel in Guilford Street, off Russell Square, when he ended his twenty-five years' service . . . it may have been longer.

When I was six, we made the long journey to London, but it wasn't until I mentioned it in the staffroom of the school where I was teaching some fifty years later, that I realised what an undertaking it had been. This was 1928 remember, seven years before driving licences were required, and when there were very few petrol pumps and even less garages on the road; very few proper roads, for that matter, mostly what were known as 'unmade', with no tarred surface.

Motorists had to learn by trial and error how to fix the engine when the car broke down, and I'm quite sure many faults were made worse through ignorance. But that was all part of owning a car, a challenge that most men must have enjoyed. The spare tyre was accommodated on the running board, where also sat a five-gallon can of petrol in case we ran out. I shouldn't think my Dad was nervous of making such a lengthy trip – he wasn't that kind of person – but we did have friends with us, a Mr and Mrs Gammack, neighbours from Rosemount Viaduct, and you never knew what could happen out in the 'wild blue yonder'. It was best to be prepared for any eventuality.

As usual, the boot was packed with all the necessities for making our own meals, plus a small 'bivvy' (bivouac) for Dad and Bill Gammack. I can't remember the make of the car that made this daunting journey, but the door of the boot was hinged at the bottom, coming down to make a convenient table for our snacks. Whatever the make, it could cover the 508 miles as easily as any Rolls Royce; we just made one overnight stop at a place called Wreay, I think, in the north of England.

After having something to eat, Dad and Bill Gammack set up the 'bivvy' for themselves and the two ladies and I were to sleep inside the car. I am practically sure, however, that I was the only one who got any sleep that night. Even in July, it was still quite dark in the dead of night, and I was scared out of my wits to be rudely awakened by unearthly howls coming from somewhere close at hand. It turned out that the tent had been pitched on, or in very close proximity to, a colony of 'forkytails' – earwigs, to give them their proper name. They were crawling all over the two demented men, and Mum even had to fish one out of Dad's ear with a hairpin. Not the best of medical equipment, you may think, but the only thing handy and it did the trick.

All thoughts of a peaceful sleep vanishing, we continued on our way, landing in London much earlier than we had expected. Of course, we took some time to find Guilford Street and Mr Schaper's hotel, where we were to be staying.

Our host was a huge mass of a man, who did all the cooking sitting on a high stool. (His great belly sort of rested on the long table, and his vast behind overlapped all round the stool, neither of which seemed to bother him, but I couldn't keep my eyes off him.) He didn't have to move at all. With three sons and three daughters at his beck and call, he had everything he needed handed to him.

His wife ran everything else in the establishment, the ordering of food, the paying of accounts, dealing with the guests, making sure that her daughters kept the rooms spotless in their role as chambermaids, and were courteous and friendly in the dining room when they were waitresses – not too friendly, of course. She kept a strict lookout for any fraternising and quickly put her foot down if there was even the slightest hint of it. Mrs Schaper was no dragon, however. She was a small, slim woman, always laughing, always bustling about but never too busy to answer questions or to have a wee chat, if that seemed called for.

(I used the man, his wife and family, and his hotel, as models in the London-based part of *The Back of Beyond,* giving them different names.)

After we were given a lovely meal we were shown to our rooms, where we decided to unpack before venturing out into the great 'metrollops' (as I mis-repeated what my Dad said). We had another nasty shock. Our suitcases were moving with forkytails. They were inside everything, the feet of socks and stockings and even inside the ladies' knickers – a rude word in those days and which were worn only under ladies' skirts; men wore short underpants or drawers (long johns).

We never came across Wreay again in any of our travels over the years, although I recently found it in a large-scale map, but it remained in our memories as 'Forkytail Hotel'. Ah, happy days!

On that holiday, we saw quite a lot of London's attractions – Madame Tussaud's, where Auntie Gwen was sent into hysterics by a young boy swinging a hanging body round in the Chamber of Horrors (the huge hook was through her stomach and blood was much in evidence . . . well, red paint) – the Tower, Nelson's Column, and so on. We also found time to go shopping in some of the big stores. I can remember Mum buying me a lovely straw sunhat in Selfridges in Oxford Street – I even had my photo taken wearing it but I lost it before we even got home.

*

Uncle Jim and Gwen Schaper became engaged shortly after we'd been there, but their cosy, happy world was soon to be shattered. I don't know the ins and outs of the operation he had to remove his tonsils, but from various accounts of it, I've gathered that a swab was inadvertently left inside. All I do know for certain is that it infected one of his lungs and by the time the trouble was diagnosed and that lung had been removed, the other lung was also badly affected. Both lungs, of course, could not be removed – there were no such miracles as transplants then – and his condition was so critical that his parents were sent for. Gwen insisted on marrying him although the doctors held out no hope for him, and the marriage ceremony was performed at his bedside.

He did survive, however, and was given enough compensation to buy a small grocery shop in Stoke Newington. But it was no real compensation. For the rest of his life he had a hole in his back about two inches in diameter, from which a rubber tube protruded. This was so that the poison from his one remaining lung could be drained out every day. Repugnant as this task must have been to her, Auntie Gwen carried it out manfully until he died, roughly forty years later. He had still not reached retirement age.

One incident comes to mind regarding Auntie Gwen. While her new husband was recuperating in hospital, she and her friend, Alice, came to Aberdeen by boat to see her in-laws (my Granny and Granda). This would have been about 1930 or '31, and their cabin cost them £1 each. I was not much more than eight, but that was when I discovered how little the English knew about the Scots.

They were both pretty girls, dark and vivacious, but it was Alice who made their visit so memorable, stunning everybody as she came down the gangway, by saying, in a disappointed voice as she looked around the people waiting on the quay, 'Oh, I thought all Scotsmen wore kilts and had red hair.'

This at a time when very few Scotsmen could afford a kilt and a redheaded man was not altogether common. My Dad had red hair though, as had his father, as had I, but then I wasn't a man. Granda used to tell us we weren't proper Forsyths if we didn't have red hair, which upset those of my cousins who didn't. Of those who did, only one actually had Forsyth as his surname. The others were either daughters of the sons, or children of the daughters, who, of course, bore different surnames.

Back to Alice. Her other gaffe came on the Sunday night when Granny set out home-baked oatcakes and a huge lump of Crowdie cheese on the table for tea, plus, of course, scones, pancakes, shortbread, strawberry and raspberry jam, all home-made. This was the usual Sunday tea, because dinner (lunch nowadays) had consisted of broth or some kind of soup, boiled beef, carrots and tatties, and maybe a jelly or semolina pudding or tapioca. There was no need for another three-course meal, but the tea-table was also laden with food . . . always.

Alice helped herself to a quarter of oatcakes – a triangle six inches at least at its widest because Granny wasn't into elegance – and bit into it without spreading it with butter or having anything to drink. After swallowing what must have been a bone-dry mouthful, she exclaimed, 'Oh, I know what this is. It's porridge in the raw.'

I'll draw the curtain there. If they had stayed for much longer, my poor Granda would have had apoplexy from trying to hold back his laughter.

Some years later, we visited the Paul family in Stoke Newington, in the house above the shop. Auntie Gwen had a wicked sense of humour and one morning, while the Italians in the ice cream shop in the street behind were all talking at the same time and flinging their hands about, my Dad said, quite innocently, 'I wonder what they're saying to each other?'

'Would you like to say good morning to them?' Auntie Gwen smiled, and proceeded to teach him a short phrase in Italian.

He was about to stick his head through the open window and repeat it, when Uncle Jim put his hand on his shoulder. 'No, Bob, you'd better not. She's taught you a string of swear words.'

There was laughter all round, but to this day, that phrase still comes to my mind occasionally. I hope I never meet any Italians, otherwise I might feel like airing my linguistic ability and end up with a broken nose.

On one of our holidays there, we went to Brooklands to the motorcycle racing, but got lost before we ever got out of London. Spotting a bobby on point duty at a junction, Dad stopped and asked for directions – in his very best English. To his surprise and our amusement, the policeman answered in the Doric, the broad Aberdeenshire dialect. 'Weel, weel, laddie, you're a lang wye fae hame.'

After a second, Dad joined in the laughter, and I was told to write down where the bobby was directing us.

The butcher's shop closed early on Wednesdays, and in the summers we mostly visited Mum's sister Nell at the various places where her farm-servant husband was cottared. Like so many farm workers, he only worked at each farm for the obligatory six-month period before going to the feeing market in Aberdeen to sign up with another farmer. They moved around a lot, mainly in Aberdeenshire, and I liked going to see them because there were plenty of cousins to play with, nine at the final count.

Eventually, however, they settled in Ellon, Auntie Nell's husband taking up the life of a peddler in preference to the hard work on a farm. This was, perhaps, a good move for him, but not for his wife and family, for they only saw him occasionally, at longer and longer intervals until his visits stopped altogether. He never supported his children from the time he abandoned them, and Auntie Nell had a hard struggle to feed and clothe them, but she was a hardy woman, fit for anything.

On one occasion, the minister came to ask why she didn't send her family to Sunday School and she answered him snappily, and completely honestly, by saying they didn't have anything decent to wear – a sentiment probably sprinkled with an oath or two. Maybe swearing was the only way she could cope with the worry of where the next meal was coming from, or new shoes for the bairns, or clothes for school, and her colourful language didn't seem to bother anybody – neighbours or friends alike came to her for advice in their troubles.

Our playground in Ellon was the north bank of the River Ythan – not a huge river by any means, but certainly deep and treacherous enough to carry off a child who fell in. No warnings were displayed, and although Auntie Nell generally said, 'Keep awa' fae the edge, mind', we didn't heed her. We could look after ourselves.

If the ball went into the water when we were playing football or rounders, or whatever, and got wedged in the weeds, one of the older boys would shin up a tree, inch along a low branch until he was over the water, and use a stick to try to fish it out. The rest of us watched with no idea of the danger involved, carrying on with the game as if nothing had happened when the ball was retrieved. Sometimes, sad to say, the ball dislodged itself and was carried away altogether, which meant the end of the game . . . unless we could rope in somebody else who could provide one. Looking back on the exploits we got up to then, I'm sure we must have had a guardian angel looking after us.

The only trouble we ever had came from people – men to be precise. Auntie Nell's upstairs flat could only be reached by going through a close that also led to the back entrance to the Buchan Hotel, and quite often, we were verbally accosted (no physical abuse, I can assure you) by one or more drunks. They could hardly stand, so we called them names back, safe in the knowledge that they couldn't chase us – Baldie, Fatty, Bandy, Baldy, Specky. My oldest cousin once tried Buggerlugs, but the cursing, fist-waving recipient wasn't as drunk as he looked, and we had to run for our lives. A whole crowd of us tore across the quadrangle, up the outside stairs and burst into the house, many more of us than actually belonged there. Auntie Nell strode to her door and, looking over the top rail, she let rip with a mouthful of oaths of her own. She ended the exchange by shouting, 'Awa' an' bile yer heid, ye drunken bugger!'

Her four sons all grew to around six feet, her five daughters all married with no scandals attached to them beforehand, so all in all, and even taking her linguisitic failing into account, she did a pretty good job of bringing them up.

Occasionally, we went to Peterhead on a Wednesday to visit a Mrs Lawrence, some sort of distant relative but I never found out exactly what the connection was – on my Granny's side, I think. Over ninety, she was bedridden, and it amazed me to watch her propped up on what looked like dozens of pillows, knitting socks, wearing a 'busk' round her middle. This was a leather pad with holes in it where she stuck in her four knitting needles (wires, she called them) to keep them steady, or maybe because she hadn't the strength to support their weight, I don't know, but by Jove, she could fairly click on. This is the house I describe in *The Three Kings*, although I couldn't have been much more than eight or nine when she died and I was writing about it sixty-five years later.

On winter Wednesdays, my father played football in the Shopkeepers' League (none of them available for Saturday games). He was a very athletic man; a photograph shows him to be in the Porthill Gymnastic Club Session 1912–13, and another in the Excelsior Football Club 1919–20. When he was not so engaged, however, he took his wife and small daughter to the Cinema House, just along from where we lived in Rosemount Viaduct.

Mum often laughed about one particular incident but I can't truthfully say that I remember it. It was during a silent film featuring

'Baby Peggy' (the Shirley Temple of her day) who often watches her Daddy shaving. One day when nobody is looking, she goes to the bathroom, stands on a chair to reach the shelf, and lifts his cut-throat razor. At that point, apparently, pre-school, I sprang to my feet and shouted, 'No, Baby Peggy! No, don't! You'll cut yourself!'

I had watched my own father shaving, and he had often nicked his face with his open razor, so I knew how lethal it could be. Anyway, I think the usherette came and warned my parents to keep me quiet, otherwise we'd have to leave. This was a threat I dared not flout, so I sat with my hands over my mouth for the rest of that adventure of my favourite film star.

There were no trips on Saturdays. The butcher's shop remained open all day; didn't close until nearly nine, sometimes. There were always women who left it until the last moment to buy in their Sunday lunch – probably their men didn't get paid until they finished work on Saturday afternoon and stayed in the pub until they reeled home fit only for bed. The Gallowgate was a poor working class area, with a diversity of employment for the unskilled – in the shipyards, the railway and the quarries, delivering coal and other commodities by cart. There were, too, some jobs in the comb works, glove factory, paper mills and Grandholm Mill, where they made Crombie cloth and tweed.

In the 1920s and '30s, of course, even those who had served their time and were qualified tradesmen found themselves unemployed, having to sign on for money from the 'Dole' ('the burroo' in local terms) or the Labour Exchange to give it its proper title. For some, that was a disgrace, as, even more so, was applying to the parish for help. It was a time for Soup Kitchens, and although I only know of the one in Loch Street, which was still going into the sixties, there may have been others.

The two universities – Marischal College and King's College – were only for those whose parents could afford to keep them there, but for some of those fortunate enough to be given that chance, there was no post open for them when they graduated, which is why so many left their home town and looked further afield – England, of course, and the Dominions.

But that is by the by. None of the Forsyths attended a university. Only the very rich attained that height. Clever boys from poorer homes stood no chance unless someone took an interest in them – a teacher or minister, perhaps, or a father's boss – and financed them to a certain extent.

*

The year before I started school, Dad rented a big wooden shed at the side of a lovely granite house outside Kintore. It wasn't more than ten miles from Aberdeen, but it was like we were in another land, another era. The house belonged to two elderly sisters, the Misses Taylor, who looked after their brother Joe. He had been gassed in the war, the Great War, that is. World War II was in the far distant future.

Joe did all the dirty jobs about the place, cleaning out the hen runs, doing what had to be done to the dry privy, making sure the midden didn't spill over, as well as growing loads of vegetables – tatties, carrots, neeps, leeks, shallots, peas and broad beans. He also looked after the rambling strawberry plants, the raspberry canes, the gooseberry and blackcurrant bushes, so that his sisters could make hundreds of jars of jam for the winter. He loved jam, did Joe, and was often to be seen with a jam sandwich, what we called a doorstep, the slices of bread were so thick. There were no sliced loaves then. A loaf was bought, often still warm from the bakehouse, and wrapped in tissue paper to be carried home.

The sisters kept the front garden looking beautiful with all kinds of flowers – peonies, red hot pokers, rambler roses, pansies, hollyhocks, antirrhinums, nasturtiums – a mass of strong colours, and honeysuckle round the glazed front door, so that the evening air held a lovely perfume, helped by the night-scented stock.

These elderly ladies had also to do the housework and keep things in general looking spick and span. They didn't wash their bedding in spring like most housewives did, but waited until the weather was more predictable. It turned out, therefore, that we were there when the blanket washing got under way, and I was allowed to tramp them in a big tub outside – a most enjoyable task – and to help to put them through the big mangle set up by the back door before they were pegged out on the washing line. Mind you, although the two Misses Taylor were always profuse in their thanks, I don't think I could actually have done much to help them.

At first, I was a little afraid of their brother. Joe shuffled about, never saying anything, just a grunt now and again, but I liked to watch the swing of his arms as he chopped sticks, or dug into the pile of coal to fill the scuttle for the fireside. The fire had to be lit every day, to heat water, to cook, and so on, so although this was the middle of summer, he never removed his khaki jacket. Sometimes whole rivers of sweat poured down his face, but all he did was to wipe them off with his sleeve.

After a while, he began to smile at me, to stand in such a position that I could see what he was doing, even holding out the axe to let me have a try – I didn't manage – and letting me hold the bowl while he collected eggs. The hens had a habit of laying wherever they felt like it, free range as it's called now, and it sometimes took quite a time to find all their hidey-holes. By the end of our first stay with the Taylors, Joe and I were best pals. Mum was anything but happy about the association, I don't think she lost her initial fear of him, but my dad laughed off her doubts.

'He's just like a child himself. He won't touch her.'

Joe never did touch me – not that year or the next.

I can't put a month to those idylls in the countryside. I have photographs of me helping with the haymaking, and in these parts, harvest isn't until well into August. It could be that the second of our sojourns there, each lasting at least a month, was at a different time from the first, but in both cases, Dad went to work in Aberdeen on his motorbike. I don't know how my mother filled her days on her own. I was too busy doing what I was doing, what I liked doing, to think about anybody else – selfish brat that I was! Maybe she rebelled at last, for our second stay was our last, though I always have happy memories of the Taylors.

I was newly ten when I was sent to my Granny's sister at Gowanhill, a few miles from Fraserburgh, for the whole six weeks of the school summer holidays. I can't really recall why, though I've the feeling that Granny thought I'd been looking a bit peaky. I had lovely auburn hair (I had, honestly, long and curly until it was cut), and the very fair skin that goes with it. I doubt if I was really under the weather, but Mum's Auntie Teenie agreed to have me and that was it.

Uncle Jimmy Christie (pronounced Chrystie by his neighbours, which I always thought was swearing) was grieve at the farm, and we had visited them a few times before, so they weren't complete strangers to me. I did feel a little weepy when the car turned a corner and just disappeared, but Auntie Teenie wasn't one to waste sympathy where it wasn't needed. 'Get your case unpacked', she told me, brusquely, 'and get yoursel' washed. You'll be sleepin' ben the hoose in Jean's bed, so you'll be a' richt there.'

I did as I was told. I washed my face, hands and knees in the basin set out for me in the back porch, and was made to scrub my neck before I was shepherded into the tiny room which was to be mine for the next six weeks. In spite of the woman's assurance, I wasn't all right in the bed. I had a problem getting into it for a start, it was so high, then Auntie Teenie blew out the candle and I was left alone . . . in the dark . . . on a bed that moved with every breath I took. Not only that, something bit my arms and legs when I shifted them. I felt the mattress gingerly, wondering what kind of beasties were there, and wasn't altogether relieved to find that it was stuffed with what felt like stalks of corn – the cause of what I'd imagined to be insect bites. I later found this to be what they called a 'caff' or chaff bed. I got to sleep eventually and also got accustomed to the animated mattress and having to pummel it every morning to raise it from the dead.

There were a few children in the same row of cottages and they were friendly up to a point, but they were much younger. Also, don't forget that I came from the big city – a toonser, in other words – and was related to the grieve, the foreman, whose word was law. But Uncle Jimmy didn't scare me. He took me under his manly wing at the farm, letting me mash neeps for the cows in a big machine that took all my strength to work. He let me try my hand at milking once, but I didn't care for the feel of the cow's udder. That and the lash round the face I got from her sharny, smelly tail was enough for me. I was definitely not going to be a milkmaid when I grew up.

Uncle Jimmy gave me a demonstration one afternoon of something I'll never forget. I was watching as he scythed down some thrustles (thistles) when he suddenly said, 'See this, noo.'

He pointed to an insect that had landed on the back of his hand and was now gorging itself on his blood. I stood transfixed as the little body grew redder and redder, and rounder and fatter, until it suddenly toppled over and fell to the ground, dead as a doornail.

'It's a gleg,' Uncle Jimmy told me, 'and it damn well serves him richt.'

I've never felt any inclination to find out if it was only the man's weather-beaten hand that was lethal or if my blood would have had the same effect, and I never will. Losing a glegful of blood would be the death of me these days, not the gleg. If you are wondering what a gleg is, I have it on good authority that it is really a horsefly.

I did make one really good friend at Gowanhill, though – the orra loon – that is, the boy who did all the dirtiest, lowliest jobs about the place. I can't remember his name, but he was quite flattered that I followed him around like a puppy, and showed me all sorts of things. He taught me how to whistle with two fingers in my mouth; how to put a broad blade of grass between my two thumbs and get a whistle from that; how to walk, then run, along the midden wall without falling in. The whistlings took me much practice to perfect, but walking the midden had to be mastered right away. I was terrified of falling in the middle of all that muck – and I never did. Isn't it marvellous what fear can make you do?

The best thing he taught me, the *pièce de résistance*, was to fill a pail to the brim with water and then spin round, faster and faster with it held out at right angles to my body . . . without losing one drop. That was a marvellous achievement, but I never had occasion to show my prowess to anybody else. There was nowhere in Aberdeen that had the facility for such an exhibition. Nor have I ever had any cause to try out my powers of whistling.

Gowanhill had a shop attached to it, run by Mrs Sutherland, the farmer's wife. Auntie Teenie often sent me up for something, probably just to get me out from under her feet, but one errand in particular sticks in my mind. 'Jist ask for a half pun o' tae', she instructed me.

I ran to do her bidding – she wasn't a bully by any means, but it was best not to get up her wrong side – and Mrs Sutherland beamed when I went in. 'What can I do for you today, Doris?' she asked, seeing that I wasn't brandishing a paper list.

'I've to ask for a haffpunnotay,' I told her, unwittingly stringing the unfamiliar words together, 'but I don't know what it is.'

She burst out laughing. It must have sounded funny me using mangled Doric words in my normally perfect English, but she managed to explain that what my aunt wanted was half a pound of tea. It was mainly through living in Gowanhill that I became so familiar with the Doric that I often use in my writing, although my Granny and Granda helped a lot, as well. Mum used to frown at them for speaking so broadly, but it was so natural to them that I lapped it up.

I did enjoy my stay in the cottar house, but I was still glad to go home. I hadn't felt homesick once while I was away, but the minute I set foot inside my own house again, I began to cry.

I had the surprise of my life that October. I was presented with a baby sister. At first, I loved the idea of playing with a moving, breathing doll, but I soon changed my mind about that. This 'doll' wouldn't stop yelling its head off if I picked it up, and I was ordered to leave it alone. Besides, it was red-faced and not particularly pretty, but it improved as the weeks passed and I got around to thinking of it as her, she . . . or even Bertha. I was soon forced to admit that she was quite bonnie after all.

The only thing was, she got all the attention. Even Granny cooed over her, and sang songs to her like she used to do for me.

Far does my bonnie Bertha lie, Bertha lie, Bertha lie?
Far does my bonnie Bertha lie, the caul' caul' nichts o' winter oh?
She lies in her Granny's bosey, bosey, bosey,
She lies in her Granny's bosey, the caul' caul' nichts o' winter oh.

It really hurt that Bertha was now being held in my Granny's bosey, although she did take me on her knee sometimes. 'You needna be jealous o' your wee sister,' she would say. 'Your Mammy and Daddy still love you as much as ever, and so does your Granda and me.'

I wasn't too happy about going to Gowanhill the next summer. Baby Bertha would have Mummy and Daddy all to herself, and they might not want me back at the end of the holidays. On the other hand, I was glad to get away from nappies hanging all over the house when it was raining, and having to be quiet if the 'wee darling' was sleeping.

Nothing had changed at Gowanhill. Uncle Jimmy still took me to the farm with him occasionally so I'd be out of Auntie Teenie's way, and on the whole, I enjoyed myself. There was a Sunday School picnic on one of the Saturdays I was there, and although I didn't attend the Sunday School, just the church, I was allowed to accompany the other cottar bairns.

This was a strange experience. The minister tended to the needs of two different parishes – Rathen (centred in the church the Christies attended) and the joint fishing villages of Inverallochy and Cairnbulg. He usually held his service in the country in the forenoons one week and afternoons the next, allowing him to go to the coast in the opposite mornings and afternoons. I wish I could have sat in on at least one service at the seaside. How did the two sets of villagers behave towards each other as one congregation, I wondered?

As far as I was concerned they were all one, because there was only the width of a road separating them, but the 'Bulgers' didn't like to be associated with the people of Inverallochy, and vice versa. The picnic was therefore divided into three factions, two of fisher folk and one lot of country bairns, including me by adoption.

The two dialects were completely diverse, the seafaring families inclined to add 'ickie' to every name and sound the 'k' in words like knee and knife. Here is a made-up example. 'Johnicke's cut his k-nee wi' a k-nife.' I was intrigued, and spent most of the afternoon trying to listen to them speaking. It was quite difficult, since those from each place kept to themselves, each group sitting apart from the other two.

On the last Saturday of that holiday, there was a wedding to attend. Meg Christie was marrying her lad. Mum had bought a lovely lemon taffeta dress for me, with a dear little cape round the shoulders and frills round the sleeves and the hem. It sounds horrible, but I was very proud of it. After the actual ceremony in the house, while the adults were drinking a toast to the happy couple and paying no attention to me, I remembered a tree along the road a bit where the branches were enticingly low.

Without a thought to my finery, I tiptoed off, scaling up that tree like the tomboy I had become when I was in the country. Alas, during my spell as a pirate scanning the horizon, I fell off the rigging and trailed back to my mother, crying my eyes out because of my bleeding knee. Mother-like, she was only interested in the three-cornered tear in my dress. Enough said.

My last holiday at Gowanhill was when I was twelve. The big house next door had new occupants, including two girls, one a little older than I was, and the other a little younger. They were tomboys par excellence and we spent every day, all day, doing things we shouldn't. We never forgot to go back for something to eat, of course, but we had a marvellous time. Auntie Teenie was so relieved to have me taken off her hands that she got out of the habit of checking if I had washed myself, and so I made a few dummy splashes with my hands in the basin every morning and night, without letting the water touch any other part of me. I only had to be careful on Sundays, because she inspected every inch of me before we went to church.

Church was the Church of Scotland at Rathen, over the hill from Gowanhill, and in the pew in front of the Christies there always sat a very tall man, so tall that I couldn't see the minister even when he was up in the pulpit. This meant that I had to find somewhere else to focus my attention. It wasn't long before I discovered that the man's head, completely devoid of hair (long before this became fashionable and probably due to alopecia) and bright red from constant exposure to the weather, was a skating rink for flies – attracting them in swarms. Time flew much quicker for me that year than normal, though I still can't believe that he wasn't aware of their antics.

At last, the service ended and we set off over the hill again, Uncle Jimmy looking most uncomfortable in his Sunday suit and the high collar that his wife starched until it was so stiff and hard that it looked to be made of cardboard. His bowler sat ill upon his bushy grey locks and his shoes, polished until I could see my face in them, clearly hurt his feet, for he grimaced with almost every step. Auntie Teenie wore a long black coat atop her Sunday sprigged frock, and her laced shoes seemed to be bothering her, as well. She must have suffered from corns or bunions, maybe both, but she would never admit to any aches or pains.

On the Sunday my parents were coming to take me home, of course, we didn't go to church. Auntie Teenie was preparing an impressive meal for them, so I sneaked out to my friends without washing at all, as I had done every day that week. When I went back at dinnertime, the Erskine was there at the door. Mum and Dad had arrived . . . and Bertha, too. I was surprisingly pleased to see her.

'Oh, you've really got sunburnt this year,' my mother exclaimed when I ran to give her a hug.

'She's hardly been a meenit inside the hoose,' Auntie Teenie nodded.

Unfortunately, as has been proved to me over and over again, misdemeanours will always be found out. When we arrived home, quite late in the evening, I burst into tears, as usual, but this time, Mum spotted the pale channels the tears were leaving behind them and rounded on me angrily.

'Just look at you! It's not sunburn – it's dirt! Go and wash yourself thoroughly, my lady! The fire hasn't been on and there's no hot water, so use the kettle I was boiling to make some tea – but bring it right back. I'm gasping for a drink.'

Meekly, I got the kettle and went into the bathroom, also taking with me the book Auntie Teenie had said I could take home with me. It had belonged to her Jean and was all about brave Belgian children in the First World War, and I loved to picture me as the heroine who saved a company of soldiers by carrying a message.

That reminds me of a story that used to be told – a joke, really. The message 'Send reinforcements, we're going to advance' was relayed along a line of soldiers, but by the time it reached the person who had to send it out by wireless, it had become, 'Send three-and-fourpence, we're going to a dance.'

I filled the sink with hot water, took the kettle through to my mother and went back to sit down and read. I've always been a book-worm, and I was oblivious to the time ticking away.

When Dad called, 'Are you nearly finished in there?' I answered, 'Nearly. Just my legs to wash.'

After another five minutes, he called again, 'Come out of there this minute. I've to get up early in the morning, remember.'

'Just coming.' I turned another page but, suddenly, the light went out.

I must admit that I have always been terrified of the dark, so, as my mother said, I shot out of the bathroom like a scalded cat, in time to see my dad shutting the door to the electric meter cupboard.

Realising that he had switched off the light on purpose, I shouted, 'I hate you!' and ran upstairs to my bed – still filthy.

I have never forgotten those words. They were the last I ever said to him.

3

Going back a few years, our Sundays were usually spent with my father's family in one of the many lovely spots that we discovered. Mostly motorcycle combinations at first, with one or two cars, the ages stretched from babies to boys and girls in their teens, plus parents in their thirties and forties. As we all grew older, so changes came in the vehicles. Motorbikes were changed for cars, big, small or somewhere in-between.

Deeside was a favourite trip, perhaps going as far as Ballater or Braemar, where the scenery is impressively beautiful, and the mountains looked down on us with benign eyes. They probably wouldn't have been so welcoming in the winter, of course, totally covered with snow. Parked in a clearing in the pine trees, we often saw animals not known in the city. In the early thirties, the Forsyth family, like so many others, went to Crathie to see the young princesses accompanying their grandparents to church. That was something we children really looked forward to. They weren't ordinary human beings like us, they were more like beautifully dressed dolls, puppets that waved to us in genteel acknowledgement of our presence and we waved back, energetically and noisily, like the ragamuffins we were.

Donside was different; still bonny but with a different feel to it. Everything was wilder, the river itself, the trees, the hillsides, the not-so-far-off mountains. But we could still find satisfactory places to eat our picnics.

We travelled all round the northeast of Scotland, into the highlands or along the coast, where we found a lovely secluded area near the village of Pennan – where the film *Local Hero* would be made many years later. We didn't go down the perpendicular road to the village – at least it looked perpendicular to me. Not very far along from there, the road we were on dipped until we were on a level with a wide bay. There was a beach, caves for us to explore, the sea to paddle in, a convenient stretch of grass to set out our dishes and eatables. We went there quite a lot after that. I was the youngest of the cousins for years, but I doggedly went whither the others went, climbing rocks, exploring the caves, scraped elbows and knees ignored. I was aware that some of the older boys looked on me as a bit of a hindrance, so I was determined to prove I could do anything they could do.

We have a photograph of us all sitting around an old seaman in a peaked cap and navy gansey, being regaled with his yarns of derring-do, smugglers and pirates, dodging the coastguards and customs men, possibly all inventions of his own. He had probably come to investigate the city folk who were making so much noise enjoying themselves, and had fallen, as so many did, for the easy camaraderie that existed between them. The Forsyths were a high-spirited lot taken *en masse*, but it was all fun with them, nothing out of place. He had likely been as fascinated with us as we were with him. Plus, each woman pressed something on him to eat and drink, and he never went away without a coin or two in his hand.

On one particular Sunday that I recall, we went inland for a change, and found a nice picnic spot at Cockbridge, the source of the River Don. There was a fairly large flat area, the burn (that was all the river was at that point), being small enough to jump across, if we were careful. There would have been at least five packed cars, with dickey seats carrying two or three kids, and one motorbike with a sidecar, so there was a fair amount of people. The three large aunties obligingly 'cawed' the clothes ropes they had brought for the young ones to skip with, while the men and the lads played football.

Completely exhausted after all the exertion, most of us hunkered down on the riverbank and laved the water up to cool our faces. There was a lot of joking going on until one of the young men, very handsome with fair curly hair, let out a roar of dismay, then jumped up with his hands clapped over his mouth.

Willie was Auntie Vi's young man – not quite twenty, she was the baby of the Forsyths – and his dentures had fallen into the fast-flowing water. Well, we all exploded with laughter and scarpered after him as he raced along the bank, except Vi, who hadn't known his teeth were false. (This has always bothered me. Had he never kissed her?) Thus ended a beautiful romance, and I often wondered if any of the men fishing downstream for salmon had had an unwelcome catch.

On another Sunday – I can't give months or years for any of our trips; they're just lumped together in my memory – we were making for Inverness. By this time, there was more traffic on the road and the men decided that each vehicle should go on its own and we would all meet up at a spot just outside the town itself. The others managed to keep to the plan, but we were held up by having a puncture . . . with a most upsetting outcome.

Firstly, Dad got one Primus going before changing the wheel. While he was so occupied, Mum pared the tatties in water we got from a nearby burn, brought them to the boil and then picked some wild flowers with me until they were ready. By this time, Dad had set up the second Primus and was frying the sausages and bacon, the smell, as my Granda would have said, going round our hearts like a hairy worm, and making our mouths water in anticipation of a lovely feast. It's strange how much hungrier a person gets in the open air.

This was when Mum lifted the pot off the heat to bree the tatties (drain the water by holding the lid on and turning the pan upside down). Picture the scene, if you can. The car was parked on the grass, she was on the sandy verge of the road, and when the steam scalded her hand she let go with a yell. The noise made my dad jump to see what was wrong, knocking against the handle of the frying pan, which landed on the ground, too . . . upside down, naturally.

So potatoes, sausages and bacon were well entrenched in the sandy ground, fit for neither man nor beast. Dad tried washing them with the can of water meant for making a pot of tea but it didn't work; a mouthful of sandy-coated tatties wasn't exactly appetising. Even a bite of one of Forsyth's best sausages (for which they had won an award a year or so earlier) was every bit as inedible, no matter how nutritious it may have been.

We had nothing left to eat; no water to make tea, only a packet of Abernethy biscuits which are on the dry side with nothing to wash them down. It was also Sunday, remember, so there were no shops open on the road. Not only that, Mum was offended that Dad's first thought had been for the food rather than for her scalded hand, so there was a distinct coolness in the air as we carried on to Inverness.

By the time we joined the others, they had eaten all their supplies and, I'm sorry to say, thought that our mishaps were absolutely hilarious. I'll leave you to guess what happened when we went home. My mother did not have the Forsyth sense of humour.

Another outing could have had a more serious outcome. The men had made up their minds to go south for a change – they always made all the decisions – and we set off for Kirriemuir, the birthplace of J.M. Barrie, the great Scottish writer. At that time, there was nothing to advertise this fact, but we had been told where to look for the little window (high up in the gable of the house where he was born) that had been his inspiration for *A Window in Thrums*. He also wrote *The Little Minister*, which, in addition to being a wonderful story, also gives a description of life in the small village at the turn of the nineteenth century. His best-known work is, of course, *Peter Pan*, still a firm favourite with children.

After having a brief walk around, we piled back into the cars to look for a place to have our picnic. Apart from going through Blairgowrie into the moors and the mountains, I remember only one incident. This road, twisting and turning in hairpin bends to avoid natural obstacles, culminated in the notorious Devil's Elbow before it reached Braemar and Deeside.

All was going well with the cavalcade of around five or six vehicles until we were halfway up the first section of the 'elbow', with Uncle Billy leading. The ascent was so steep (one in three or even less) that it was first or second gear all the way, and the engines were loud in their protests. It sounded as if they were about to blow up at any moment and the cars would be catapulted right back to the foot of the hill, if they weren't smashed to pieces before that. Auntie Ina, Billy's wife, a thin nervous type even at the best of times, was so scared that she opened the door of the Lagonda and got out – quite easy because it was just crawling.

'You stupid idiot!' shouted my father, coming up behind her, and before she (or my mother) knew what was happening, he had lifted her off her feet and held her under the arms on the outside of the car until we reached the top.

I don't know how Dad managed this dangerous operation, driving with only one hand on the steering-wheel and two almost hysterical women bawling in his ears with fear, but manage he did. When we reached level ground once more, two separate marital disagreements took off, as one husband berated his wife for her lack of confidence in him, and one wife lambasted her man for putting his wife and daughter in danger. The other drivers and their passengers all came out and stood by, content to watch because there was no chance of fisticuffs. Happy days!

We took Granny and Granda out on occasional Sundays – just by ourselves. It wasn't that they didn't want to join the happy-go-lucky Forsyths, merely that Mum thought it best for her parents to enjoy peace and quiet when they were having a picnic. We sometimes went up Brimmond Hill – which I can see these days from the window of my sixth floor flat. In the 1920s and '30s, or even as late as the '50s, Brimmond was well away from the city, and it certainly was peaceful there – if you could find a comfortable spot where the heather didn't penetrate your clothes and you didn't keep sliding downwards.

Although I tended to be a bit of an extrovert then, I enjoyed those quiet afternoons with my beloved Granny and Granda . . . and my Uncle Doug; the baby Mum didn't know about, remember, and, being born on Hogmanay 1919, only two and a half years older than me. We were brought up almost as brother and sister, as you shall see, later.

I don't know which of the Forsyths, or their spouses, hired the huge wooden building at Cullerlie Farm in Garlogie. The hirer is a mystery because all the clan took advantage of it . . . and at the same time, so there must have been some squeezing in.

Dad often took Mum and me out to visit – I don't think we ever stayed overnight, Mum wasn't the kind to 'muck in' like that. She was always dressed neatly, and had me dressed to the nines, so we stand out like sore thumbs in all the photographs. I can't explain this side of her, because we also have snaps which show her, and me, looking like unkempt tinks, having a few days in Keith with one of her friends.

Mrs Reid, whose mother we stayed with in Keith, lived on the same floor as us in Rosemount Viaduct and they had two daughters, Margaret, almost a year older than I was, and Patsy, almost a year younger. We were all great pals, the two husbands included, but sadly, they emigrated to New Zealand around 1927.

Mrs Reid (I don't know her Christian name) corresponded from Wanganui (I was so intrigued by this name that I used it in *The Brow of the Gallowgate*), and after she died, Margaret kept sending Mum a card at Christmas with a little note enclosed. These, too, eventually stopped, whatever the reason.

I have some photos of us at the Aberdeen beach – no longer the draw that it once was, although the council is doing its best to bring it into the twenty-first century and appeal to holidaymakers once again. I can't understand why it went out of fashion. There were deck chairs for hire, bathing huts to change in, and, if you didn't feel like forking out money for these luxuries, there were acres and acres of beautiful, soft, golden sands where you could stretch out to sunbathe, with space enough to disrobe with a towel to hide your modesty. But the facilities gradually disappeared; the sands lost their smoothness, even the block of toilets degenerated into something out of a horror film.

But I must come down off my high horse. Like all old people, I am probably looking back to only the good things. There must have been bad things, too. The weather, for instance. To enjoy a seaside holiday, you must have decent weather, and until this year, Aberdeen certainly could not lay claim to have much of that. The summer of 2003 must surely go down in history as the longest period with wall-to-wall sunshine, up into the 80°F, high 20°C. If this is attributed to global warming, long may it continue.

SCHOOLDAYS

5

When I was four, a chatterbox who wouldn't stop asking questions, Mum decided that I needed a teacher's discipline, but the law said that I couldn't start school until I was five. The Demonstration School, however, not far from where we lived in Rosemount Viaduct, was a different kettle of fish. It had been established as a training ground for student teachers, who would (hopefully) absorb the lessons being demonstrated by the fully qualified professionals. It accepted children of four . . . provided that they passed certain criteria. I was expected to be able to talk fluently to the person assessing me (Mum wasn't allowed in the room), but as my Granny could vouch, I could talk the hind legs off a donkey, so that was no problem. I was expected to know the names of colours, fit different shaped blocks into their respective places, draw a man and a house – the man needed a head, two arms coming from just below the head, and two legs, and the house required a door, two windows and a chimney – all of which tests I sailed through. Perhaps I was over-confident, but that seemed to be what they were looking for, and my education began in the August of 1926.

Apart from the short nap we were supposed to take after lunch, nothing else of the nursery class remains in my mind. From the following year, we were taught to read phonetically; that is, we were given different symbols for different sounds. Our alphabet has twenty-six characters, but these do not represent every sound we use, so the extra symbols we were taught stood for 'ch', 'wh', 'th', et cetera. I'm afraid that the only one I can recall now is 'the' – an oval with a line across the middle; the Greek letter Theta, I discovered when I was much older. This was much the same method as the Initial Teaching Alphabet that was hailed as a great breakthrough in the sixties, forty years on.

The ITA was abandoned after a year or so, because of complaints that the children were unable to spell properly. I was not affected in this way because we moved to Hilton Drive when I was seven. The 'Dem' was too far for me to travel and as we were now in the catchment area for Woodside School, that is where I was sent. I therefore learned to spell in the age-old manner.

I had three teachers at Woodside, but the first was by far the best. Miss Deans was patient, explaining things so that even the slowest pupils could understand and made all her lessons interesting, even sums – though I was never all that happy with figures. She gave us little plays to act, an activity I loved, having always been a wee show-off. She read us good stories, and gave us other titles to look out for. As a result, I've always been a bookworm, reading any kind of book I could lay my hands on. My parents fortunately encouraged me in this, buying me many of the children's classics as Christmas and birthday gifts.

When I was ten, Dad bought me a set of Arthur Mee's *Children's Encyclopaedias*. I read them over and over; they were like a bible to me, even when I was grown up. I still have them, very much the worse for wear, and still dip into them for reference.

Miss Downie, our next teacher, was also nice, slightly firmer, which was only to be expected since we were that bit older. The last teacher we had, however, Miss Dow, had a strict rule – no talking in class. The punishment for breaking this rule was . . . the tawse, known to us as the strap; the belt as the kids called it when I was teaching, although it was only the headmaster who used one then. They have been banned now, unfortunately. Like hanging, the threat of the belt was a deterrent, yet I must admit to being unable to hold my tongue, so I was at the receiving end of Miss Dow's strap on many occasions . . . with long weals up my arm to prove it.

A little story here, before I finish with Woodside School. Bear with me – it *is* relevant. Not long before I retired, it must have been around

April or May of 1982, I had an appointment with my dentist for four o'clock. To get there from where I'd parked the car, I had to pass a small charity shop and, because I was a few minutes early, I was drawn in to have a look at the books. The place was so packed with people that I couldn't get near the shelves. I didn't buy anything, but I did get quite a shock. There, behind the counter, one of the volunteers, was Miss Deans – the only time I had seen her since I was eight – fifty-two years earlier. She was busy serving, and I was disappointed that I couldn't get near enough to speak to her, but guessed that she wouldn't have known me, anyway.

Half an hour later, face numb and feeling sorry for myself, I was on my way back to the car when who should I see again but Miss Deans. She was standing on the pavement at the corner of a street – shades of George Formby – obviously waiting for someone. Nobody else was about, but I felt so shy suddenly that I just smiled and said, as best I could with my mouth full of tongue, 'Lovely afternoon', or something like that and walked past.

She grabbed my arm to stop me. 'Wait. Don't I know you?'

'You taught me at Woodthide Thchool when I wath about theven, Mith Deanth,' I mumbled. 'A long, long time ago.'

'Yes, of course. Doris Forsyth. I never forget any of my star pupils. Did you make good use of that brain of yours?'

'I'm jutht about to retire from teaching at Hathlehead Primary,' I told her proudly, if not altogether clearly.

She beamed at me, a truly radiant beam, making me feel like a tiny tot again, being praised for something well done. 'Ah, here is my lift. My neighbour collects me on the days I take my turn in the shop. Goodbye, my dear. I'm so glad to have met you again.'

As the car drew away, I stood for a moment, thinking. She hardly looked any older than I remembered her from my childhood, yet she must be a fair age now. Then, feeling so much better for the encounter, uplifted in fact, I crossed the road to our Datsun Sunny.

Only about two weeks later, her death was in the evening paper. It was the surname that caught my eye, then the little notice said 'retired teacher', and although I had never known her Christian name, I knew instinctively that it was *my* Miss Deans. No age was given, so I tried to work it out. She had seemed fairly old to me when I was in her class, but anybody over twenty is ancient to a seven or eight-year-old. She may have been newly graduated, which would have put her in her early to middle twenties then . . . but no! There had been no raw edges about her. She was too mature, too experienced and had too much self-confidence . . . she had definitely been teaching for years before 1929. Say she'd been thirty then – that made her eighty-one when she died. I strongly suspected, however, that she was nearer ninety . . . if not over it, yet she'd still had all her faculties.

I was a week late in starting at Rosemount Intermediate School in 1934, which I will explain in a moment. We had moved from the house in Hilton Drive in 1933. The Housing Department had decided to carry out a Means Test on all its tenants, and had issued the forms necessary to get this information. My father wasn't the only man who refused to divulge his income, with the result that there was a large influx of families to the new estates of private housing springing up in all suburbs of the city.

I was still at Woodside School when we moved into the villa in Mid Stocket Road in October 1933 (bought for £640, with a deposit of something like £25 and the balance, plus interest, payable over sixteen years). Because I was just a few months away from sitting what was known in Aberdeen as the Control examination, which had to be passed before going on to a higher school, be it a Secondary or the stage in between, called an Intermediate.

Those who didn't pass had to remain behind, to try again the following year. One girl in my class had failed three years running and left school altogether at fourteen, never having got beyond Primary 7.

Dad hoped that I would do well in the Control, because he wanted me to go on to the Central Secondary. I wasn't keen on this; Doug, Mum's youngest brother, was already a pupil there and was slaving at homework every night until the early hours.

Dad and I had a bit of a squabble, but I remained firm, so my name was entered for Rosemount Intermediate, where, after three years, a pupil could transfer to a Secondary if he or she proved capable of it. I suppose Dad thought I would see sense by then . . . and I may have done, if fate hadn't intervened. I was sent to Gowanhill again in that summer when I was to make the transition from one school to the next. It was, if you remember, my last visit there. Dad was killed in the early morning of the day after I came home; killed on his motorbike on his way to the shop to make the mince and sausages ready for opening at eight. The only other vehicle on the road at that time of day was a newspaper van, and it must have been a million to one chance that they both came to the same crossroads at exactly the same moment – no road-marked warnings then, no traffic lights.

Two policemen rang our bell about 7 a.m. on 23rd August to tell my mother that her husband had been involved in an accident. They asked her if there was a man she could ask to accompany her to the hospital where he had been taken, and she told them to ask Mr Forbes, a neighbour and friend. His wife came round with him and volunteered to take me to Ord Street to be with my grandmother. Mum wouldn't let her take Bertha.

Only then was I shaken awake and told to dress quickly – still not washing off the dirt from my holiday. I put on the school uniform Mum had laid out for me – navy gym tunic, square-necked and with three box pleats front and back, square necked white blouse, navy interlock knickers with elastic in the legs and a pocket for a hankie. Under that, of course, a Chilpruf vest, a hand-knitted vest and fleecy-lined liberty bodice with suspenders to hold up my long black woollen stockings. (Yes, it was summer, but my mother had little regard for changing seasons, and this naturally became a bone of contention between us as I grew older.)

Mrs Forbes walked me to Ord Street, not very far, where she explained what had happened (a few whispered words) and left me, too young to understand fully what was going on. Mum came there in the afternoon to say that the police hadn't been strictly honest with her. Dad had been dead on arrival at Woolmanhill Hospital, and she had been sent to identify his body.

Granny and Granda took me home on the late forenoon of the funeral day – shining with cleanliness, Granny made sure of that –

where some of the Forsyths had already arrived. I was glad to see my cousin Isobel Mackay, my Auntie Jeannie's daughter, because she was only a few months younger than I was. Before I could think of what we could play at, or amuse ourselves with, Granny ordered us to sit down and not make nuisances of ourselves. All the seats were occupied, even the wooden, padded-topped stool where we kept our slippers, so we sat on the floor between the sideboard and the window, not really a very comfortable place. There was only a square jute carpet in the living room, the cheapest until Dad could afford something better. (It remained there for many years.) The wide surround was varnished wood, but that cold surface was all that was available to us, the only two children amongst a whole houseful of adults.

We sat quietly, watching the stir as people moved around getting the table set and so on, until I remembered that there was a pile of *Children's Newspapers* in the lounge. Thinking that they would keep us quiet and save anybody accusing us of being nuisances, I rose quietly and tiptoed through, only to be brought up short at the sight of the coffin. No one had told me it was there – I hadn't thought about such a thing – and I stood, paralysed in horror, looking down on my beloved dad, his eyes closed and his hands crossed over the satin shroud that covered the rest of him, although I didn't know then that it was called a shroud.

It was some minutes before the great band of steel that had clamped round my ribs and was constricting my breathing snapped as suddenly as it had appeared, and I ran into the narrow lobby sobbing hysterically, straight into Granny's arms. I could understand now what had happened and she was the one person out of all the people there who had the time and the experience to comfort me properly. Hers was the next coffin I saw, in 1942, of my own free will when I went to pay my last respects to a wonderful old lady.

Uncle Jack turned up on the morning of the Sunday after his brother's funeral. From what I took in, he was worried about what would happen to the shop. He would have to take on a man to replace Bob, so Maisie would get less than before, because she would be a sleeping partner, not contributing to the running of the business. That agreed on, he offered her £5 for the Erskine sitting in the garage that had come with us when we flitted in, only ten months earlier. 'I'm doing you a kindness, Maisie,' he murmured. 'You wouldn't get anything if you tried to sell it anywhere else.'

Not yet capable of rational thought, my mother gave him the keys to the car and accepted the tissue-thin white Bank of England fiver. He was lucky. If Granny and Granda had only arrived sooner, Uncle Jack wouldn't have got off so easily.

Mum spent the afternoon discussing with her parents the options open to her. Dad had left no will, and in Scottish law at that time, any moneys belonged to the widow, but property had to be divided between any children of the marriage. There were no 'moneys', of course. In addition to the deposit on the house, Dad had spent quite a lot in doing up the garden, making steps up from the gate (a task that my granda and one of their lodgers finished), and making alterations to the house. The upstairs bedroom had a box-room, a walk-in cupboard that he had transformed into a sort of workshop for himself.

Mum had been bemoaning the fact that Dad's had been a butcher's shop. 'If it had been anything else, I could have gone and served in it,' she said a few times to her parents, and Granny had to remind her that she had an infant to look after – Bertha had not yet reached the age of two. It was Granda who came up with what seemed the perfect solution to her problem of making enough money to live on and also pay the mortgage. 'You could mak' the hoose work for you?'

She wasn't too happy with his suggestion that she take in lodgers, but it was the only way round a thorny problem, and she eventually answered a few advertisements in the *Evening Express* put in by men looking for lodgings.

I had better continue with my schooldays. I turned up at my new school a whole week after the other pupils. Dr Cormack, the headmaster, had been notified of the reason but, as I was to find out, had told only some of the teachers. I was to have a different one for each subject, and during the morning, not one asked why I had not attended the previous week. I was also very grateful that no mention was made of my bereavement. It was still much too raw to talk about.

On that first Monday afternoon, we had to go to the Cookery Department, a separate building at the other end of the tarred playground. I can't remember what the Cookery teacher was called, though maybe it's just as well, for we started off on the wrong foot. She glared at me once we were all seated. 'You're new!' she barked. 'Name?'

Her tone flustered me. 'D . . .Doris,' I quavered.

'Stand up when you speak to me, girl! Do you not have a surname?'

I got to my feet. 'Forsyth.'

'Your address, Forsyth?'

Gathering that she needed this information to make up her register, I gave her the number in Mid Stocket Road.

'What does your father do?'

Not expecting this question, I mumbled, without thinking, 'I haven't got a father.'

Her hand crashed down on the table in front of me, narrowly missing my thumb. 'Don't be ridiculous, girl! Everyone has a father.'

By this time, I could sense a wave of sympathy coming from the others, none of whom I'd got to know yet, and who were obviously too scared of the dragon to say anything in my defence. 'My father died last Monday,' I whispered, struggling to keep back the tears, 'but he was a butcher.'

This clearly rattled her. In other circumstances, I believe she would have passed some derogatory remark about butchers, but I think she realised that she had pushed me far enough.

I never got to like her any better in the three years I had her . . . nor she me. Any time I opened my mouth to ask something, she pounced on me for talking, giving me hundreds of lines to write – 'I must not talk in class' – keeping me behind after school, to tidy up what had already been all washed and cleaned, and so on. Luckily, I got on well with all the other teachers, 'Fatty' Copland for Maths (self-explanatory) and 'Patchy' Ross for English (she had black hair with a white patch sweeping back from her forehead – most unusual then).

Our Music teacher was Mr Innes, who introduced us to many of the classics and endeared himself to us by pirouetting around while a record was playing on the wind-up gramophone. He was really fat yet he did very well as the Sugar Plum Fairy.

We had a Sewing teacher who taught us how to make several different kinds of seams (by hand, no sewing machines yet) and different ways of finishing hems. The first item we made was a lapbag, with our initials embroidered on, where we would be keeping the sewing and knitting we were working on. It was made of good strong cotton, calico maybe, and I used mine for years after I was married to keep my clothes pegs in.

The first item of clothing we made was a pair of knickers, beautifully shaped but so big that they would have held two or three of us at a time. Mum had had to pay for the material, of course, so I was forced to wear them . . . most uncomfortable. Then came a thinner cotton blouse, which didn't turn out too badly, followed by a pair of pyjamas also erring on the large side and which I had to wear. The last thing I made, in my third year, was a dress. We were allowed to use sewing machines at this stage, and we had to provide our own material for this. Somehow, my mother managed to get hold of a piece of navy Grandholm flannel – quite expensive, but made to last a lifetime. If this did not quite last a lifetime, I wore it for many years as a dress, altered it to a skirt and bolero, and years later, cut it down to fit Bertha.

I can't recall exactly what we knitted, a scarf first I think, then socks, then gloves, but I knitted a vast variety of articles over the years for my family and myself – in garter stitch to begin with, graduating to stocking stitch, Arran, cable and finally achieving the more intricate Fair Isle.

Other subjects were History, Geography, Religious Education and Gym. The Gym teacher was called Miss Marr, who told us that her brother had been with Shackleton on his journey to the North Pole, which made us regard her as something of a celebrity.

I was interested in everything and soaked up the lot like a sponge. Not long into my first year, Miss Ross (a dear soul for whom I'd have done anything to please) put me forward for a bursary. I had to pass an examination to show that I was worthy of this, of course, and was awarded £60, to be paid as £20 for each of three years.

It may not sound much today, but it was quite a help to my financially-challenged mother, who got no compensation for my father's death because there were no witnesses to the accident so early in the morning. She got no widow's pension, either. Paying insurance stamps was not compulsory at that time, and being self-employed Dad had opted not to. He had never dreamt that he would be dead at the age of forty, leaving behind a widow and two children. This was also why he had not made a will.

My favourite teacher – I'm sure you have guessed – was Miss Ross. I stopped calling her Patchy, it wasn't respectful. It was she who taught me to recognise many, many wild flowers, which wasn't her subject at all. Apart from instilling far more than the rudiments of grammar into us, she also gave many of us a real love of poetry, introducing us to the weirdly enchanting *Abu Ben Adam*. To prove how much this poem affected us, I must jump to the present day.

Less than a year ago, I was put in touch with the person who had been my best friend at Rosemount. Hilda Glennie, née Mathieson, had a beautiful contralto voice even at the age of thirteen and had been in one of the operatic societies for years and years. I hadn't seen or heard of her since around 1968 or so, but some things come about in peculiar ways.

When my husband came home from his second stay in hospital in 1999, we were asked if we needed help in the house. As a result of osteoporosis, I'm not too steady on my legs and I wasn't able to do everything that I should, so we accepted the offer. We were allotted a carer to do housework for one hour per week – paying for the service, naturally. After several different ladies had come and gone – through no fault of mine or theirs, let me hasten to say, just a general moving around, apparently – I got a real treasure, who could go through the whole house like a dose of salts and leave each room spotless and shining.

June told me one day that she also attended to Hilda Glennie, who had contracted a debilitating disease some time earlier and needed almost constant care. She had seen her reading one of my books and had told her she came to me, too. Hilda, severely disabled as she was, managed to type out a letter to me on her computer, a long, laborious process. Almost her first words were about Miss Ross – 'that dear lady we all loved so much'. She said that *Abu Ben Adam* had been her favourite poem of all time, and quoted it in full from memory. She even quoted bits from essays I had written and been forced to read out to the class . . . none of which I remembered.

I sent her a long reply, still reminiscing about our schooldays and our dear Henrietta Ross, but I was to get another wonderful, heart-wrenching surprise. Hilda phoned to congratulate me on my eightieth birthday – June had told her the date. I had a houseful of people, my family was giving me a party, so I couldn't talk to her for long, but I rang her the following day, and we spoke for well over two hours. A gift of the gab? Who, me? I'd say that Hilda and I were equally gifted.

She reminded me that she was younger than I was by a couple of months, so I asked our 'go-between', June, to find out the exact date. When the time came, I tried to phone her on her eightieth birthday, but got no reply and had to try again the next day.

'They were giving me a party,' she explained.

'They' were the wardens of her sheltered accommodation, and apparently there had been sixty people present. Her daughter had helped, and she had obviously enjoyed herself, although she didn't seem to be quite her usual jolly self. I suspected that she was very touched by the kindness shown to her, but the next time June came to me, she said that Hilda had had another stroke and was in hospital. She was there for some weeks, and I assumed that they couldn't let her out because she lived alone, but the next I heard was that she had died. Poor Hilda a truly genuine woman. I'm glad that we were able to renew our friendship even for such a little while. It meant a lot to me . . . and to her, I'm sure.

*

The grant I was awarded meant that I could not leave school at fourteen as the law allowed, but had to stay on for a third year. I had passed the Day School Certificate (Lower) in second year, and this gave me the chance to get the Higher version. I don't know how these exams compare with today; perhaps the Higher Day School Certificate would have been on a par with the 'O' level, or what is now called Standard Grade. On second thoughts, perhaps not.

At that time, all pupils, except me, could leave at the end of the term after their fourteenth birthday, unless they were intending to get the qualifications needed to go on to a Secondary School, so some of my class left at Christmas 1936, some at Easter 1937. Few were left of our original class of thirty plus for the summer term, and I supposed no one knew what to do with us now that the exams were past. At any rate, a school trip to London was arranged by the Education Authority in May. Mum couldn't afford to let me go, but Miss Ross, who was accompanying the ten girls, told her that one person could go free for every ten who paid. She managed to persuade my mother, who wasn't keen on the idea of accepting charity, to let me get the benefit of the free place. (I didn't realise until I was teaching myself that the free place was actually meant for the teacher accompanying the party, and that Miss Ross must have paid for herself.)

We had a lovely time, staying in a small hotel, a first for all of us, and going to see the sights on foot, by bus or by the underground railway. The tube was a number one favourite. One of our days was spent at Regent's Park Zoo, and we got special treatment, being allowed into several of the enclosures. When we were walking round inside the penguins' area, along with our penfriends from a London school, a great shout of laughter came from the people standing looking down on us. Looking round to see what was so funny, we discovered that the penguins had lined up in twos like us, and were following on behind. But, when we came down to the pool, they sidled past us and jumped in.

Inside the Reptile House, the keeper took out a huge snake (python, I think, but I'm not sure) and said we could handle it. We were all too terrified to touch it, but he made us stand in a row and placed the huge creature along our shoulders. If there had been such a thing as a video camera at the time, this would have made a hilarious film, because when we realised that the animal wasn't cold and slimy as we'd thought, one by one we let ourselves touch it. It was quite warm, actually.

All too soon, the day came for us to go home, and we were all packed and ready to leave just after breakfast. A small bus had been booked to take us to King's Cross Station, but someone phoned the hotel to say that it had broken down and that all other vehicles were already in service.

Miss Ross, unflappable as ever, said, 'There is only one thing to do, girls. We must use Shanks' pony.'

The expression had to be explained to us, and we set off reluctantly, each lugging quite a heavy suitcase, and moaning about the weight. Our chaperone merely said, over her shoulder as she hurried along in the lead, 'Just be thankful that we do not have very far to go, but we have no time to spare.'

Tired out after a week of constant walking around, we had to lay down our cases quite frequently, otherwise we'd have collapsed from sheer exhaustion. Don't think we were lily-livered or shy of hard work; we were nothing like most of today's delicate maidens. We had stamina, as a rule, but stamina can only go so far, and we had reached the end of ours.

As Miss Ross waited for the umpteenth time for us to move on, she suddenly had a brilliant idea. It was 1937, remember, but there were few motor vehicles about, mostly small cars. There were however, dozens of . . . horse-drawn carts. Stepping into the street, she held her hand up to a leather-aproned man sitting at the front of a canvas-covered wagon. 'We are stranded,' she began, softly, fluttering her eyelashes a little, although she must have been well over forty. 'The transport we had arranged failed to turn up and my girls are so exhausted, as you can see.'

We took the hint, and I'm sure that carter had never seen a set of 'so exhausted' girls, their heads lolling, their eyes regarding him pathetically. Miss Ross pressed on hopefully. 'Would it be asking too much of you to take us to King's Cross?'

Doffing his flat bonnet, he ran his hand over his balding head. 'Our train leaves in forty minutes,' she urged.

She, or we, must have appealed to something of the chivalrous Olde English Gentleman in him. Slapping his cap back on, he laid the reins down and jumped on to the pavement. 'Come on, then,' he smiled, going round to the back of the cart and holding back the canvas flaps. ''Eave yer cyses up first, young lydies, then 'op in yourselves.'

With his help, we didn't take long to get on board, placing our cases so that we could sit on them – by good luck the cart was empty. Miss Ross had to rely on help from the man, and sat down beside us, looking more flustered than we had ever seen her . . . looking more *attractive* than we had ever seen her. 'This will be something to tell your parents,' she smiled. 'We have travelled by all the usual means of transport, but I should not think that any of them have ever been taken to their destination by a horse.'

Then her expression changed. 'Oh, dear! I do hope all this weight is not too much for the poor animal.'

To our relief, the man shouted back to her. 'Nao! Ivy's used ter 'eavy weights. We work fer a brewery.'

We reached King's Cross in plenty of time, and although Miss Ross tried to press a ten shilling note into the man's hand, he wouldn't take it. 'That's me good deed done fer todye,' he grinned.

Our last three weeks at Rosemount were spent in a furnished flat at the top of Skene Square Primary School. The model 'house' was used by many of the primary schools for Housewifery Courses, which I must say, did me the world of good. There were only eight of us, the other two must have been off ill, or on holiday, perhaps, and we had to be there at half past eight (half an hour earlier than school) and we would finish at half past three (half an hour earlier than school). The teacher was called Mrs Sheriffs, a dainty, cheerful person who made us feel as if we'd known her for ages.

The first thing she did was to pair us off and explain how her course worked. 'Each pair will take turns of every task. We'll give them numbers. 1. Clean bathroom and outside stairs.' Our exchanged looks of horror at this made her smile. 'It's not so bad. You'll have to keep your bathroom clean when you are married, so now is the time to learn how to do it. 2. Strip bed, remake, clean bedroom. 3. Clean out and light fire, clean living room. 4. Make breakfast and lunch for yourselves and rest of pupils, leave kitchen as you would wish to find it.'

Now we had to draw lots to see who would do what first and then set to the task. Mrs Sheriffs came round to inspect and advise each pair on what they were doing, rightly or wrongly, and we could talk to each other as much as we liked, provided we did it quietly. There was a comfortable atmosphere, and when we were having lunch, which was sometimes not as appetising as it should have been, we could speak to Mrs Sheriffs herself.

I got very friendly with her – no, I wasn't one of those who tried to ingratiate themselves with their teacher, and come to think of it, she was equally friendly with all of us. There were two who were inclined to be shy, but she got through to them as well. She asked us what we wanted to do when we left school, and gave suggestions to those who hadn't thought about it. I hadn't really thought about it myself, but Miss Ross had inspired me towards creative writing, so I took in some of my stories for Mrs Sheriffs to read; short schoolgirl-type plots. She told me I should think of taking up writing as a career, but it would be over fifty years before I was able to take her advice.

Whoever was finished their allotted task first had to clean the silver with bathbrick or some other little job that only needed doing occasionally, but after lunch, we had to sit down in a circle and add a bit to the large rug that several schools had taken a hand in. The design was stamped on the canvas and the rug wool was cut into the appropriate lengths – I found this activity quite soothing.

We got out half an hour earlier than normal, and there was a large grocery shop across the road, which, I discovered, sold a pennyworth of soft brown sugar in a poke. Now, I'm not too sure about this, but the bus fare from where I lived to get me to Skene Square School was either a ha'penny or a whole penny. Whichever, I bought a poke of the delicacy (if I have a bag of this in the house nowadays, I still dip my finger in like I did as a child) and then I walked all the way home, revelling in the sweetness and making sure that I wiped off all evidence of it from hands and mouth before going into the house.

The two in the kitchen were always last, of course, because they had to clean up after the meal, but we all had to take our turn at that. On the whole what we were served was quite palatable and I don't know how the others felt, but I thoroughly enjoyed every minute of my time in that flat . . . well, maybe not so much when it came to cleaning the bathroom.

My 'housewifery' course prompted my mother to shanghai me into helping her with the washing. 'You've got a washing machine,' I objected, not that I ever paid much attention to this side of things.

'It still needs somebody to turn the handle,' Mum said, firmly.

And so I was initiated into this weird and wonderful – and back-breaking – chore. The cumbersome piece of apparatus – bigger than a modern automatic, and much, much heavier – was dragged out on its sturdy legs from its hidey-hole under the sink and the procedure began. First, a hose had to be attached to the hot tap; the water was heated by the coal fire but it never came anywhere near boiling point. Then Mum went down on her knees to light the gas ring underneath the monster. I was terrified of matches and gas rings, so she didn't even think of asking me to do it.

While the water was being brought up to the necessary heat, the dirty clothes were sorted out; whites in one pile on the kitchen lino, light colours in another, dark colours well apart, otherwise sheets and towels would be liable to turn blue, or red, or whatever got in with them by mistake. The piles were quite big; one or two of the lodgers put their things in too, although some took their laundry home to their mothers at the weekends. Then the ropes were put out, starting at one of the four poles on the drying green, continuing round the square and then diagonally across.

Now began the actual washing. The lid had been placed on top of the clothes, and the handle was ready for turning, its wooden knob at the end of the agitator that came up through a hole in the middle and lay across the top in an L shape.

The process wasn't as simple as turning a handle round and round, unfortunately. I had to push my hand forwards and back, forwards and back, ad infinitum, which moved the bottom part of the agitator through the clothes, churning them hither and thither. After less than five minutes, my right arm was so sore that I had to turn round and use my left arm, and so on until the slave mistress deemed that the clothes would be clean enough and I could stop.

But this wasn't the end! Oh, dear me, no! With a pair of wooden tongs, white with so much immersion in water, I had to take out each article, let it drip for a few minutes, then put it in a pail to be emptied into the deepest sink. The old tenements only had one sink because the washings were done in an outside washhouse, but houses built in the thirties, forties and fifties usually had two, one much deeper than the other. This one was used for the first rinsing in cold water and left until the second load went into the machine. I won't go into every little detail, you'll surely have got the idea by now. After each load was taken out, some more water was added to the receptacle until the final load must have been put into almost lukewarm water. The originally boiling water was too precious to empty out and gas was too expensive to light the ring again. The miracle was that, even using the same water over and over, which must have resulted in it being decidedly murky, all the clothes came out spotless.

I can laugh about it all now, but to be perfectly honest, I didn't carry out this operation very often. I was never a great lover of housework of any kind.

I left Rosemount School (with a Dux medal) on my fifteenth birthday, but I didn't go on to the Central where my Dad had wanted me to go and where Dr Cormack, the headmaster, advised my mother to send me. I had to start work in order to bring as much as I could into the household coffers.

LEISURE TIME

6

In writing about my schooldays, I completely forgot about what I did when I wasn't at school. Until we moved to Hilton Drive when I was seven, it was a case of reading *Fairyland Tales*, an upmarket booklet for teenies, then progressing to *Rainbow*. At Hilton, with other children as companions, I didn't read so much, though being that bit older, I did read the *Children's Newspaper* when Dad started buying it for me.

The Hilton houses, newly built when we moved there, had a patch of grass at the back (a drying green shared by the four tenants) and a small garden each to grow vegetables. In our block there was usually at least one girl of my own age, probably more, and two or three boys, so the drying green was too small for playing boisterous games. Hilton Drive, however, although a busy thoroughfare now, was relatively traffic free then; only the odd cart or car could be seen and my father's motorbike, which he kept in the cellar when he wasn't using it.

I can't say where the coal was kept (I wish I had written this before my memory grew so temperamental); in a separate bunker, I would think. At any rate, there was masses of room in the cellar for a whole gang of us kids to play there if it was wet. The bigger boys spun ghost stories that scared the life out of the smaller ones and gave me night-mares, or we played card games (no gambling), or cowboys and Indians – where the Indian braves took great pleasure in tying up the palefaces. There were one or two naughty boys who revelled in leaving us lying on the filthy ground with our hands and feet tied up, but I think somebody's mother gave them a good 'talking to' – probably threatening to get the bobbies to them if they did it again – which stopped this practice for a while at least. I must point out here that there was never any real maliciousness in these 'hooligans', some of them thirteen or fourteen, and nothing even bordering on the inde-cent was ever attempted.

If it wasn't raining, we played in the street – games I think I've mentioned earlier, and Dad sometimes took his motorbike to bits to clean it. This, as it turned out, was not only a stupid thing to do, but also very dangerous. Even with the door propped open, it was quite dark down there, but he was never stuck for ideas. He had taken a candle and a saucer down with him and set them on an old cardboard box. The flickering light couldn't have been very much help to him, but he was apparently managing fairly well until a gust of wind from outside blew the candle over. You are probably ahead of me. The fumes of the petrol ignited, setting fire to the old cardboard box as well.

While this was going on, I was in my room – we lived in one of the upstairs flats – trying hard to light a match from the box I had sneaked through from the scullery. It was a task I had never attempted before and I was determined to master it. I had gone through nearly the whole boxful, some breaking, some just refusing to light, when I suddenly struck lucky but got such a shock that I dropped the match, at practically the same time as I heard Dad shouting from below 'Maisie! The house is on fire! Get out! All of you, get out!'

Panic-stricken, I ran through to the living room, at the front of the house, where Mum, who had been sitting reading with the windows closed because she had let our canary out, jumped up, grabbed her handbag first and then we ran out.

What follows may sound too far-fetched to be true, but – Brownies' honour – it's the gospel truth. It's a scenario that could well be used in the 'What happens next?' part of *You've Been Framed* on TV, and I bet very few would guess correctly.

There we were, four households standing, white faced, in the small front gardens that were the responsibility of the downstairs tenants to look after. I believe that my face would have been whiter than any of them. My thoughts were running guiltily on the lines of, 'Dad's set the house on fire from the cellar, but I've maybe set it on fire from my bedroom, as well.' It was a dreadful feeling, but I was only about ten and too scared to say anything.

We weren't left standing for long. Dad had managed to put out the fire in the cellar by closing the door and smothering the flames with an old curtain we girls had been using for dressing up. His face black, his teeth gleaming white, he smiled a smile of relieved pride. 'Sorry about that, folks. It was my fault, but you can all go back inside now.'

The other three men – it must have been a Sunday afternoon – wanted to make sure that the danger was over, so they went round to inspect things, while the women shook their heads at each other and made for their own doors. Before Mum and I even got to the foot of the stairs, we came face to face with a sad apparition – well, the apparition wasn't sad, but we were when we beheld it. The downstairs cat had my canary in his mouth. We never found out if the bird had escaped or if the cat had gone in through the door my mother surely hadn't closed when we ran out. Whichever way it was, I was heartbroken at the death of my pet. An hour or so later Dad made a little coffin for it, packing it round with cotton wool. I made a little gravestone from a piece of folded cardboard and wrote the one word 'Beauty' on it and we had a solemn funeral at the bottom of the garden, laying my dear yellow Beauty to rest under the fence that separated our garden from the next block's.

To save leaving anyone left wondering, the match that I managed to light had gone out when I dropped it. Thank goodness.

Just a week or so after this, Mum presented him with another daughter. She wanted to call the baby Roberta after him, but he wouldn't hear of it. She suggested Bertha next, and although he said it reminded him of the German gun 'Big Bertha', he agreed. I think Bertha got quite a lot of teasing about the gun when she was older.

*

At Mid Stocket, my pastimes changed to a certain extent. There were not so many children around for a start and most of those who were there attended private schools. The girls went to St Margaret's or the Girl's High, and the boys to Robert Gordon's College or the Grammar School. We did play together sometimes, the surrounding terrain more suitable for hide-and-seek and that kind of thing. At the other side of the road from our house there was a market gardener's place with dozens of places to hide; places where today's youngsters could let their budding passions loose, but, at the same age, we weren't interested in anything like that. Oh yes, there was the odd little crush on one of the opposite sex, resulting in some innocent teasing, but nothing more than that . . . not until we were a good bit older, anyway.

Mostly we girls stuck with our own type of amusements, skipping, bouncing a ball against a wall and doing all sort of things (clap your hands, hop on one leg, touch the ground etc.) before it came back . . . unless you fell over or couldn't catch it. Then you were out and it was somebody else's turn.

We could enjoy ourselves without having to break rules, although Betty, one of my two best friends, and I did fall foul of the law one Saturday afternoon. I didn't have a bike – I had a fairy cycle with solid tyres at one time, which Bertha fell heir to, then Sheila, then Alan – so we used to whizz down the long hill with me sitting on the carrier of hers. Great fun, most exhilarating . . . until we narrowly missed running into a bobby pushing his bicycle up the steep slope. Cowed by his angry shout, Betty jammed on her brakes and we waited until he came back down to deal with us.

He pulled out a notebook and pencil. 'Don't you know it's against the law to ride two on a bicycle?' he growled.

'Y . . . yes,' we whispered, our knees knocking at the thought of what might happen to us.

'Do you make a habit of breaking the law?'

'N . . . no . . . no.'

'Well, I need both your names and addresses.'

In those days, nobody thought of lying to the police (perhaps an odd one or two villains, but not the general public) so, heads down in shamed disgrace, each of us told him where we lived. Having noted the information, he said, 'I'll be talking to your parents about this.'

Then he went back, retrieved his own bike from the side of the road and continued on his way.

Without saying anything to each other, Betty and I turned round and went back up the hill, she pushing our 'steed' and me trailing dejectedly along beside her. He had put an end to our fun and we had the worry of having to admit to what we had done. I had only my mother's reactions to fear, although she could deliver a fairly substantial wallop, whereas Betty had both a father and mother to tell, and her father was a tall, well-built man known to have quite a temper.

When we came to our house, I went inside leaving Betty to carry on round the corner to hers, and sat down quietly, making Mum instantly suspect that something was wrong . . . as mothers usually do. So I had to tell her, but just as I finished, the doorbell rang. It was the policeman.

'Is this where Doris Forsyth lives?' he asked, in his most official manner.

'Yes,' Mum nodded. 'What's she done?' I had just told her, but she thought I'd been keeping something back . . . again, as mothers do.

'Two on a bike. Has she not told you?'

'Yes, she was telling me when you came to the door.'

'Good for her. Now, nothing more will be done about it. I wanted to make sure they gave me their right addresses, that's all, and give them a bit of a scare. It usually stops them from doing it again. It's quite dangerous, you know.'

My mother was actually smiling when she came back to the living room. 'I'm glad you told the truth, anyway,' she said, lifting a ten-ton weight off my shoulders. 'I suppose you heard what he said, and he's right. It *is* dangerous, so don't do it again.'

Just as a matter of interest, that same part of Mid Stocket Road, a long, very steep hill, was superb for sledging, we discovered not long after this, and as far as we knew, there was no law forbidding it. The older boys, from about fourteen up and from all nearby streets, each packed five or six of us younger girls at their backs, and with a push of their feet, off we went. It was the most exhilarating, hair-raising experience, whizzing down and down with nothing to stop us. That's

what made those 'joy-rides' all the more memorable. There *was* no
way to stop – no brakes, no nothing . . . except feet, and it was too
dangerous to go right to the bottom, more than twice as far again.
I'm talking about the middle thirties here, and although there were
no Corporation buses in this area, Rover buses ran a service that came
up Rosemount Place and King's Gate then turned into Richmondhill
Road to join Mid Stocket on its way back to Rosemount Place.

You can understand why we couldn't chance going beyond
Richmondhill Road. The air was whooshing through our ears and we
were making too much noise ourselves to hear if there was a bus
anywhere near, and if it came out of that side street right in front of
us, there was nothing we could do except run into it. This is why we
(the youths) perfected a way of pulling one side of the reins (a piece
of rope) and broadsiding before we reached this point, usually
resulting in bodies hurtling off and skidding to a halt in a gutter,
hopefully out of any vehicle's path.

Then we had to pick ourselves up, thump ourselves free of ice and
snow, check for any broken bones and set off on the long trudge back
to the top of the hill to repeat the procedure . . . over and over again
in the pitch blackness of the winter nights. These thrilling, daredevil,
addictive adventures were brought to an end when the Corporation
decided to create another bus route to cater for the private houses that
had sprung up around the top end of Mid Stocket Road.

Betty and I compared notes the following morning on our way to
Sunday school. She hadn't got off so lightly as I had. Terrified of what
her father would do, she didn't tell her parents anything, and they only
heard it from the policeman. He could see that her father was really
angry and tried to defuse the situation by saying, 'It's nothing to
worry about. I'm just checking that she gave the right address, so
that's the end of it. Don't be hard on her.'

Her father didn't take that advice. He gave her one good wallop
for not telling him about it, and another for doing it in the first place.

I had started going to Sunday school with Betty at Craigiebuckler

Church. That began at 10 a.m., then we joined our Mums and Dads in church at 11. Going home, my parents and I went to see Granny and Granda and collect Bertha – Ord Street was about halfway between the church and our house, and Betty and her parents carried on by themselves.

Once she took in lodgers, of course, Mum was too busy cooking lunch to come to church, and I went to Ord Street on my own after the kirk service. Granny had lodgers, too, so I enjoyed myself there just as much as at home; more, really, because the maternal eye wasn't frowning at me for speaking too much, chatting up the young men. Mum was a great believer in the 'Children should be seen and not heard' maxim, but Granny wasn't so strict. Perhaps she hadn't been so lax with her own children, but grandchildren are usually given more leeway.

A rather humorous experience springs to mind here. I was thirteen or so when two of Granny's lodgers took me to see a menagerie in the Tivoli in Guild Street. Maybe in their late teens or early twenties, Jimmy Collins and Wattie Donald worked in Rubislaw Quarry and were probably not very well paid. They took the cheapest seats, in the Balcony, and 'Way, way up a 'ky', as Dave Willis, the well-known comedian used to sing. To reach them, we had to climb and climb and climb what seemed like endless flights of stairs, then, after we reached the top and got our breaths back – even before that, because there was a queue of people behind us – we went cautiously down the steps between the tiers of seating. This was an almost vertical descent, causing me much worry in case I fell. There was nothing to stop me catapulting over the balcony rail and landing in the orchestra stalls.

Luckily, none of us did, so we settled onto our not-very-comfy seats just one row from the front. Wattie had bought a bag of Soor Plooms, boiled sweets that last a long time, adding to our enjoyment of all the different animal acts. During the interval we remained where we were, observing the people in the stalls squeezing past the others in their row in order to get to the bar. The orchestra, too, took a break here, so we had loads of time to look around us. Then a bell rang, the drinkers came back in twos and threes, the lights dimmed and the orchestra struck up the introduction for the first act of the second half. I'm ashamed to say that I can remember only one from the whole show, the one the entire audience was waiting for, the finale, the *pièce de résistance* – the one that will never fade from my memory.

The curtains opened slowly. The stage was filled by a huge cage, with a low tunnel-like entrance from the side. The drums began to roll. A united gasp of admiration came from the enrapt audience as the lion (or lioness) appeared. We had to crane our necks to see properly, and the magnificent animal had only padded a few steps when the tumult began. It was some seconds before we three realised why the orchestra and everybody in the stalls were running out shouting. Then we saw that the tunnel had come adrift from the cage itself, and the beast was not inside either of them. He (or she) was going across the front of the stage, stopping occasionally to look into the auditorium as if wondering whether or not it would be possible to jump the gap.

The Dress Circle was also emptying, and the Upper Circle, but we in the Gods sucked our Soor Plooms smugly as we looked down on the panic-stricken activity below. No lion, or lioness, however well trained, could climb all those flights of stairs to get at us. The safety curtain had come down almost immediately, but there was no real danger in any case. Those responsible for looking after the animals had managed to coax him, or her, back to the side, while other workers were making sure that the tunnel was securely attached to the cage this time.

The act went on. The tamer cracked his whip. The lion leapt on and off various sizes and shapes of stands, giving a loud roar occasionally to prove that this was no mean feat. Then the trainer put his head into his charge's mouth. All hearts almost stopped, then picked up speed in horrified expectation of what could happen. Dare I say that at least one of the spectators actually felt a little let down when the possibility didn't happen and the curtain came down with no further mishaps? That was my first, and most exciting, visit to the Tivoli, giving me much to boast about on the Monday at school.

I'd have been around fourteen when I started taking an interest in boys. This had to be kept secret from my mother, still she couldn't keep tabs on me every minute of the day, especially when I was at school. So Betty and I would stand chatting to our two Romeos at the corner of Wallfield Crescent and Rosemount Place nearly every afternoon. Mine was called George, hers was Patrick.

We were making good progress one day, laughing and joking and getting to the stage where we had more or less paired off. It was Betty who spotted them – my mother walking towards us holding Bertha by the hand. They were quite a distance away but had already seen us, so it was no use trying to avoid Nemesis. I had been caught redhanded and I would have to face the consequences. She would go on and on at me as if I'd committed some terrible crime . . . in front of George. In actual fact, the degradation was even worse than that. She took me by the scruff of the neck and yanked me to the bus stop. Betty, staunch friend that she was, ran to catch up with us, and the last we saw of the boys, through the rear window of the double-decker, they were doubled up with laughter. So ended that little liaison.

I was never allowed out on my own after that. I had to take my little sister with me. I wasn't exactly at the stage of making a date with anybody, but one day, when we were out for a walk, we met a boy I knew who walked nearly all the way home with us. Now, Mid Stocket was originally a country road, and just down from our house there was still a romantic trysting place, known as Lovers' Lane. There were well-worn stone steps up to the path that wound amongst the trees, and steps down at the other end – or vice versa, depending on the way you came. There were also a few wooden benches, presumably for lovers to rest . . . and perhaps have a few kisses, not that Philip and I were on those terms. We sat down for a wee while, with Bertha squashing in between us, a plump four-year-old, and that's when it dawned on me that she presented something of a danger to me. Then I remembered the pennyworth of pandrops (mint imperials) I'd managed to buy by saving a couple of bus fares. Surely there was one left? Ideal for a bribe.

'I'll give you a sweetie if you promise not to tell Mum about Philip,' I said, after he left us and we were almost at our gate. (By the way, the railings and the gate were removed during the war to be made into munitions, and were never replaced.)

I should have known, shouldn't I? Tell a kid that age not to do something, and it's the first thing they do – a natural perversity. I had barely closed the door behind us when she piped up, righteously, 'Doris gave me a pandrop not to tell you she was in Lovers' Lane with a boy, but it was all fluff from her pocket.'

She got a fond pat on the head. I got a thump on the back. Fate can be so unkind!

A WORKING GIRL

7

Having just had the usual Saturday and Sunday free, I set off on the Monday morning to take up my as yet unknown duties as office girl in a small wholesale confectioner. At my interview, Mr Steel had asked, amongst other things, if I had good teeth. Wondering what that had to do with my ability for the position, I said I had.

'You won't have if you work here long,' he smiled.

This puzzled me. All the boxes and jars in the store would be sealed – it was a wholesale business, not retail – so how would I get a chance to sample anything? I was soon to find out. I may be besmirching characters here, but telling this tale won't land the people concerned in trouble, because they would be well over a hundred if they were still alive. Let me explain.

The only other person in the tiny office was around forty years old (in 1937), but was really friendly and very helpful. We sat at one long desk in front of the painted-over window – we couldn't see out, and no one could see in. There were two drawers at each side, one shallow for keeping pencils, pens and their nibs, a round ruler, paper clips and elastic bands, the little necessities, and one very deep, in which Evelyn kept the thick ledgers and an equally thick cash book, plus the large bottle of ink from which, like in school, we filled our inkwells. In mine were the slimmer daybooks (sales and purchases) and a small receipt book for cash sales.

I think a cleaner did come in at six, but if anything was spilled on the floor during the day, or brought in on people's shoes, I had to sweep it up or wash it off. If I had done all the clerical work I was supposed to do, I was allowed to have a wee shot on the typewriter. I was very slow at first, but with Evelyn's help, I was soon able to make a passable job of typing out invoices, two-fingered, perhaps, but still passable.

Being office girl and general dogsbody, I had to take the daily takings to the bank every day. This entailed going to the foot of Windmill Brae, crossing the railway bridge into The Green – a dangerous place to be walking at night but not altogether a salubrious area at any time of day then, although it is far more upmarket now – then up the long flight of stone steps at the side of Boots' the chemist. That took me up to Union Street and the North of Scotland Bank. I might point out here that I was only fifteen all the time I worked for Mr Steel – a child entrusted with sometimes hundreds of pounds; admittedly, mostly in cheques, but there were often quite a number of five pound notes, even tenners, neither of which were all that common then. Mind you, I was so young that it never crossed my mind that I could be in danger.

In those days, there were no breaks in the working day. I'd been told to start at nine in the morning, that I'd have an hour off for lunch – only time to wolf something down quickly before I'd to catch a bus back – and finish at six. There had been no mention of time off to have a cup of tea and, accustomed to having fifteen minutes playtime morning and afternoon at school, I was slightly worried as to how I would survive. I'm happy to say that I did much more than survive.

That first day, Mr Steel and the two reps had gone out on their daily round to collect orders from the shops, Evelyn, my superior and mentor, sent me up the brae to an Ice Cream Parlour, it may have been called the Washington Soda Fountain, for two bottles of lemonade. She must have paid for them, because I didn't have any money. Then, wonder of wonders, she said, 'Go through to the store and ask Jim for two cakes of chocolate.'

Jim Hay wasn't my senior by very much, and he went to the end of a shelf, lifted the lid of one box and handed me two cakes of Fry's Five Boys. I was to find out that he opened one box at a time and used it until it was empty, then started on another. That way, there was only one open box to camouflage. After about a fortnight, we got Cadbury's Dairy Milk instead (my all-time favourite), and then, perhaps, moved on to Rowntrees. I asked Evelyn how much I'd have to pay for this, and she said, seriously, 'Ach, pay at the end of the week, a penny ha'penny wholesale price instead of tuppence.' (In today's money, that would be roughly a quarter of a penny instead of half a penny, for a two-ounce bar.)

We nibbled at our chocolate, washed it down with a few 'scoofs' of lemonade and then stashed the bottles at the back of the tomes in our deep drawers. Being a working girl was going to be heaven.

At the end of the week, I opened my pay poke, a marvellous feeling, and said, 'How much am I owing for the chocolate, Evelyn?' I knew it was six times a penny ha'penny because we worked six days a week (Saturdays until one o'clock), but to my amazement, and delight, she smiled, 'I can't remember how many we've had. I'll start keeping a note next week.'

My spirits rocketed in the following weeks. No note was ever kept, and for the whole year I was there, we each consumed ninepence per week of the profits – less than five of today's pence – not that such reckoning entered my head.

To those who say we were stealing, all I can say is that it didn't seem like it at the time. Others, more broadminded, may only wonder how we didn't get sick of chocolate – on the contrary, I began a lifelong obsession for it – but after a while, Evelyn said to ask Jim for two tins of condensed milk instead. These were the smallest tins that Nestles made, selling in the shops at two old pence, but, like the chocolate, the wholesale price was one and half – not that we paid for them, either.

In writing this, I do feel ashamed, and guilty, about what we did but I was only fifteen remember, and at that age, you didn't argue with your immediate boss. You didn't argue with anyone older than you . . . except your mother, and you could guarantee that you'd be punished for that.

In addition to what we took without permission, there were the legitimate perks of the job. New lines were constantly being introduced, and a box of the newest was always set on a table behind us for customers (the retailers) to sample. Evelyn and I usually had a few to see how they tasted, but we once devoured practically a whole 12-lb box – but perhaps I'm exaggerating. Maltesers weigh very little, so 12-lb would have needed a gigantic container. At any rate, whatever the weight, we disposed of most of it. This would have been in late 1937 or the first half of 1938, and even a handful at a time wasn't enough for us. Thank goodness most of the shopkeepers had managed to sample one or two before we finished the box altogether, and Mr Steel was very pleased with the orders that flooded in. Maltesers had taken a trick with the general public, too.

Evelyn had another job – at the dog track on Saturday afternoons – and when she asked me if I would like to make a bit of extra cash, I jumped at the chance. Four shillings (twenty of today's pence) for two hours? When I was only getting seven and six (just over 37 pence) for a whole week's work?

The track was approximately where Asda is now at the Bridge of Dee, so I'd to take the tram down Holburn Street and come off at the terminus. Evelyn was actually quite far up the hierarchy of employees here, so she showed me where I had to stand and then left the girl at the next position to explain what we had to do. It was simple enough. We were in the same wooden building as the totalisator (don't ask) and we paid out to those who had placed their bet on the winning dog via this machine.

Perhaps ten of us stood at a long counter with a sliding hatch in front of each person, which we had to open to pay out, and close to check our cash and get ready for the next race. There was a bonus in this, a little something that Evelyn hadn't mentioned. Many of the 'punters' left a tip, sometimes as small as thruppence, but helping to add up to quite a decent sum at the end of the two hours. Some were more benevolent. If there was an odd amount in their winnings, anything up to half a crown, they didn't pick it up. In contrast to this, those who had really big wins usually didn't leave as much as a penny.

I soon realised that the big winners were part of a syndicate, and every member of that syndicate had to get his exact share supposing the total amount was into the hundreds of pounds. Even the odd amounts had to be shared, nothing for the person who paid out the cash.

We come now to the incident I mentioned. It took place in July, on the last day of the Glasgow Fair week, and the place was packed with Glaswegians – loud, jokey men . . . unless they were crossed in some way. Then they became even louder and horribly aggressive. We workers weren't allowed to watch any of the races – the premise being that if we won something people would say we had inside knowledge. In reality, we knew nothing about the dogs themselves, or of what happened on the racetrack, but on this occasion, having everything ready for the next payout in plenty of time, and being truly curious as to what went on, I opened my hatch to take a wee peep.

The noise was building up, the electric bunny was flashing round with the hounds in hot pursuit. Every man there was shouting at the pitch of his voice to encourage the dog he had backed. Suddenly, and most unexpectedly, a jacket was thrown on to the track right in the path of the leading greyhound. The poor terrified animal jerked to a halt, and the others, puzzled at what was going on, pulled up beside him.

The last dog sauntered past them all to come in first!

We found out later that the jacket had been thrown by a man whose dog, ahead for most of the way, was being beaten in the last seconds of the race, but he couldn't have envisaged the result of his action.

Over the din made by men outraged because their dog should have been first, came the announcement on the tannoy. 'The winner is Wandering Boy.' This was probably not his name, but all the names were similar to that.

I had never heard a rabble like that which started now (never since, either), but it hushed hopefully as the next announcement started – 'The first dog past the post is adjudged to be the winner, no matter what happened on the track. That is the rule.'

Despite the renewed roars of objection, we inside the booth were instructed to obey the order, and paid out to only a handful of men, who had taken their lives in their hands to push through the angry mob to claim their rights. All winnings paid, we closed our hatches double quick before the horde of menacing, threatening, waving arms reached us.

Terror-stricken and shaking with fear, we young lassies expected the wooden walls to be knocked down and a vengeance-seeking crowd to swarm in and take all the money . . . and perhaps finish us off, as well. We wanted to turn and flee . . . but we couldn't! Each hatch, window and door was mobbed by furious monsters and, after an hour or so, even the most self-confident of us were tearfully wailing that our mothers would be worrying about us not being home.

Then someone had the bright idea of pulling the night watchman's camp bed out of a cupboard and setting it up under the skylight. This was on the part of the roof nearest the road, an outside area blocked off from the public. There was no shortage of young male volunteers to push us upwards from the back, and ignoring where their hands strayed and what we must have been displaying, we scrambled out on to the corrugated iron, slid down and tore off without looking back.

I don't think this incident was ever reported to the police. The manager hadn't wanted any further trouble, nor would he have courted any adverse publicity, so it wasn't in the local newspaper, either. It did, however, leave a lasting memory with me, and, I'm sure, with the other girls, too.

My mother *had* been worried about me, but that didn't stop her from walking into me for being late home. She didn't believe my excuse . . . not at first, anyway.

There was another benefit to the two extra hours I was working each week. Even giving Mum a couple of shillings extra, I still had enough along with the tips, to buy a coat for myself for the first time. I took a few weeks to save up the twenty-five shillings (£1.25), but, by Jove, I was proud of it.

(I am writing this in August 2003, so imagine my astonishment to see, in the magazine of Scotland's *Mail on Sunday*, a picture of that same coat, a brown belted tweed, with the instructions to today's young ladies to look out for 1940s style coats – the latest fashion at £140. I bought mine in 1938. I wish I had kept it!)

I would likely have worked at the 'Dogs' for years, but I was forced to leave for the good of my health. For some inexplicable reason, it was almost eighteen months before I contracted scabies, a most annoying and irritating affliction. Having suffered the terrible itch between my fingers for over a week, I went to the doctor, who told me to wash myself with sulphur soap only, and to change my vest daily, ironing the clean one before putting it on. That applied to both my vests, of course.

'And you'd better give up that Saturday job,' he added, darkly. 'Even when you think you're clear, you could be infected again.'

The trouble did clear in a few weeks, but I took the doctor's advice. When most people had seen me scratching, they had kept well away from me, as if I had a dirty disease . . . which I suppose it was. It originated from handling money – a new meaning to the description 'filthy lucre'?

I had been working for Mr Steel for almost a year when he told me he wouldn't mind if I looked for another job. 'I can't afford to pay more wages,' he explained, 'so I change my office girls every year. They get better jobs easily enough.'

Naturally, Mum thought that my work hadn't been up to standard, but she did eventually come round and I took to scanning the Situations Vacant column in the evening paper. There was no shortage of jobs, and I was soon accepted as junior clerkess by Van den Berghs and Jurgens (Stork Margarine). The wage was 12/6 (an increase of 5/-, or 25p) and would be increased yearly . . . if I passed The Royal Society of Arts exams in Shorthand, Book-keeping and Typing, at Elementary, Intermediate and Advanced Levels.

This office was situated within the Coast Lines sheds on Jamieson's Quay, as I mentioned earlier, and the atmosphere was completely different from Steel and Co. There was one lady of indeterminate age – we did discover it eventually – two juniors, at newly sixteen I was most junior, and one clerk aged seventeen or eighteen. Miss Murray had a beautiful antique rolltop desk, with dozens of fascinating cubbyholes inside, while the rest of us sat at a long high counter on high stools, with feet dangling and whatever we were working on spread out in front of us on the sloping surface. There was also one typewriter on a table facing the door, for the use of all. Miss Murray and Hazel had an early lunch break, from 12 to 1.30, so George and I had to wait until they came back before we had ours.

Being in the Coast Lines sheds meant that one or other of the four storemen was always liable to pop in, but George still managed to make the most of boy being alone with girl. Let me stress, however, that nothing really out of place happened, just a tentative touch here and there – above the waist, of course – a shy hurried kiss (sort of), and there was always lots of suggestive remarks made by the storemen. I didn't complain – I quite liked it – physical and verbal.

Working so much amongst older men extended my vocabulary, and Mum was soon objecting to the more than risqué jokes being bandied around our table. I could give as good as the lodgers, the jokes . . . and the swearing, I'm sorry to say. Mind you, the words we used would be regarded as pretty mild today.

One of my first duties, repeated daily, was to type out address labels for the deliveries. Each box had to have its destination marked clearly, for the benefit of the carrier, wherever it was going.

I was getting on well when I came to an order slip for four boxes Stork for Maud Home, Maud. Knowing that Maud was a lady's name as well as being the name of a village in Aberdeenshire, I typed out four labels for Miss Maud Home, Maud. How was I to know that Maud Home was a Mental Hospital in Maud? You can imagine the hilarity my labels caused. I was teased about it for months.

It must have been around a year later that a new junior was taken on, and the typing of the labels was no longer my responsibility. All went well for a week or so and then – I could have kissed her – Peggy made out a whole set to 'Mr. H. M. Prison, Peterhead.' Now even I would have got that one right, but I didn't join in the laughter. I knew how it felt to be at the receiving end.

While I was still the youngest in Van den Berghs and Jurgens, as in Steel and Co., I was sent to the bank every day. I also had to post the mail at the Post Office at the corner of Regent's Quay and Market Street. This dual task entailed a double journey – along Jamieson's Quay to South Market Street, along the edge of the harbour then crossing Regent's Quay to push the letters into the slot in the wall. Then I'd to come back, pass the end of Jamieson's Quay and carry on along South Market Street to the bank at the corner of Palmerston Road. It was like completing a rectangle when starting from half-way down one side.

The money to be banked was in cheques and paper money mostly – there was once a £50 note, a real rarity in those days and the only one I've ever seen to this day – and some coins, so they were put safely inside a strong manila envelope.

Oh, no, I hear you thinking, she couldn't have? But yes, one day I did. My head likely full of the remarks the boys on the coal boats had shouted as I passed, some quite complimentary, I rammed all the envelopes in my hand well down into the letterbox. Then, realising what I'd done, my blood ran cold and I crept into the Post Office itself to ask if they could give me that special envelope back.

'You can't have it back,' said one assistant. 'Once it's gone through that slot, it belongs to His Majesty's Mail.'

'But it wasn't *meant* to be in His Majesty's mail,' I wailed.

'You put it in the box, so it becomes mail.'

'Is there no way to get it out again?'

'No.'

One of the men behind the counter took pity on me, however. 'If you come back at three, and ask the postie who empties the box, he might look for it and hand it over, but I can't promise. It's really against the law.'

But I needed it before three – that's when the bank closed – so I trailed back to Jamieson's Quay and confessed what I'd done. I must have looked pretty woebegone by this time, so Miss Murray just said, 'Go and tell the bank you'll be late with our deposit, then go back to the Post Office and when the postman comes to empty the box, ask him nicely if he'll give you our envelope back. If he does, take it to the bank, and if he doesn't, my head will roll, as well as yours. The deposit slips have to be date stamped with the correct day, or Head Office will go mad.'

Luckily, when the postie came, he saw the funny side of it, found the big envelope and handed it over with a smile. 'Keep your mind on your job after this, lass.'

'I will, and thank you very much.'

Very relieved, I started to retrace my steps once again, but my ordeal did not end there. For a change, I crossed to the other side of the street before heading for Palmerston Road, and having passed Waterloo Goods Station and a large granite block belonging to A.R.Gray, I came to a row of shops with tenement houses above them. I must explain here that this was long before tights were invented and because I had discarded the liberty bodices as childish, and refused to wear a corset or a suspender belt no matter how much my mother ranted, I kept my stockings up with wide black garters.

I was nipping along quite smartly – it wasn't ladylike to run, but it was after three thirty – when horror of horrors, one of my garters snapped, my right stocking slid down my leg and I grabbed at it with my right hand – the hand that was carrying the bank money. As I've already said, there was only a handful of coins inside, but they spewed out on to the paving slabs like an avalanche and I was just about to gather them together when I saw some trawlermen rolling towards me. There is something very distinctive about the way trawlermen walk, just like the waves rolling. There would be hell to pay if any money went missing, but I was in an awkward position, bent over with my hand again clamped round the calf of my leg to prevent stocking and garter from falling out below my skirt. This garment, thankfully, was one I'd made myself and was fairly long . . . if not very elegant.

There was only one thing to do. Opening the nearest tenement door – there were no security entry systems then – I stepped inside and stood with my back against the wall, thankful that I'd come that way instead of along the side of the harbour where the dock workers and ships' crews would have been revelling in my predicament . . . and I'd have had nowhere to hide.

I considered taking off the loose stocking altogether, but I couldn't walk around with only one stocking on. Apart from looking ridiculous, I'd be frozen. Secure in my isolation, I lifted my skirt and took hold of the home-made garter. I always bought the elastic and sewed them myself, because the ones in the shops were too fancy, and too expensive. The problem wasn't as bad as I had feared. It was just my stitching that had come undone . . . but I had no needle or thread to fix it.

I did have enough sense to think of a solution, though, so I held the two ends together and tied them into a firm knot, took off my shoe and stretched the restored garter over my foot. Then I pulled up the errant stocking that had reached my ankle, and just as I was about to pull up the garter to secure it, the street door opened. I don't know who was the most surprised, the two men or me. My skirt was up round my waist – I was wearing a pair of interlock directoire knickers (not at all sexy but it *was* winter) – and my stocking had descended to my ankle once more, as if needing the garter for support, which, of course, it did, didn't it.

It was the older of the men who spoke; the younger was too intent on looking where he shouldn't. 'You dropped your money, lass, so we picked it up for you.' He couldn't hide the mischievous glint in his eyes.

'Thank you.' I sheepishly accepted the envelope of paper money and the handful of coins.

His eyes went to the floor. 'That's the worst o' wearing garters, but I see you managed to tie it in a knot.'

'Yes, thank you.' I didn't know what else to say.

'I could tie it flatter than that, if you like?'

'It'll be all right the way it is, thank you.'

'Rightio, then, but maybe you should check the cash is a' there?'

It was, all the cash and all the notes and cheques, so they went off, both grinning like Cheshire cats.

I didn't think it was funny, especially when I had to work for another two and a half hours with the garter almost stopping my circulation and a knot digging into my thigh. I wished now that I'd let that man make his sheepshank or whatever it was; it would have been flatter. But the experience didn't make me stop wearing garters, nor did my mother's dire warnings of, 'You'll be as fat as your Auntie Jeannie by the time you're forty if you don't wear something to keep you in shape.'

She wasn't far wrong in that prediction, though. I did start to gain weight in my forties and, try as I would, I never lost the three stones I put on the first time I stopped smoking (for four years), nor the other two I amassed after the second time (six years). But that was all in the future.

… AND WAR!

8

When I reached seventeen, my wages . . . sorry, salary was increased to sixteen shillings weekly, paid through the bank once a month. This wasn't nearly so handy for me, but being able to tell my friends that I was now earning a 'salary' more than made up for the inconvenience. After attending evening classes over the winter, I had passed the Royal Society of Arts exams in Shorthand, Typing and Book-keeping at the Elementary stage, and was determined to go on to the Intermediate and Advanced stages, as well. As it happened, circumstances altered my plans, but more of that later.

I was given two weeks off with pay in August, and having saved a few bob, I decided to accept Auntie Gwen's offer of a free holiday with her. The last holiday I'd had was my week in London with the school, but this was something in a different category. My aunt was far more modern in her views than my mother, and she wouldn't stop me from doing whatever I wanted.

I made the trip myself by train; I knew about travelling, I'd been in London before. This was, of course, 1939, and there were already barrage balloons flying overhead, Air Raid Precautions stations built, trenches being dug. It astonished me that London was preparing for war, when there no sign of anything in Aberdeen. But on one of my solo outings in Lee Green something else intrigued me and I went running back to tell Auntie Gwen what I had seen.

'There was a big box in one of the shop windows, and it had pictures on it that moved. Like a film, but not a film, and a crowd of people were standing watching. It was a lady singing into a microphone, and when the manager of the shop came out, he told us this was called television and soon there would be one in every home.'

I was so excited that Auntie Gwen left the pastry she was making and ran with me to see what this new invention looked like. She was equally as impressed as I was, saying, 'I hope it's not too expensive when it's on sale. I'd love to have one, but your Uncle Jim's a proper Scrooge. Won't let me buy half of what I want.'

Aware that my mother thought Gwen was a wasteful housewife, I always regarded her with deep affection. She was fun, she didn't worry about tomorrow like most women. 'Tomorrow'll take care of itself,' she was wont to say. Maybe she shouldn't have married Uncle Jim. On the other hand, maybe it was a good thing she had him to keep her from being a spendthrift.

The war, of course, put paid to the introduction of television for some time, but I'll always remember the preparations for war and the entertainment from a box.

On the first Sunday in September, listening to Neville Chamberlain on the radio, we learned that Britain was now at war with Germany. Mum was quite shocked – hadn't he assured us only a year before that there would be peace in our time? – but it didn't worry me unduly. Aberdeen was much too far north for German bombers to reach – and we could carry on as usual.

There were changes, however. With petrol and diesel in short supply, all buses became mere shuttles, and we had to transfer to a tramcar at the bottom of Mid Stocket, a staggered junction where four streets met. It was a windy corner, and there seemed to be a competition between the drivers of the two kinds of transport as to which would arrive at the crucial stop first. Our bus service (for the duration) consisted of only one vehicle that went to the crest of the hill then turned and went back, generally in time to see the tail end of a tram sailing down Rosemount Place. With sometimes almost twenty minutes to wait for the next one, this left the passengers going to work in rather a nasty mood.

Soon after the outbreak of war, all the docks were cordoned off by high railings, and those who worked within the area, or had some message there, had to show a pass to get through the gates. This involved inventing some ingenious excuses for not having it with you, but this applied more to the female sex than to the men. Let me explain.

Women and girls are prone to changing their handbag to match their outfit, so if we had been out somewhere the evening before, it would be ten to one that we grabbed the bag we had been using then . . . but our permit was inside another. The harbour police were very efficient, but I discovered, after weeks of passing the two men who took alternate shifts, that it was quite safe to flip any old envelope at whichever was on duty that day, and he would let me past because he recognised me.

This was a bad practice, of course, and encourage me to be quite careless. Standing at the gate one morning, inevitably, was a strange policeman, who demanded a proper look at my pass.

The lie came automatically to my lips as I looked down at the envelope I was holding out. 'Oh, I'm sorry. This is a letter from my cousin, and I thought it was the envelope I keep my pass in.'

'You'd better find the right envelope, then,' he said, sharply, 'and be quick about it. I haven't got all day.'

I glanced along at the clock on one of the buildings on Regent's Quay. Five to nine! Time for desperate tactics. 'I left it in my other handbag,' I pleaded, 'but you'll have to let me in or I'll be late for work.'

'That's your lookout,' he . . . snarled, I think, would be the best description.

'Please, I'll get into trouble.'

'You can't come in till I see your pass.'

'I told you . . . it's at home.'

'So? The quicker you go and get it, the quicker I'll let you through.'

In tears now, I ran back up Market Street, had to wait ages for a tram in Union Street because it was past the rush hour, and then wait another ten minutes for the shuttle bus at the foot of Mid Stocket Road. It was almost ten o'clock before I arrived home, and, while I retrieved my other bag from where I'd thrown it the previous evening when I was dressing to go out, I had to suffer my mother's sarcasm about not paying attention to important matters.

'The only thing in your head now is the boys you meet,' she added, hitting the nail squarely on the head.

Thankfully, the problem bobby said not a word as he glanced at my pass before letting me through – he likely didn't even remember me – but it was still quarter to eleven before I raced into the office and had to undergo another lecture from Miss Murray.

None of this taught me a lesson, I'm ashamed to say. I left my permit at home several other times but never again came up against the policeman with no heart.

One day in the spring of 1940, I was one of a tramload of passengers on our way back from lunch. I was on the top deck chatting to a neighbour when a peculiarly staccato rat-a-tat-tat noise started, growing louder as it came nearer. We craned our necks to find out what was happening, but before we had time to see anything the driver rammed on his brakes and yelled, 'They're machine gunning us!' He sprang off the vehicle and ran inside a shop for shelter. We had just rounded the corner into Union Terrace, with sunken gardens along the left side, a few shops and offices at the other side, not forgetting the Caledonian Hotel, the most prestigious in Aberdeen at the time. We could see the tracer bullets now as well as hear them, and as everyone else seemed paralysed in horror, my gallant companion leapt to his feet to take over the duty that should have been the driver's.

'Keep calm, everyone,' he said, his voice as steady as the Rock of Gibraltar, 'there is no need to panic. The gunfire's not so near now, so I think we should take the chance to get off the tram . . . in an orderly fashion!'

Knowing Freddie quite well, I could recognise his inner tension, but his quiet assumption of authority did the trick, and in a few minutes all passengers had been safely evacuated. We could see a German bomber being chased by several Spitfires, from Dyce

Aerodrome we learned later, and what turned into a dog-fight was far enough away for us to stand on the pavement and watch.

A cheer went up when smoke started belching from the huge Heinkel, yet every person there was conscious of what could happen if it crashed. Its direction suggested an area of dense housing near the Bridge of Dee, with a probable high death toll. Word soon came out that it had actually landed – whether by some miracle or due to the pilot's expertise – on a partially built ice rink, and there had been only one fatality . . . the pilot himself.

It turned out that he had been on a lone spree of destruction, starting an hour or more earlier. Having lost sight of the rest of his squadron, or whatever they call it in Germany, and still with his load of bombs intact, he had swooped in from the sea, dropping one after another. His first few fell between the Torry Battery (a fort built to repel the French during the Napoleonic Wars) and the house of one of the civilian workers there. The blast caused much damage to the house and its inhabitants, and killed several soldiers.

The next stick of bombs he released landed on and around the Boiler Room in Hall Russell's shipyard, where many of the men were sitting out in the sun enjoying their dinner 'pieces'. Nearly all were killed, and there were many casualties in other areas of the yard, too. All this had taken place with no alert sounded and no defence mounted.

Only then, it seems, did the enemy pilot come farther inland to avoid the 'Spits' that he knew would soon be after him. He reached the very outskirts of the city before turning and trying to make for the open sea again, but he'd been spotted and attacked by the Spitfires in the Rosemount area somewhere. There were many casualties, dead and wounded, on that, our first taste of real attacks.

The sting in the tail of this incident came, for my family, later that same day. No information was ever given out on the wireless, for obvious reasons, but the news was circulating throughout the city in no time, embellished each time it was passed on. The woman who shared a landing and a lavatory with my granny had been shopping in the town and when she got home, she couldn't wait to tell the things she had heard. According to her, half of the harbour had been flattened and Hall Russell's had been blown to smithereens.

She pulled herself up short. 'Oh, I'm sorry, Mrs Paul. I forgot your Doug worked there.' She tried then to undo the harm she had done. 'Ach, it's maybe just a rumour. I ken there was bombs, for I heard them, but maybe there wasna as much damage as folk say. Dinna worry, Mrs Paul. Doug'll be fine. You'd have heard by this time . . .'

She left it at that, but she had said enough to make Granny sick with worry – for her son, an apprentice draughtsman with Hall Russell (he eventually rose to become Managing Director), and also for me, her granddaughter who worked in the harbour area.

Thankfully, all Hall Russell's workers, blue and white collar, were allowed to go home once a check had been made on who was still all in one piece. Doug was in a somewhat dazed state but he was able to tell his mother that, as far as he knew, the harbour had not been bombed. He also reminded her that I'd have been on my dinner hour at the time, and well away from the harbour.

Relieved that her worry had been for nothing and with her mind completely at rest, Granny packed Doug off to bed and lit her gas iron to get on with her ironing before making the tea.

When Granda went home around five, she told him how worried she'd been and how good it was that neither Doug nor Doris had been harmed.

'Oh, aye?' he said quietly. 'So you was worrying about Doug, and you was worrying about Doris, but you never gi'ed a thocht to the poor auld man.'

It turned out that he and his fellow gardeners in Ben Reid's Nurseries at Hazlehead had also been machine-gunned. This must have been on the farthest point of the orbit the German pilot had made. 'We'd to jump the dyke,' he went on, 'or the beggar would've got us.'

In late 1939, when one of our 'boys' volunteered for the RAF, Mum was left in something of a financial quandary. As she once observed, 'I can't even buy a thruppeny raffle ticket at the door.' Worse was to come. My darling Granny suffered a stroke.

I must say something here about our family doctor, who passed away many years ago. Agnes Thomson was, I suppose, fiftyish – or looked fiftyish to me. She was a tall, mannish woman who always wore a grey tweed costume and could scare the living daylights out of me, but she had a heart of gold. There was no National Health Service then, and doctors charged 2/6 (two shillings and sixpence or twelve and a half pence in today's currency) for each consultation or call-out . . . and these did not mean the five or so minutes like we're allowed nowadays.

It must have been quite late at night when they discovered something was wrong with my grandmother. Besides Granda (who was absolutely lost and didn't know where anything was kept), and Doug (at twenty-one, he was useless, too) there were three other men in the house. Of these three lodgers, it was Forbes Copland who took charge. Not one of the others would have known how to use a telephone supposing there had been one anywhere near, so I don't know who was sent for the doctor – Doug, probably, on his bike.

However the doctor was told and she arrived at Ord Street in no time at all. I can't give you a blow by blow account of what went on, but I can remember Granda saying, the next afternoon, 'That woman's an angel. She sat and held my Nell's hand for hours. It was her that pulled her through.'

I can well believe that. Dr Agnes was sharp, abrupt and seemingly unfeeling when there wasn't much wrong with you. She slapped my thigh once because I drew back my leg when she was pulling a verucca out of my foot. I can see her point, though. I did bleed all over her carpet. But she was an anchor to cling to if you were really ill. Plus, I know for a fact that she didn't charge for her all night vigil with my granny . . . and probably not for many of her other patients in similar circumstances.

It took Granny a while to regain her power of speech that first time, and the use of her hands. What she never recovered was the use of her legs. For a few weeks, Forbes, with my Granda press-ganged to help him, made a pretty good job of providing breakfasts. My mother went there every day to do what she could and to make something for the tea. At last, Granny was forced to admit that she'd never be fit enough again to look after her lodgers, and asked Mum if she would take over.

At that time, before the National Health Service, if one member of a family was unable to look after herself, another member was expected to step in and do the needful. With Granny's other daughter living sixteen miles off, the duty fell to my mother, a mere twenty-minute walk away.

This meant, of course, that she had to be with Granny until Granda came home at five. Doug – I only called him Uncle Doug when I wanted to annoy him – like all office workers, didn't finish until six. So, for the best part of three years, my mother looked after two houses, doing all the cleaning, the laundry and the cooking for her parents and young brother, and her own lodgers (two originally Granny's).

I had been going out with more than one of these young men – not at the same time, of course and nothing serious – but I was especially attracted to one of Granny's, an apprentice mechanic with William Tawse, Contractors. Jimmy Davidson was two and a half years older than I was, a month older than Uncle Doug, who was born on the last day of 1919. If I remember correctly, Jimmy first came from Laurencekirk to work in Aberdeen when he was seventeen, but he was twenty when he was called up in February 1940. He did his training in the RAOC at Chilwell, then was attached to the Seaforths as a fitter and we corresponded all through the war. He also came to see us every time he was home on leave.

Johnnie, another of Mum's lodgers had volunteered for the RAF not long after war was declared, and then, some time after Jimmy left, Bill was called up and Forbes, twenty-eight years old by this time, also had to go. And so we were left with Jock, a man in his fifties, who had been one of Granny's longest residents. One lodger, of course, was not enough to keep the household going, although I was able to give my mother a bit more board money by now.

I don't know whose idea it was, but two problems were solved at one stroke when Granny, Granda and Doug moved into our house.

Mum didn't have to run back and fore to Ord Street any more, and had three new lodgers to replace those she had lost to the war.

The many men who were being called up had affected me too. Because there were not enough teachers available, the evening classes were stopped after my first year. Thankfully, Lever Brothers (the parent company) still honoured the age-related salary scale, even though I couldn't continue with my studies.

Another little true anecdote here. A coal company called Adam Brothers was next to the Coast Lines in Jamieson's Quay, and I got quite friendly with a young clerk there. We had the same lunch hour, and sometimes found ourselves walking along the quay together. Andy was tall, slim and quite good looking, so when he asked me out, I agreed to go to the pictures with him. (On a Friday night, the day he was paid, because there was no 'going Dutch' in those days. If a boy asked a girl out, he knew that he'd have to pay her into the cinema or wherever he took her.)

I was eighteen now, but my mother still considered me too young to be going with boys. I had always got over this by saying I was meeting Betty and Kitty, so I did the same this time, too. The date went off quite well, and I enjoyed it up to a point, but there was no magnetism between us, and I didn't want to let him believe that there was. I was trying to let him down gently when I saw him on the Saturday morning – we just got Saturday afternoons off – and said my mother had given me a row for coming home so late the night before.

Shortly before this, Auntie Gwen had taken her two children, Jean and Michael, to Aberdeen away from the Blitz, and they stayed with us until practically the end of the war; she, herself, went back to London to be with Uncle Jim. At that time, Bertha would have been eight, Jean Paul would have been about eleven and Michael about five or six. That Saturday afternoon, I decided to give the kids a treat, and took them to His Majesty's Theatre to see *Snow White and the Seven Dwarfs*. Even Jean was inclined to cover her eyes when the wicked

Queen was on the screen, and the two younger ones were almost under the seats in thoroughly enjoyable fear. They liked to be scared out of their wits.

We sat through one and half shows, and came home just in time for tea. As soon as I set foot through the door, Mum said, 'I've had a visitor. He came not long after you went out, and he was here all afternoon, but he couldn't wait any longer. Do you know who it was?'

Thinking it was one or other of the ex-lodgers on leave, I shook my head and kept smiling, but her next question, shot out abruptly, made me shake at the knees.

'Who did you say you were out with last night?'

'B . . . Betty and Kitty.'

'Oh, yes? And what picture did you see?'

This was easier, so I told the truth; I can't recall what it was now.

'And did Andy enjoy it, as well?'

The words dripped with sarcasm, her eyes had narrowed as she waited for me to try to extricate myself from this awful situation. But she knew that I knew that I'd been rumbled, and what could I say?

A little disappointed that I wasn't giving her a chance to wipe the floor with me, she went on, 'You told him a lie, as well as me.'

I could explain that. 'I didn't want to go out with him again . . .'

'You told me he was a coal dunter.'

'I never said Andy delivered coal.' I was quite put out by this. I was being accused of something I hadn't done.

'You said he worked in Adam Brothers, and you didn't say he worked in the office, so what was I supposed to think?'

(Today's girls will be sore pushed to believe this account, even toned down a bit, but I swear that every word is true, and I don't think I was the only girl of that age to be in the same boat.)

The kids, who had dashed out to the garden to play until tea was on the table, came in now and saved me from any further tongue-lashing.

Not long after that, Andy was called up and wrote to me several times from his different postings. Then, maybe a couple of years later, there was a photograph of him in the *Evening Express*. He had been killed in the first thousand bomber raid on Cologne, but not, as you may expect, anywhere near Germany. They had completed their mission safely, had returned across the Channel safely, and all the crew were killed when their plane collided with another above their own aerodrome. It was very sad and I felt it all the more because of the shabby way I had treated him. He was a nice lad.

Back to 1940. It soon became clear to us that German pilots were concentrating on the docks, and there were no air raid shelters anywhere near Jamieson's Quay. The sheds were repositories for sugar, cattlecake, locust beans and various other commodities, most of them in sacks stacked in high piles. It was the head storeman's brilliant idea to remove the central sacks from several of the piles, leaving vacant covered areas to which we carried our chairs when the sirens blew an alert. Then, setting our ledgers on the seat, we knelt on the cement floor to do our work, sometimes for only about ten minutes if it was a false alarm, but sometimes for well over an hour or even longer.

Could this be why my knees aren't what they should be nowadays?

We had some terrifying moments during air raids, although now that I come to think of it, we shouldn't have been so scared. After all, we were on our knees, and what better position could we have taken up? I have a strange feeling that at the worst moments, when we thought we were about to be sent to Kingdom Come, we did actually put up a prayer. I have heard many ex-servicemen, including my Jimmy, admit that they prayed during attacks by shellfire or bombs even if they had never been inside a church, or had only gone when forced to as a child.

*

It may have still been 1940 or into 1941 when we heard the sound of feet marching along the quay towards us. Visions of jackboots and German soldiers with pudding-basin tin helmets flashed into my too imaginative mind, but curiosity made us all go outside to see what was going on. It was a battalion of Seaforth Highlanders on their way to the

North Boat (actually bound for Shetland, I discovered later), and we smiled to them as they passed, perhaps blushing if any of them winked.

Then my heart gave a jolt. There, about the middle of the line, was Jimmy, a big grin on his face at the astonishment on mine. We couldn't speak to each other, couldn't even touch hands because of the sergeant beside him, so our eyes had to give the message instead – a message that should have been obvious to both of us.

It was obvious to Miss Murray, Hazel, Peggy and Helen, who had replaced George when he was called up. There was little work done for some time, discussing why these young lads were being sent north, when all the fighting would be across the English Channel. Then the others settled down again, but I couldn't. I felt as if I had lost the most important person in my life; as if he were on his way to hand-to-hand combat with the enemy. He wasn't of course, although by this time, Norway was occupied and what was called the 'Shetland Bus' had been set in motion. This brought Norwegians away from their oppressors, but also took many of the men back to join the underground fighters, plotting against the enemy, doing their utmost to drive them back to Germany. I know very little about this but what I do know was that Jimmy and his comrades slept in the huts the fisher girls had used when they followed the herring, but he always said in his letters that he wished he were in the heart of the fighting.

Our correspondence continued, of course, and he visited every time he was on leave, and although it was wartime, we still managed to enjoy ourselves . . . other girls for him, other boys for me . . . nothing serious. We were too young to be serious.

It was different now. I was over eighteen and Mum could hardly stop me from going out with the cousins who turned up every now and then. It was quite funny, really. One of the storemen observed one morning, 'I saw you going into the Majestic wi' a sailor last night?'

'That was just my cousin,' I replied, knowing it was a question. It had been the son of one of my father's sisters, Tommy Duffus, who had joined the Royal Navy.

Perhaps a few weeks later, another of the men said, 'I saw you going into the Palais wi' one o' the Brylcreem boys on Saturday.'

'That was my cousin,' I replied again. It had been Douglas Mackay, Auntie Jeannie's son. The RAF lads were often called the Brylcreem boys. It wasn't a compliment, though. It was a suggestion that they thought themselves better than any of the other services, which – I'd better whisper this – they still do.

The crunch came another morning. 'I saw you wi' a different lad last night, though he wasna in the forces. How many cousins are you going out wi'?'

'That wasn't a cousin,' I said, without thinking. 'That was my uncle.'

'Aw, come off it! Pull the other leg, it's got bells.'

I had spoken the truth. It was Doug Paul I'd been with, and there was definitely nothing between us. What happened was that we sometimes used to mention that we'd like to see such-and-such a film and we arranged to meet inside the foyer. He paid his own ticket and I paid mine. We'd been brought up almost like brother and sister, and we were always quite comfortable with each other, whereas the cousins were apt to hint that they wished we weren't cousins. I don't think they did, really. Going out with Douglas Mackay always meant going to the Palais de Dans. Tap dancing had proved to be of little interest to most of the girls he had met while he was away, so he'd been forced to develop some skills in the ballroom. I wasn't really a good dancer, but when I was with Douglas, I could do all the intricate steps you could think of – even scissors steps to the slow foxtrot. I think, of all my escorts, I enjoyed my evenings with him most.

In those days, early in the war, going dancing meant wearing a long dress unless you were in the Women's Services, and I had been given a lovely pink taffeta from Tina Forbes, who lived round the corner from us. She was a few years older than me, and gave me another evening dress later, lemon with yards of material in the skirt. I felt like Ginger Rogers on the dance floor. It was even more fun going home – no buses after midnight. It was a fair distance to walk, so we took short cuts through back streets, humming the tunes the band had been playing, until we came to the long climb up Mid Stocket. The houses set back from the street, we could give rein to our high spirits.

Singing quite loudly, not that I was any great shakes as a singer either, we would waltz up the middle of the road, or do a bit of tan-going, or quick fox-trotting, and in my long dresses I felt on top of the world. We must have annoyed all the residents in the houses we passed, but we didn't think of that.

Going back to the subject of air raids, one unusual incident springs to mind here. We finished work at 6 p.m., and it was usually pitch dark by then during winter, so we were quite surprised to see a red glow in the sky when we came outside one night. There had been no alert, but there had been several bad air raids where the bombers had sneaked in and no sirens had been sounded. Unsure of whether to go back inside or chance going home, we huddled together trying to place where the fire was, and Miss Murray narrowed it down to somewhere near the beach. We knew that the gasworks couldn't have been hit or the whole of the city would have heard the explosion. That was a relief. There weren't many houses in that area, so what could be burning? At any rate, the bombers had missed the actual harbour, spread widely though it was.

We made our separate ways home after a while, quite unsettled to know that we could all be wiped out with no warning, but that was the kind of war it was – no quarter given or taken. Civilians were in the front line as well as the armed forces. Our sleep was interrupted that night, as it so often was, but, despite the all clear not being sounded for over an hour, we heard no enemy activity. This was sometimes called 'a false warning' which made you think a mistake had been made and there had been no bombers in the vicinity at all, but we had a marvellous defence system and quite often the bombers were repelled before they ever reached the city. It is well known that Aberdeen had the most air raids in Scotland, but not the worst, thank goodness. Glasgow and Clydebank had that dubious honour.

We learned next day that the fire *had* been near the beach, practically on the promenade itself, but it was not a result of bombs. The Scenic Railway in the carnival on the Queen's Links had gone on fire for some reason – they didn't think it was sabotage – and it was very fortunate that the flames hadn't attracted enemy attention earlier, when they were at their fiercest.

We were still making use of our makeshift shelters, but had a visit one day from an official from Lever Brothers, our head office. He wanted to know how we were coping and was amazed when he saw what we had to do. In Port Sunlight, they had presumed – if they had thought about us at all – that there was a shelter in close proximity. He promised to do something about it, but we'd been promised all sorts of things before – a new typewriter, a new handbasin to replace the cracked one in the cloakroom, etc. – but nothing had materialised. What could he do about this, anyway? He couldn't order the Town Council to build an air raid shelter especially for us, for heaven's sake. Could he?

9

We had discovered Miss Murray's age by accident. Before George was called up, he used to tease her by asking her when she would have to register – the morning paper regularly printed details of when the different age groups had to register for conscription or warwork. On the point of coming out with what would give away her age, she always broke off. 'You'd do anything to know how old I am, wouldn't you, George Logan? But I'm not telling you.'

There had been nothing nasty about question or answer. It had actually developed into a standing joke between them, but when he was called up, none of the girls had the nerve to continue with it. We were dying to know – for the simple reason that she was so cagey about it – but we didn't have the guts to ask. Then we noticed that she blanched while poring over the relevant page one morning. We had noticed before that she flipped through the pages and only read one thoroughly, so when she went for lunch that day, Hazel, Peggy and I grabbed the paper and discovered that the forty to forty-five age group of women were next to register. So now we knew at long last, if not her exact age, at least to within five years of it. I have never understood why she was so reluctant to tell people herself. I've always been quite open about mine; in fact, I'm quite proud these days to tell people that I'm over eighty.

*

It must have been late 1941 or early 1942 when Miss Murray read out the latest communication from Head Office and left us all flabbergasted! We were to be moved out of Jamieson's Quay altogether. This was a way of solving the problem of our safety that none of us had foreseen, and we girls weren't at all sure if we liked the idea. We had grown accustomed to, even quite enjoyed, the banter we got from the seamen and dock workers, and their wolf whistles set us up for the day.

Not only that, where would we get the sugar for our tea? Since it was put on ration, Charlie, the head storeman, used to poke a pencil into one of the sacks of sugar, fill our bowl and then close the hole by rubbing his fingers over it a few times – like a magician passing his hand over and making something disappear. This was repeated, on a different sack, each time our bowl was empty. It didn't occur to us that this could be regarded as stealing – it was on a par with Evelyn getting Steel's storeman to provide us with bars of chocolate. At least we got a teabreak in Van den Berghs – just as well, for there were no shops anywhere near us.

There were no shops close by in Bon Accord Square, either. It was a lovely street, with Georgian buildings all the way round and a massive rectangle of lawn in the middle. What had originally been private houses occupied by wealthy Aberdonians were now given over entirely to offices – all kinds of businesses, from solicitors and private consultants down to lowly margarine manufacturers. Strangely enough, the caretaker of our particular building was Mrs Logan, George's mother, a fact that he dwelt on each time he came home. 'Why couldn't they have moved here when I was working for them? I'd just have had to get out of bed and come upstairs to work.'

It was a great change from the Coast Lines sheds. We had one huge room on the ground floor – Mrs Logan's premises were below that – and the window was shaded by heavy wooden louvered blinds that had more than likely been there since the place was built, and were ideal for the blackout. There were several other offices in the same building, but it wasn't exactly the kind of place where people mixed. Each little group of staff members kept to themselves, and if you met someone on your way in or out, you just exchanged a nod and a 'Nice morning' or 'Nasty weather today'. That was all.

I don't know if it was the same all the way round the square (round a square?), but I always got the feeling that the men – only those over the age for conscription were left – and women who worked upstairs considered us a flight beneath them in more ways than one. Our new abode was certainly more opulent than our last.

Not long before we moved from the quay, I had gone into the Labour Exchange on my way home for lunch to volunteer for the WRNS – I don't know why I chose the Wrens – but I was refused on the grounds that I was employed in the distribution of food. This apparently exempted me from other war work. Accepting that I'd never have the excitement of being in uniform unless I changed my job, I settled down to remaining an ordinary civilian for the duration. Hazel and I went out together as often as we could afford to, going to the pictures straight from work then to one or other of the little tea-rooms on Union Street, whichever we happened to be nearest.

Hazel always made for a seat where she would be in full view of at least two young servicemen (one for herself and one for me), and she usually managed to find an escort home. I, of course, was left with the one she hadn't fancied. If an alert was in force – when no buses ran – I was glad of a companion on my long weary walk home in the pitch blackness, but if there was no air raid, I said I'd prefer to take public transport. It was perhaps no quicker, considering the time I had to wait sometimes, but it was safer – much safer.

Then Hazel met a Canadian airman one night and things changed. She made a foursome date, a blind date for me, and I was dragged along to the Ice Rink in Spring Garden. She was an accomplished skater – she and her sister went there regularly – and the boys, being Canadians, were almost as good as professionals. I, on the other hand, was an absolute novice. It was my first time on ice, and I spent more time on my backside than on my feet. I wasn't the only one, I'm glad to say; there were lots of others in the same boat.

Thankfully, there was half an hour allotted for speed skating, so I sat down on a bench to watch, my soaking rear end getting colder and colder as the minutes passed, but still glad of the rest. Then it happened! As they whizzed round, Hazel and her partner were letting each other lead for a few minutes then changing over, and on one change, coming from behind her, the boy didn't leave enough space between them and his skate came right up the front of Hazel's leg. He went to hospital with her in the ambulance, and I was left, feeling sick at what I had seen, with the other boy. I can't remember either of their names, but 'my date' saw me home and even supported me right into the living room because I was still shaking. Shocked at our story, Mum gave us strong tea to steady our nerves and didn't give me her usual lecture about picking up strange men.

After a while, she asked, 'Have you told Hazel's Mum what happened?'

I hadn't thought of that, so out we went again, but by this time, the sirens had blown and there were no buses or any kind of public transport running. We walked all the way to the foot of Bon Accord Street, around three miles I'd think, though it felt much longer than that. We had hardly spoken to each other at the rink and we couldn't find much to say now. It felt really strange.

Mrs Lamont was much older than my mother, Hazel was the youngest of three, but despite the shock we had given her, she thanked us and offered us tea, which we refused very politely. When the 'All Clear' blew, my escort said that he had better go, otherwise he would miss the last bus to Dyce Aerodrome, and he'd have to report what had happened to his friend.

We walked up to Union Street together, and along as far as Union Terrace, where I caught a tram, thank goodness they were running again, and he carried on to the country bus terminus, I suppose. Sadly for me, by the time I reached Mile End, the last bus up the hill had gone and I was left to walk the rest, which was quite scary, with no lights of any kind. I was never so glad to get home as I was that night.

Hazel was off work for some time, but as soon as her leg healed, she went back to the ice rink . . . without me. I couldn't have gone back supposing I'd been offered a thousand pounds. I never saw 'my'

Canadian again, and Hazel never saw hers after he left the hospital. She thought their squadron must have been posted.

It was early 1942 now, and we two girls continued to go out together, being 'picked up' by various young men in uniform – there were very few young civilian males left in the city. Yet it wasn't on any of those occasions that life suddenly changed for me. I was waiting at the bus stop across from my house when a naval officer stood up beside me and started talking. He was actually Merchant Navy not Royal Navy but I didn't know the difference then, and I learned that he was a 2nd Officer on one of the Ben Line ships and was about to start studying at Robert Gordon's College in order to get his First Officer's ticket. He was lodging just round the corner from us.

After a few days, he asked me out. I didn't have to think about it. In fact I was very flattered that a man so much older – six years is a big difference when you're nineteen . . . or it was then. The uniform, I suppose, also played a large part in making me accept – none of the other boys I knew had any gold braid. We went out twice a week for months. I was still writing semi-love letters to Jimmy, and going out with him when he came to visit us, also with the cousins when they were around, and, of course, 'Uncle Doug'. I didn't have any deep feelings for Sandy, but . . . he was an officer.

The more I saw of him, the more I grew to like him and when he asked me to marry him, on the day he was notified that he had gained his First Mate's ticket, I readily agreed. He had already bought an engagement ring, which fitted perfectly, but he had to report for duty in two days. Mum, still somewhat Victorian in her attitudes, seemed to be quite happy about my commitment. Her daughter was doing well for herself, wasn't she?

His ship sailed to Oran with supplies for the troops there, but he had also made arrangements for the wedding to be in just over a month in Rathven Church, near his home village of Portgordon in Morayshire. Bertha was only ten, but she was allowed to be brides-maid, and Sandy's brother was to be best man.

We had a week's honeymoon in Preston, where his ship was being refitted, and then they were ordered to join the Murmansk convoys. Unfortunately, in Russia the winter had already set in although it was only October, and they were ice-bound for eight months. It was a long time before I saw him again. Meanwhile, I still went out with Hazel . . . and nothing else changed much either. I did tell all my escorts straight away that I was married. They respected me for it, and I felt smugly righteous at being so honest when so many other married girls were jumping from one lover to another.

Then, it must have been into our autumn that same year, Mum had gone out one evening and I was in what had once been our lounge, now Granny and Granda's living room.

It would have been around seven that evening in late October 1942 when the bell rang. I answered it and was quite disturbed to see Jimmy on the doorstep. This was the first time I'd seen him since I had written to tell him I was married – a 'Dear John' letter – and I had been dreading his next visit.

To let you understand why what happened next came as no surprise to me, I had better make it clear that Jimmy had lodged with my granny before coming to Mum, and that Granny had always had a real soft spot for him. She had understood exactly how he was feeling, and her words were meant kindly, although she couldn't possibly have foreseen the eventual result.

She was propped up in bed by about a dozen pillows, as she had been for some time now, and she held his hand much longer than necessary when he greeted her. Then she looked at me with her eyebrows raised. 'You two should go oot for a wee walk, and nae be penned up in here wi' an auld man and his useless wife.'

I didn't know what to say, but Jimmy smiled. 'What about it, Doris? It's a fine night, just a bit cold.'

Granda, probably shocked at his wife for suggesting it when she knew we had once gone steady, now issued a warning, 'You'd best keep walking smartly.'

So off we set, each uncomfortably aware of the other and afraid to broach the subject uppermost in our minds. We did keep walking smartly, for most of the hour or so we were out, but we also managed to work round to a point where we knew our feelings for each other were still the same. The first shy kisses became longer and we ended up by breaking away in dismay. We couldn't carry on like this.

My mother was in when we went back, not looking at all pleased with us, and it was just as well that Jimmy had to leave to catch the last bus to Laurencekirk. I think, however, that Granny had done some diplomatic talking while I saw him to the bus stop, because the maternal telling off I expected never materialised.

I must confess that the interlude really unsettled me. I shouldn't have agreed to it. I ought to have known what could happen. In fact, it was fortunate that it hadn't gone any further. It very nearly had. I did feel guilty, and I'm sure he did, too, so our letters were more stilted after that.

As I said earlier, Granny died in December 1942, and we were all shattered. I cried myself to sleep every night and wondered how on earth I'd get through the funeral. I had no one to lean on. Sandy was still away, Mum was comforting Bertha, Doug had his father, my Granda, to turn to. I was feeling at a very low ebb that day, and couldn't believe my eyes when Doug went to answer the door and brought Jimmy in. He was home on leave again, and had come to see us in a forenoon to save any further embarrassment. It was he who was embarrassed, and deeply upset when he heard about my Granny, for he had loved her nearly as much as I did.

Feeling that he was intruding, he made to leave and, wonder of wonders, it was my mother who asked him to stay. He stood at my back and held my hand all through the funeral service, squeezing it so hard at times that it was quite painful. We didn't care that everyone had noticed, we needed each other and he was glad to be there for me.

Nothing was ever said about it. My mother must have realised that I wouldn't have coped with saying goodbye to my darling grandmother if he hadn't been there.

Doug's wedding had been booked for the week after, when he would qualify as a draughtsman. He and Reta had planned to ask the

driver of the beribboned taxi to take them from the church to Mid
Stocket to give his mother the bride's bouquet, but they wanted to
postpone the marriage. Granda, however, was adamant that Granny
would have wanted them to go ahead – which we all knew was true –
and so they did.

*

Everything was going quite smoothly at our new premises in Bon
Accord Square. There were no storemen to tease us, and we all felt
quite proud to tell people that was where we worked. It gave a better
impression than saying, 'Inside the Coast Lines sheds', but there was
one real drawback. By this time, the city was being assaulted regularly
by incendiary bombs and we had to take our turn at fire-watching.

Looking back on this, I am amazed that the safety of several
buildings with a caretaker in each was placed in the hands of two
flippertigibbets of twenty years old. Peggy had a caliper on one leg,
Helen was pregnant and Miss Murray wasn't asked. I think she must
have been over forty-five by then. I suppose each office had to supply
at least two for this duty, and Hazel and I had no choice.

It wasn't as bad as we had feared. We had to spend the night in the
room above our office, a huge hall of a place with a wide open fireplace
. . . and yes, we were allowed to use it. I suppose Mrs Logan would
have had to make sure it was burning properly for us, and a whole
pail of coal was always standing at the side. There didn't seem to be
any shortage here, not like at home, where Mum practically counted
each lump of coal to make sure nobody had sneaked one into the
grate. (She also counted the bags of coal the men delivered in case
they cheated her.) Two camp beds were also provided for us, with
pillows and blankets. This struck Hazel and me as a poor kind of joke
when we saw them first. How could you go to bed and sleep if you
were supposed to be watching for fires?

I can't remember how often we had to take our turn, perhaps once
every ten days, and we were allowed to go home at half past seven in
the morning and not start work until ten. We regarded this as quite a

bad deal. Were we supposed to stay up all night then only get an hour to go home for breakfast and snatch forty winks?

We did try. We sat on the typists' chairs at first just talking about this and that, mostly boys, I expect, then after a while, we had to lie down to give our backs a rest. We didn't fall asleep the first time. We didn't know what to expect and had our pails and stirrup pumps at the ready beside us, but it was a tremendous effort to keep our eyes open. Neither of us smoked then – it was a year later before I was persuaded to try a cigarette and was hooked – so we had nothing to help us keep awake.

Half past seven took a couple of years to come round, and we made our separate ways home after reporting to Mrs Logan. Hazel, fortunately for her, lived in Bon Accord Street, only a short walk from Bon Accord Square, whereas I had to walk a good bit down Union Street to get the No. 5 tram and change at Mile End for the bus.

The only blessing for me was that the bus stop was right outside the door of Murdoch the baker, who sold the best morning rolls I have ever tasted (an Aberdeen speciality found nowhere else), and the smell wafting up my nostrils was too tempting to resist. I went home armed with a bagful, still hot from the bakery and . . . oh, how I long for one now. (The poor excuses that most modern bakers offer as rolls are more than twice the price, less than half the size and nothing like the taste. There are one or two near exceptions with regards to the last.)

Feeling like going to bed after I'd had my breakfast, I had just a short time to rest before starting on the journey back to work. Needless to say, as we were dog-tired by the end of the day, we didn't think too highly of this procedure, and decided that we would play it differently next time.

So, on our next turn we chatted for a while, read for a while, and then lay down to sleep. Why stay awake when nothing was happening? We would hear if the sirens blew an alert . . . of course we would. In the morning, we went down to report to Mrs Logan before going home. 'Another peaceful night,' Hazel ventured, because we both knew by the woman's expression that something had happened.

'There was an alert on from two till four,' she said sarcastically. 'A couple of fine fire-watchers you are.'

Hazel and I looked at each other, ashamed that we had slept through the crucial period, but Mrs Logan laughed suddenly. 'I'd have come up and wakened you if anything had been going on, but there wasn't a sound.'

Safe in the knowledge that she would keep us right, we went to sleep every time after that.

Hazel and I were on duty on Hogmanay, would you believe, but we didn't really have anything to celebrate and we went to bed as usual. When we went down to the basement the following morning, however, Mrs Logan said, 'Peggy and her sister came to first foot you about half past twelve, and they threw gravel up to the window but you must have been sound asleep. The noise got me out of bed to see who it was, but they wouldn't let me go up to waken you.'

We had been caught out again, but that didn't make us change our ways.

*

Still on the subject of fire-watching, we did have one very interesting evening, but I will have to give you the lead up to it first. Granda, heartbroken at his wife's death and with his health going rapidly downhill, developed pneumonia and was sent by Dr Agnes to Woodend Hospital towards the end of January 1943. It wasn't too far from Mid Stocket and Mum went to see him on the Wednesday afternoon.

When I went home at teatime on the day of her first visit, she told me about a poor Norwegian sailor who was in with appendicitis and had missed his ship. 'Your Granda says he can hardly speak any English,' she went on, 'and he can't read it at all, and he doesn't get any visitors.'

I didn't need much persuading to accompany her on the Saturday afternoon. It was exciting to think I would meet a real Norwegian –

they were always tall, blonde and very handsome, weren't they? Besides, I had managed to get some books and magazines for him from the Norwegian Reading Room in Bon Accord Terrace, which I passed on my way to and from work every day. Quite a number of Norwegian ships called at Aberdeen then, and the council had set up this facility for them, a library with everything they could wish to read, in their own language.

Fridjof Hougland (I used his name in *Time Shall Reap*) was even better looking than I had imagined, and although we did have a problem understanding each other, it soon became obvious that he understood more English than he could speak or read. He did manage to tell me his name, and I told him mine (I was married by then but I'll come to that later), about the Reading Room and where I worked. I also gave him a humorous account of the fire-watching activities . . . or non-activities, as they were.

He hadn't been able to tell me anything about himself, so I was quite unaware that he had been in hospital for some weeks and was almost ready to be discharged. I got a shock, therefore, on my way back from lunch on the Monday, when I turned into Bon Accord Terrace and spotted him standing outside the Norwegian Reading Room. I eventually understood him to be saying that he was returning the magazines and books, but he had wanted to see me to thank me. In fact, he wanted to thank me by taking me to the pictures, and I was tempted to accept.

I knew that my mother would go off her head if I, a married woman, as much as thought of going out with a foreigner and I did have a legitimate excuse not to go. 'I'm sorry, but this is my night for fire-watching.'

This was double Dutch to him, and I tried to explain while he accompanied me down to the office, but I knew he didn't understand. He had just taken my hand in his to say goodbye when Hazel came round the corner, her eyes popping as she watched him walking away.

'Who's he? Oh boy, I could go for a gorgeous hunk like that, Doris, and you don't need him. You've got a man already.'

Despite this being so, I must admit that I did wish I hadn't been duty-bound that night, but, on the other hand, I felt proud of myself for refusing him.

Hazel kept on asking me about him that night, and I was telling her as much as I knew when we heard a low whistle coming from the street below. We both ran to the window, defying the blackout regulations by opening the wooden louvered blinds to look out, and there he was, looking up and smiling his thrilling, heart-stopping smile.

'We can't let him in,' I told Hazel. 'What would Mrs Logan say?'

''I don't think she can say anything,' Hazel laughed, desperate to get to know him. 'Anyway, she doesn't need to know.'

He was very quiet when I took him up, and she did most of the talking, but I was conscious of Fridjof's eyes on me . . . too conscious, as Hazel told me after he had left. Before going, he said, shyly, 'You come wiss me tomorrow, Dorees?'

He had obviously learned some new words, but . . . 'Oh. No, I can't. I'm sorry. I should have told you before. I'm married.'

'Yes? You can come?'

'I can't. Don't you understand?' I pointed to my wedding ring, but oh, how I wanted to go. How could I, though? Anybody could see me.

It was Hazel, bless her, who settled it. 'Of course she'll go out with you,' she told Fridjof, then turned to me. 'Don't be so daft. Who's going to know?'

I went to the pictures with him the following evening. I also went with him to the room in Forest Road that he had booked for the night. I salved my conscience by assuring myself that it was on my way home and he was only being friendly. As it was, we sat closely together on the bed, we cuddled a little, we kissed a little . . . and then I forced myself to break away. I wasn't an innocent young girl any longer; I knew what this could lead to.

Fridjof saw me home, it wasn't far, and I could understand from his expression that he was letting me know in his own tongue how sorry he was that he wouldn't see me again. He had been ordered to join another ship the following day. I, too, was sorry, but it was probably – most definitely – better this way.

It was some time later before I realised how foolish, and how lucky, I'd been. In that situation, most young men would have tried, and likely succeeded, to overcome the girl and taken their pleasure. I'd heard other girls saying that foreigners were out for all they could get and were never heard from again. Fridjof, however, had proved that he wasn't like that, and although I never heard from him again, I never completely forgot him.

Although Douglas Mackay was now in the Middle East, he still wrote to me. Tommy Duffus, though, had married a girl he met in the south of England and I never saw or heard from him again. Doug Paul (Uncle Doug) was living with his in-laws in King Street and we didn't see much of him after his father died. It was only Jimmy, then, who was a regular visitor, at around three-monthly intervals. We still corresponded, but there were no more walks or outings. That would have been asking for trouble.

Sandy was at sea for long periods at a time, but he also had quite long spells at home, and we sometimes had a week or two in Portgordon with his parents, who were much older than my mother. Old John Thain, over seventy, had been a sailmaker, and I got on very well with him. He was a couthy man with a droll kind of humour, and he seemed to like me, too. His wife, I don't think I ever heard her first name, was anything but couthy. She had no teeth, so her mouth always seemed to be set in disapproval. She was fairly tall, well-built and walked with a straight back, lashed into her corsets, no doubt. The fisher style of life was different from what I'd been used to, and I never felt fully at ease there.

The Sabbath was a complete day of rest. No work of any kind was done. Sunday dinner had to be prepared the day before, usually a big pot of some kind of soup, often Cullen Skink, a delicacy made with smoked haddock, milk and potatoes.

Although I knew deep down that I still loved Jimmy, I never once thought of separating from my husband. That would have caused a proper scandal.

Life went on through 1943. One mundane day after another, only lightened by my evenings out with Hazel and the likelihood of being taken home by a young man I wasn't particularly taken with and who wasn't particularly taken with me.

They were brief, platonic relationships in the main, sometimes with just a goodbye kiss, sometimes, thankfully, not even that, but there were one or two who got a bit fresh and could be stopped with a slap on the hand. There was also the odd one who wouldn't take no for an answer, and it was quite a struggle to get free.

Things never went further than that, so I suppose I should have counted myself lucky.

With no young men needing lodgings any more, my mother turned to older men – travellers for commodities sold by nationwide firms, or representatives of various companies, in Aberdeen to check on branches in the area. Dealing with a class above the mechanics, lorry drivers and young clerks, she no longer referred to her lodgers. They were boarders now, or paying guests, but they were quite happy with the facilities she had to offer . . . and the food. Give Mum her due, she was a good cook.

However, it became more and more difficult to find boarders, and they usually only stayed for a week or two at the most and the next thing I knew was that there were four strapping land girls in the house.

They were like a breath of fresh air to me, but a headache for my mother. She had to try to remove make-up and nail varnish from mirrors and bedroom furniture, even from the mats and congoleum on the floors. They were a jolly lot, though and provided lots of fresh vegetables and, even more welcome since they were scarcely available in the cities, eggs.

Breakfasts and teas were accompanied by tales of boyfriends, good and bad, and I avidly listened to what 'he' had said and done the evening before. They were certainly not shy, and some of their accounts left nothing to the imagination. That shocked their landlady but I found it fascinating. I was even a touch jealous that my 'love life' had not been so exciting. If I remember correctly, only one romance was still blossoming when they left, a few months later.

Mum said she wasn't going to take females again. They were too messy.

MOTHERHOOD …

10

Aberdeen's worst raid came in the summer of 1943. It started when dozens of bombers came across the North Sea from Norway, sweeping into the city like a plague of locusts. It was around 9 p.m., still dusk as they took different directions to wreak most havoc. Almost every area was affected, churches, schools, hospitals and, of course, large numbers of houses left in ruins.

Even St Peter's Cemetery, where Granda Forsyth and Uncle Billy were buried, was hit. Doug and his wife lived in King Street, not far from St Peter's, and I can remember Reta telling me that they had been to the cinema and had just gone into the lobby of their tenement building when one of the bombs exploded almost on the doorstep. When they looked out – the door had been blown off its hinges – they saw that bits of tram rails had landed on the tops of the houses at the other side of the street. In her parents' top floor flat, a hole had been made in the roof, probably from similar debris falling there.

Damage was done throughout the entire city, and hundreds of people were killed or wounded in that one night. Because no other attacks had been on anything like this scale before, I had often ignored an alert if I was already in bed, but this taught me not to be so blasé.

I had been even more foolish on one occasion about a year or so earlier. The siren had sounded early in the evening, and we listened for about half an hour to the distant thuds of bombs, as we usually did. None of the enemy planes would waste their ammunition on Mid Stocket; there was nothing of any importance near us at all. So we were extremely taken aback when the noises came nearer . . . and nearer. We could hear the bombs whistling down in quick succession, one very close before the noise grew fainter. Strangely, there was no explosion from 'our' one, so we presumed that it had been a dud.

Granda, who had been taking his life in his hands by standing outside smoking his pipe, poked his head round the living room door when everything was silent again. 'I'm gaun ower to see where that closest ane landed. 'Twas jist ower the road.'

Granny, this was just a few months before she died, went mad at him, and did manage to persuade him to wait until the following day. And so, after breakfast, he took Bertha and me across the road, through the gate into the nearest field but we could see nothing. Positive that he hadn't been wrong – he was a quiet but very determined man – Granda took us into the next field, and there, sure enough, was a huge crater. The bomb had sunk into the newly ploughed soil without exploding.

I suppose we three were lucky in our foolhardiness as there could quite easily have been a tragedy, and a bomb disposal squad was soon on the scene to defuse it. Following the path of the bombs, all of which had exploded except 'ours', the experts were able to state that the target had actually been Foresterhill Hospital, not that far from us as the crow (or a bomber) flies.

Foresterhill Hospital was built to replace Woolmanhill, the old Infirmary in the centre of town. The new site was chosen to allow for expansion and was to be something of a showpiece. So modern and innovative, in fact, that the king himself, Edward VIII, was asked to open it in the summer of 1936 – a new king, before his coronation, to be forever associated with the new hospital.

Edward, however, declined the honour on the grounds that he had a previous engagement, and the then Duke and Duchess of York performed the duty. Imagine the resentment felt by all residents of the city when it came out that the king had actually been in Aberdeen that day to meet Mrs Simpson at the Joint Station and take her to Balmoral. I know that I, who had practically worshipped the man before, went right off him then. I felt no sympathy when he had to abdicate. He wasn't fit to be a king, anyway. On the other hand, I admired the Duke of York, a man I had hardly heard of (I was only fourteen) for stepping into the breach that day. What's more, he turned out to be the perfect king, especially for a Britain at war.

Fast forward again to a little later in 1943. Life went on with Sandy coming home very occasionally and Jimmy putting in an appearance more often; only now, with Granny and Granda both gone, there was no one to encourage me to go out with him – the exact opposite, in fact. My mother made sure that we were never on our own; she even came to the door with us when he left.

It was into December before I knew for sure that I was pregnant – legitimately. I had not been unfaithful to my husband and we'd been married for over a year. I was only allowed to work until the fourth month, then Miss Murray hinted that I ought to leave . . . for my own health, of course. The thing was, in those days, it wasn't seemly for girls in that condition to be flaunting themselves in public. Mum, around the same age as Miss Murray, was in full agreement with her, and so I had to leave Van den Berghs. No more firewatching. No more going out with Hazel or Peggy or . . . anybody else, especially not boys.

I didn't really need the money, I got quite a decent allowance through the Ben Line, but I did miss the freedom (such as it had been). My only companion when I ventured out now was my mother.

To hide my broadening figure, I bought a 'huggy' coat, a silver grey plush fabric, something like fake fur, but not meant to look realistic. It was perfect in the cold weather, not too bad through spring, but in June, even warmer than usual, it was absolutely suffocating. In addition to how I felt, I must have looked like an elephant in a sheep's fleece stretched to its utmost.

To make things worse, there was no 'bringing on' a birth in those days. The infant would come out when it was ready. Well, this infant took a jolly long time to be ready, and it was three weeks past the given date before Sheila emerged – three long weeks during which I was practically sewn into that huggy coat. I wasn't even allowed to go into the garden without it . . . in case the neighbours saw me.

My husband had insisted on booking me into a private nursing home – money no object? – and I was in there for two whole weeks. At that time, women were meant to remain in bed for at least seven days before being allowed up for short intervals that increased gradually for the next seven days. To be honest, though, I'm not sure if this was general practice or only in that nursing home. After all, at £100 per week the longer they kept you the better for them. Being treated like a lady was very nice, so I didn't complain at all.

We were between boarders when I went into hospital, but I was to get quite a surprise when I went home. I had better give you the story of how this came about.

A battalion of the Royal Artillery that had been in Malta all through the siege had been given one week's leave when it ended. Sergeant Albert Rees, however, felt that one week in Carmarthan with his wife after being away for so long was not enough, so, when they were posted to our Torry Battery for a respite, he asked his CO if it would be possible for him to take her to Aberdeen for a couple of weeks. Told that it would be fine as long as he found lodgings for her, Albert asked a man standing next to him in a pub one night if he knew of anyone who might take her.

He had approached the right person, the postman for our part of Mid Stocket. The man gave him Mum's name and street number then added, 'Mrs Forsyth used to take lodgers, but I'm not sure if she still does.'

Albert told me the next part of the story himself, as he always regarded it as extremely funny. He had rung our doorbell and put his request very politely to the lady of the house (he *was* a proper gentleman), but when she didn't answer him straightaway, he felt rather apprehensive.

Then she said, somewhat curtly, he thought, 'Are you English?'

Guessing that she must have had trouble with an Englishman at some point, or more than one, neither of which was the case, he smiled, 'No, we're Welsh.'

She obviously relaxed. 'That's all right, then.'

Albert and Eiddwen were in the house when I took home my baby, and they practically took her over. They had been longing to start a family, but it was to be many years before we got the ecstatic letter that their dream was about to come true.

As it happened, Eiddwen didn't stay with us for two weeks; she stayed for well over a year, although she only saw Albert when he was off duty. She wasn't much older than I was, and we became as close as sisters – closer than I was to Bertha at that time, for she was still at school. Eiddwen would come shopping with me in Rosemount, quite a distance to walk with a pram, and a real struggle coming back up, so it was good to have someone to take turns. We chatted to each other on those outings, although Eiddwen could speak very little English and I knew no Welsh. Bertha and I did eventually learn one or two Welsh songs from Albert, and a few Welsh phrases, but she remembers more than I do.

Eiddwen learned a bit of English and Scots, but there was one word that she could never get right. When my Auntie Ina was visiting, she often said, 'Give me the bairn for a wee while', and the Welsh lass was determined to air her knowledge. Her attempt misfired, delighting everybody, and Sheila was henceforth known as the 'brain'.

One day, Eiddwen asked me why my mother didn't like English people, and I had to tell her about the failing that many Scots had. There was no special reason for it, it seemed to be an inborn dislike, especially in older people, maybe a hark back to the countless battles between the two countries, culminating in our defeat by the English at Flodden, and followed long afterwards by their victory over Bonnie Prince Charlie and the Jacobites at Culloden.

Albert amazed Mum and me on the first Sunday morning he was in the house by volunteering to take the baby out for a walk. When I started to make the carriage-hung pram ready, he said, 'No, no, just give me her shawl.'

This was a product of my mother's knitting, beautifully lacy, done on fine needles with two-ply Shetland Floss, and was large enough to wrap round his shoulders as well as the infant. Thus adorned, he sallied forth in his shirt sleeves, into an area where such a thing was unheard of, was actually looked upon as something only the hoi polloi would do. It was also something that the child's own father would never have done. He never as much as took her out in the pram when he was at home, come to think of it.

Albert was a beautiful pianist – he played the organ back home in the Bethesda Chapel – and both he and his wife had lovely singing voices, so we had many musical evenings, which were repeated when they returned three years after the war for a holiday.

I may as well relate a far more recent little incident here that made a great impression on me. We hadn't seen Albert and Eiddwen for well over twenty years when we paid them an overnight visit in Cross Hands one July on our way to see Sheila and her husband in Surrey. The next morning, a Sunday, Albert, Eiddwen, their daughter Anne and Albert's brother (who turned up unexpectedly after breakfast) gathered round the piano to sing for us, hymns, anthems, operatic pieces, changing from one to the other with hardly a break. What made this even more enjoyable was that they each sang a different part – tenor, baritone, soprano and contralto, and we were surrounded by the soaring sound of a whole wonderful choir. It was truly a marvellous experience and we could have listened to them all day. As it was, we had to leave after two hours. We had promised Sheila that we'd be there in the afternoon – and we didn't want to miss her birthday.

We kept in touch with the Rees family by mail, and sometimes by phone but we didn't see them again for more than another twenty years, when we flew to Cardiff (via Belfast, would you believe, on a 29-seater) to celebrate Albert's eightieth birthday. We were accompanied by Bertha and her husband, Bill Jamieson, who had gone to see them several times, by motorcycle in the early years, later by car. It was quite an emotional reunion, reminiscing about their time in Aberdeen when we were all young. Next day, they took us to the house they shared then with Anne and her family. On that Sunday, it was only Albert who sang to us, as Eiddwen was not in very great health. Sadly both have both passed on since then.

I seem to jump back and forth like a flech (a flea with a kilt), or, as my Granny might have said, 'Like a hen on a hot girdle', and now I must return to 1944, again. Sheila didn't see her father often – he was on several long dangerous missions, and Jimmy had gone across the Channel on D Day plus 4 (I didn't know the exact day until years later), so I couldn't help worrying quite a bit about both.

This was made all the worse by receiving no mail. Sandy had never been a prolific letter writer – I took it for granted that he'd been kept too busy while they were at sea – but Jimmy's letters had come regularly when he was in Shetland, Yorkshire and even Brighton, where they trained for the invasion. He had often said he wished he could be sent abroad, and now he'd got his wish and he was in the heart of the fighting. When would he have time to write?

I occupied the long days by keeping my two rooms clean. After Albert and Eiddwen left, Mum had let Sandy and me have the lounge as a sitting room and the back bedroom, which was like having our own little flat. That worked very well when Sandy was away. I paid a rent for the two rooms, and board for my meals. When Sandy came home, of course, I wanted to make our meals, and as is often the way, two women in one scullery (as we called a kitchen then) spelled constant strife. And there was constant bickering between Mum and me. I realise now that I was selfish, expecting everything to be done for my convenience. I can't remember ever taking a turn at cleaning the bathroom or the scullery, which I really should have done, and I was annoyed when my mother nagged at me about niggly little things. The resentment built up between us until I decided I'd have to move out altogether.

Finding a house was absolutely impossible, but I eventually heard of a room to let in a house not very far from Mid Stocket. It was empty, so I had the pleasurable task of furnishing it. Furniture wasn't rationed but it was cheaply made and marked with a double, blocked-in 'C', the 'Utility' mark. Everything was 'Utility' then, even the sheets and blankets, everything you could think of. Having plenty of money at my disposal now, I didn't even think of buying anything secondhand. Limited for space, I purchased two chunky armchairs covered in brown Rexine, a small dining table, two upright chairs, a double bed and a small bed for Sheila.

Next to my room at the top of the stairs was a fair-sized walk-in cupboard that I was allowed to use. It served as a scullery (I'd to fetch the water from a tap outside), as a larder, as a sideboard to keep my dishes and cutlery, as a place to keep towels and spare bedding. It was also where I had to cook, on a double gas ring. When I think back on it, it was a dangerous set-up in such a confined space.

Although Mum hadn't been too happy about me moving out, we were still on friendly enough terms, so I went to visit her quite often. Two of her prewar lodgers had come back by this time, Johnny Elphinstone and . . . Jimmy Davidson, and I was quite glad that I wasn't living there any longer. It would have been awkward to see him every day.

Sandy was still in the Merchant Navy, his peacetime job as well as wartime, and we only saw him between trips. I should have realised that this was building up to another dangerous situation.

… DIVORCE

11

If I thought that living with my mother was bad, I found that living in a strange woman's house was much worse. I don't suppose Mrs Campbell (I'll call her that) was actually picking on me – it could have just been her way – but she seemed to be constantly reprimanding me for something. I would need to remember that she needed to use the washing line sometimes, as well as me. She didn't need her afternoon rest disturbed by my daughter making a noise. Would I please be careful of her linoleum when I was carrying heavy things up or down the stairs? And so on.

I couldn't really see what she had to complain about. I had to wash quite a lot; children could get dirty in five minutes, especially when they were outside making sand pies in the plot of earth she was allowed to play in. My daughter was very well behaved . . . as a rule. I was always careful of her linoleum, and her wallpaper when I was going up and down the stairs. Of course, I was still in my early twenties, and it wasn't until I was much older and had a house of my own that I could see her point . . . and my mother's. At that time, however, I took Sheila out as much as I could, for there were many lovely walks in the vicinity.

I often landed up at Mid Stocket. I didn't admit to my mother that I didn't enjoy living away from home, but it was good to have two young men to talk to. Both Johnny and Jimmy must have realised how unhappy I was. Johnny had bought a motorbike and came across one night to take me for a spin. Sheila was sleeping and she never woke up in the evenings, so I asked Mrs Campbell if she would mind listening for her. To my astonishment, she gave a smiling nod.

I believe now that this was actually the start of my slide downhill. Tearing along the country roads at 50 or 60 miles per hour, with my hair streaming out behind me and my skirts blowing up over my knees – I hadn't yet taken to wearing trousers – was a taste of freedom I'd never experienced before. It never entered my head that I shouldn't be doing such a thing, that my husband probably wouldn't like it . . . or if it did, I ignored it.

I rode on the pillion several times before Sandy came home for almost two months and unknowingly stopped that pleasure . . . any pleasure I had in the little nest I'd made. He wasn't happy with the room, he wasn't happy if I asked him to look after Sheila while I went to the shops, or did a washing. This was a most complicated business anyway. I'd to bring up a pail of water, boil it on the Primus and rub the dirtier items between my knuckles until I was satisfied that they were clean. Then it was a case of wringing by hands, going down to empty the basin in the outside drain and filling it with clean cold water for the rinsing.

This process had to be repeated three or four times until everything was hanging on the line. Sometimes, when white towels still had stains, I laid them flat on the grass still dripping with soapy water. This usually took out stains, particularly if it was sunny, and it was safer than using bleach, a hint picked up from my mother with regard to nappies.

My suspicions that Sandy wasn't the fatherly type proved well founded. As soon as he decently could after breakfast, he was off on some excuse or other, dressed in one of the light-coloured suits he favoured, which made him stand out from the usual navy blues, parson greys and browns other men wore. I'm quite sure that he wasn't involved with another woman, but he did like to meet people, to go into a bar and chat with other men, to go into a café and have a laugh with the waitresses. I resented being left alone so much. After all, I was on my own with our daughter when he was at sea, and I felt that he should take over some of the responsibility when he was at home.

Storm clouds were gathering. I was now at a stage where, like Rhett Butler, I didn't give a damn. Why should I sit in every evening, knitting, sewing, reading or listening to the wireless, when my husband hadn't taken me out once while he was home?

(Incidentally, I had gone to see *Gone With the Wind* by myself when I was eight months pregnant with Sheila – a marathon four-hour sit. Thank goodness there was an interval.)

When Jimmy started coming to see me, giving me books he knew I'd like to read, I welcomed him with open arms, figuratively speaking. I did wonder sometimes why Johnny had never come back – I missed the motorcycle runs – but I didn't care too much. And so things went on for some weeks.

The scene is set, isn't it? A small room, a little girl asleep in her crib, a double bed and a young man and woman trying not to show how they felt about each other. At first, we did sit in the armchairs and discuss books we'd enjoyed reading and it was just a goodbye kiss at the door. That couldn't last, of course.

Books were forgotten eventually. The kisses began when he came in and things just built up without us as much as thinking that what we were doing was wrong. Very, very wrong. As wrong as it could possibly be.

Nemesis had to come. Jimmy had told Johnny the first time he came to see me, which was why the motorcycle runs stopped, then he foolishly confided that we loved each other. Johnny was well known as a ladies' man, so this news hadn't really upset him, but his pride probably got a knock. Whatever prompted it, he 'clyped' to my mother; told her exactly what was going on and sat back to watch the fireworks.

I needn't go into great detail. Mum had a blazing row with Jimmy and told him to leave her house. Then she came to tell me what she thought of my 'carry-ons', and forbade me to see Jimmy again. Also, she said she would tell Sandy the minute he came home. Which she did.

I should have been ashamed of myself when my husband confronted me, but I wasn't. I was sorry I'd hurt him – I hadn't planned it, it had just happened; the usual excuse, I suppose – but that was us finished.

I don't like re-living that horrible time. I know I had only myself to blame for being in such a situation, but it's easy to be wise after the event. In any case, I don't think my marriage to Sandy would have lasted very long anyway. We weren't really suited and we didn't have the same interests; he was a born bachelor, finicky, moody and only used to mixing with his own kind of people. I was inclined the other way; I could, with my usual gift of the gab, hold a conversation with anybody. It was better that we split up then than go on until we came to hate each other.

I didn't know until my mother told me later that Sandy had gone back to Mid Stocket and told her what he thought of me. I was all that was bad; a whore enticing men to come to bed with me, but I needn't think I'd get away with it. He would never give me a divorce. Jimmy Davidson would never be able to marry me, though he waited till his hair was white as snow and he'd a beard right down to his feet. I think this is what tempered Mum's anger at me . . . a little bit.

Really upset after she told me what had happened, I still had to face up to everything. My allowance was stopped. Even when Mum and Auntie Ina both told me I should write to the Ben Line and claim something for Sheila, I wouldn't. I had hurt Sandy enough already, and in view of what he'd said about me, I wanted nothing more to do with him.

The thing was, how would I exist with not a brass farthing coming in? Because I'd never been in a position, before I married, to buy more than the necessities of clothing, I had spent more than I should – not a fortune, by any means, just too much. I had made sure that Sheila had the best of everything, shopping mainly in better-class shops, with the result that I had saved very little. There was nothing to do but climb down and crawl back to my mother. I sold all my furniture and household items for £100, which would keep me going until I found a job. Mum was willing to look after four-year-old Sheila to let me go out to work . . . and she could also make sure that Jimmy and I had nothing more to do with each other.

Fate, however, still had something up its sleeve with which to clobber me. Some months earlier, the doctor had informed Woodend Hospital that I needed a D and C, and the appointment they sent was for the week after I moved back home. That was all right, Sheila would be well looked after, so I went in without a qualm.

The examination took place the day before the operation, and imagine how I felt when they told me they couldn't operate because I was pregnant. The doctors and nurses saw nothing strange about this, I was a married woman and pregnancy was only to be expected.

BUT! This pregnancy hadn't been expected, and Mum and Auntie Ina were coming to visit me the next afternoon, supposedly after the deed had been done. It was a different deed that had already been done though, and I couldn't sleep for worrying over how to break the news to them. When I tearfully told them, afraid and ashamed, their shocked expressions, the way their eyes darkened and their mouths pursed up told me to prepare myself for a tongue lashing such as I'd never had in my life before.

It probably wasn't a good thing that they were forced to bottle up their anger in the hospital and in the street on the way home, for it kept building up. The explosion was therefore all the greater when we went into the house, and I think I had better draw a veil over what was said. It's not something I want to resurrect. I can still feel the deep burning shame that I felt then.

*

I had the worry now of not being able to take a job, and it was a worry with no money coming in. I had to do something. Even though I was terrified of what the doctor would say – Dr Agnes would have torn a strip off me and sent me away with a flea in my ear, but she had died a year or so before – I forced myself to go and tell him my predicament. He listened, handing me a hankie to staunch my tears, then told me to go back to the waiting room and sit until all his patients had gone.

For those who don't remember, or are not old enough to know how it used to be, there was no system to let people know whose turn it was. Patients came in and sat down, and if you were smart, you counted how many were in front of you and made a mental note of their faces. Then, when the last of them was called in, you knew you were next. If you didn't pay proper attention, some unscrupulous person who came in after you would jump the queue. The point is, of course, that there wasn't a queue. You sat down anywhere in the room and had to keep your wits about you.

There were honest people too, of course, who said, 'I think it's your turn now', or 'You were before me', and that was how it was that night. Two people at different times tried to tell me it was my turn, and I had to say that the doctor told me to wait till last. I sincerely hoped that neither of them realised why.

I had been there, the second time, for about half an hour, when I finally went though to the surgery. The doctor said, 'I shouldn't really do this you know.'

I knew it was against the law to perform an abortion, but I thought that this only applied to unqualified people, back-street quacks, not real doctors.

Noticing my bewilderment, he smiled. 'It's frowned on because it's dangerous, you see.' Then he told me to lie down on the couch. I don't know exactly what he did, but it was a few days later before the foetus came away.

Although Jimmy had gone, Johnny was still at Mid Stocket Road and made things quite awkward for me by giving me sly glances as if to say, 'I know what you've been up to.'

To get away for a spell, I took Sheila to London for a holiday, paying for only one ticket because children under four could travel free, and I assured myself that it would be all right. How could they tell I was lying if I said she was still within the age limit?

The ticket collector in King's Cross would never have picked up on it if my own daughter hadn't spilt the beans. I answered his query, 'How old is the little girl?' by saying, 'She's only three.'

Sheila, bless her little cotton socks, beamed at him proudly, 'No, I'm four.'

I looked the man straight in the eye. 'She means she'll be four on her next birthday.' He accepted that. He wasn't to know that her next birthday was not for another 345 days, when she would be five, not four. He did, however, have the hint of a twinkle in his eye as he waved us through.

The other little incident wasn't so nerve-wracking. In fact, it was quite funny. On the Sunday, Uncle Jim's children were making ready for Sunday School when Auntie Gwen said, 'Why don't you take little Sheila with you, Jean?'

I don't think Jean was very pleased, but Sheila was determined to go. When they came home, however, Jean was hopping mad. 'I'm not taking her with me again! D'you know what she did?'

'Not until you tell us, dear,' her mother smiled.

'When we stood up to sing our first hymn, she sang, too.'

'What was wrong with that?'

'She didn't know any of the words.'

This made me guess what was coming, but I waited to be told.

'She sang a different song. Stone Cold Dead in de Market! I could have died!'

I had to explain that this was the song Sheila had taken a fancy to since she'd heard it on the wireless, but the words weren't exactly suitable for church, because the last line went, 'She killed nobody but her husband.' Mind you, I don't remember any more of it, but in spite of Jean's mortified expression, we adults couldn't help laughing.

Our return journey was made with no query as to my daughter's age.

It must have been well on in 1948 when I started as a clerkess in McDonald's Garage in Craigie Loanings, an offshoot of the Scottish Co-operative Wholesale Society. The SCWS also had a Funeral Under-taker's business in Bon Accord Street under the name of Campbell's Motors, supplying extra funeral cars when needed. Apart from McDonald's being a garage with mechanics and petrol pumps, there was a large area of parking spaces to let out. There were very few private garages in the area, the houses (of silvery grey granite) had been built before the advent of motor cars. We also ran quite a good taxi service – Rolls Royces and large Austins for weddings and funerals as well as ordinary run-of-the-mill hires.

Because the garage was open all day every day (24/7 as they say nowadays) there was a night clerk who took over from me at 6 p.m. and handed back to me at nine the following morning. It didn't register with me then that he worked a fifteen-hour shift to my twelve (less dinner hour and a half), but I expect he got a higher rate of pay. Our salaries were paid directly into the bank from Head Office in Glasgow, so I don't know how his compared with mine. I wouldn't have cared whatever it was, for I didn't envy him working through the night, often on his own in the vast garage empty of other human beings.

Petrol was still rationed then, and being short when I counted the coupons at the end of the day was devastating. It was actually far worse than being short in the money tally. Several customers, even regulars such as businessmen, tried to cheat us, and occasionally succeeded. They would engage me, or whoever was on the desk, in conversation while John the garage-man was filling their tanks, maybe take us out to see a new car they'd purchased, then jump in and drive away without handing over the required amount of coupons. Their petrol would probably have been charged to an account, and there was really no way of proving their guilt.

I can remember many times when Ian helped me to check my sales, and when I helped him to check his, trying to match the vehicle numbers on the coupons to the customers who had charged off. There was even one teatime when we were so engaged and a doctor came in to park his car. Dr Fraser (not his real name) always came in for a wee chat, and when he saw us feverishly engaged in checking petrol coupons, he said, 'Are you short, Ginger?' He always called me that although I considered my hair to be chestnut or auburn, not ginger.

But I was never angry about it. He came to my rescue, and Ian's, more than once by telling us to take what we needed from the supply that he'd 'banked' with us. Doctors were allowed much more fuel than ordinary people, and he sometimes didn't use all his in the time allowed.

Dr Fraser featured in a humorous incident early one New Year's Day. Hogmanay was the busiest night of the year for taxis and I was asked to work on until the pressure eased off. It was three in the morning before Ian and I were able to stand back and draw an easy breath. The phone had been ringing continuously and there had been a steady stream of people walking in looking for a taxi, as well as motorists coming in for petrol. No law against drink-driving in those days.

Waiting for a taxi to take me home was like waiting for it to rain pound notes. I had given up hope and was about to hoof it all the way up Mid Stocket when Dr Fraser bounded in. 'My God, Ginger!' he exclaimed when he saw me. 'What the bloody hell are you doing here at this time of night?'

It was almost half past three by this time, so when he learned of my predicament he said, 'I'll take you home . . . as long as it's not too far.'

I ought to have recognised the signs, but I was dog tired, so I got into his car and off he drove – up the little bit of Craigie Loanings, along Westfield Terrace and across the ragged junction at Mile End into Mid Stocket. That took longer to type than it took the good doctor to drive. He could have been on a racetrack, the speed he was going, and it was lucky that we met no other drivers under the influence. The Stocket is a long, almost straight hill, so we shot up there like a bullet from a gun until we reached the part where a small road goes off at the side to a row of three old, low houses. This was likely the original road, before it was straightened out.

This was when I recognised how inebriated he was. Slowing down only a little, he drove into this side road, then – and this is not one word of a lie – he wove in and out of the trees that separated him from the road he should have been on. Back where he should be, we had only to pass the Lovers' Lane and Oakbank School (a reformatory) and I was home. I told him when to stop and I got out of the car on shaky legs, well aware now that I was very fortunate to still be in one piece.

It was two days before I saw Dr Fraser again. He slouched into the office from the street door just after midday, nothing like his usual bouncy self, and bent over the counter to rest his head on his arms. 'Christ, Ginger, I feel bad.'

Guessing that he was suffering from a hangover, he'd likely been drinking since I saw him last, I said, sympathetically, 'I hope you didn't catch the cold when you took me home the other night.'

His head lifted a little, and he looked at me with bleary eyes. 'Did I take you home? I can't remember.'

'You did, and I was really grateful. You saved me having to hike up the hill in the pitch dark on my own.' I have never lost my fear of the dark.

He was frowning now, apparently dredging his memory. 'I've been having this queer picture of me driving through trees – like I was going in and out the dusty bluebells. Would that be right?'

'Yes, just after Richmondhill Road there are three old houses . . .'

'On a side road. Was that where I was . . .those trees?'

I couldn't help giggling at him. 'You shouldn't be working today. You should be in bed.'

Another groan. 'I'm just out of my bloody bed, Ginger. There's nothing wrong with me that a nip of whisky wouldn't put right . . .' He broke off, shaking his head.

'No, I couldn't even face a hair of the dog that bit me. I was paralytic last night, and the night before, but never again. I swear to you, Ginger, never again.'

He heaved himself up as nearly erect as he could. 'I'd better go and get the jalopy out. I've patients to attend to, and I can diagnose just as well drunk as sober.'

'You're not fit to attend . . .' I began but he was on his way into the garage. I opened the hatch into the washing bay where one of the drivers was hosing down his Rolls. 'Bill, get round and stop Dr Fraser from taking his car out. He says he's got to attend to his patients, but he can hardly stand, he's so drunk.'

Fortunately, Bill was able to persuade him to get in the passenger seat to be driven home, and it was another two days before he came in again, stone-cold sober.

There was one mechanic in the garage and one apprentice, as well as six drivers and a garageman, and Ian, of course, so I was the only female among all those men. Most of them teased me, but not one made any advances, for which I suppose I should have counted myself lucky. The thing was, we all got on very well together. Then Mr Thomson engaged another girl for the office. Kathleen was a great help, a cheery well-built girl who also had the gift of the gab, and we became really good friends.

When Jimmy Balfour offered to teach her to drive, she talked him into giving me lessons as well. He had an old Morris, with the starter button on the floor, and I never felt easy with it. It became the routine that I drove myself home and Kathleen then drove herself home . . . to Rosemount Place. I was a nervous wreck each time I'd to take the wheel, but Kathleen wasted no time before she applied to sit a test. The day before she was due to try, Jimmy B. asked me if I would mind letting her drive me home as well, and on the way up the hill, he barked at her to stop.

This 'emergency stop' almost had my head going through the soft roof and Jimmy B. flying through the windscreen. Then, as my house was also on a side road apart from the main thoroughfare (another part of the original road), he told her to go in from the upper end and face downhill. This meant that she had to manoeuvre the small car round a hairpin bend, and both her passengers had their hearts in their mouths when she almost didn't make it, stopping within half an inch of a low garden wall – a neigbour's, not ours. There had originally been railings on top, but they had all been removed to make munitions during the war. The promise to replace them when the war was over was never kept.

Despite those near mishaps, Kathleen sailed through her driving test, while I decided to put an end to the lessons that scared me out of my wits . . . and, I'm sure, had the same effect on Jimmy B. As a matter of interest, he emigrated to Australia not long after that. Two mechanics were taken on in his place, coincidentally both called Bob, and then, to replace Kathleen, who found a job with better pay, another two girls, Annie and Priscilla, known as Pat. In our teabreak one morning, I discovered that Annie's father knew most of the Forsyths and wanted to meet me.

I was invited to her home for tea, a quaint, round, little building that had once been the lodge to Woodside House. It turned out that her dad had practically been brought up by my father's sister Maggie, and I became a regular visitor there, with Sheila.

Bob C. had taken a shine to Priscilla, and I went out with Bob W. several times, but he, strangely enough, also emigrated to Australia. Why was it that men couldn't seem to get far enough away from me?

The hectic pressure of work at McDonald's was beginning to tell on me, even with two girls to help, so I applied for a job in Cordiner's Garage on North Esplanade West, where I started early in 1952. This was much farther away from home and I had quite a long walk from the bus – down Bridge Street, College Street and South College Street, then under the arches of the railway line to emerge onto the Esplanade itself, a beautiful wide street alongside the River Dee. There was only one other girl in the office and although she was younger than I was, we settled into a friendly, easy relationship. There was only the garage to worry about, no taxis, and we sometimes spent time looking out on to the river, even going outside to watch the university boat crews practising in the sunshine.

There was one blot on the landscape, however . . . isn't there always? Most of the businesses near us were fish-curing yards, and you had to watch your step because of the fish 'bree' sloshing about on the pavements. Not only that, in the summer especially, the stench was terrible. But, like everything else, you got used to it after a while, and the fish girls were a cheery lot.

Irene lived in Torry – once a fishing village on its own separated from the city by the Dee – and she often asked me to walk along to the Victoria Bridge with her, for company really, but as she put it, 'Just for a laugh.' It meant that I had much farther to go to catch my bus – along South Market Street, passing Jamieson's Quay where I had worked at one time, and up the steep hill of Market Street, but I didn't mind. It was good exercise for me.

I'd been working on the Esplanade for almost a year when I had the biggest (and best) surprise that I could ever have had. A solicitor's letter informed me that my husband had applied for a divorce and that the hearing was set for such-and-such a day in Edinburgh. I did not need to attend unless I wanted to contest it. Contest? Why should I want to contest it when it was what I'd been longing for since 1947, the action that Sandy had sworn he would never take. (It transpired that he had met someone else – someone he wanted to marry.)

The big day came a month or so later; the wonderful day when I received the actual notification that I was free. The final decree, because there is, or was at that time in Scotland, no *decree nisi* to come first. I floated on air down the long slope to work that day, and went into the office waving my piece of paper Chamberlain style, wishing that I could tell Jimmy there and then, but suddenly wondering if he, too, had met someone else by this time. The more I considered it, the more positive I became that he had, but there was no way of finding out. I had no idea where he was living.

Life carried on, but I wasn't interested in anything. What had I to look forward to now?

12

Whether or not Johnny Elphinstone felt guilty for the mayhem he had caused in our household – knowing him, I shouldn't think so – shortly afterwards he suddenly decided to emigrate to Australia. My mother had now to find two new lodgers. Placing an advert in the *Evening Express*, she was very lucky in the two young men she chose out of the many replies she received.

Alex and Raymond were trainee dispensing opticians. Clean-cut and well dressed, they were like a breath of fresh air after the strained atmosphere that had been hanging around us for so many weeks. They were nearer Bertha's age than mine and gave us ongoing accounts of the girls they met, why they asked certain of them out and whether or not they wanted to continue the relationship. Alex, from Dundee, very musical, joined the Lyric Opera Company, and although none of us were keen on opera, we thoroughly enjoyed their presentations of *The Bartered Bride* and *The Merry Wives of Windsor*.

He also played the trumpet, rather loud for our living room but we didn't mind. In fact, both Bertha and I made an attempt at playing it, but only succeeded in making horrible sounds that had Mum shouting, 'Stop that row this minute, before you burst my eardrums.'

Now I come to what can only be called a string of coincidences. It was June 1953, a time when the whole country was celebrating the Coronation of Queen Elizabeth (Second of England, but only First of Scotland). Then came Derby Day. I always had a wee flutter on this classic race and also the Grand National, the only two I bothered with, and had made my choice from reading one of the storemen's *Daily Record* racing page. To be sure that I wasn't too late, I took an earlier bus back to work so that I'd have time to go into the little newsagent in College Street to place my bet. The buses ran, I think, every fifteen minutes, so I was allowing myself plenty of time. The man looked at me in a pitying way when I told him to put a shilling each way on Pinza – probably the favourite, though what did I know? – but he gave me the betting slip without saying a word.

'I'm sure this is going to be a lucky day for me,' I told him as I went out.

My business had only taken a minute or two, and it was a glorious summer day, so I ambled the rest of the way to work. It wasn't what anybody could describe as a perfect setting. College Street continues as South College Street, with a high wall on both sides; Pirie Appleton, Notepaper and Envelope Manufacturers, on the left, and the Gas Works on the right; something to do with gas, anyway . . . or electricity. I was astonished, but quite pleased, that there was so little traffic. As a rule, that stretch of road was very busy – leading to several fish yards and also to the Suspension Bridge over the Dee to Torry. (Less romantic than *Over the Sea to Skye*.)

Well, there I was, having a slow stroll on my own with nothing to distract me from my drab surroundings, when a small grey van came shooting through the arch. A small grey van? My interest was aroused. A Rubislaw grey van. It must be a William Tawse's van, the place where Jimmy worked. (I've never found out whether the firm called this colour Rubislaw Grey because their yard was in the Rubislaw area of the city, or because it was right next to Rubislaw Quarry, but it doesn't really matter, does it?)

These thoughts took a mere instant and I was delighted to see that the driver *was* Jimmy, so I waved my arms frantically to draw his attention. But things never work out that easily, do they? The small van flashed straight past me. My thumping heart took a nosedive as I turned away to continue my journey. Had he honestly not noticed me, or had he seen me and didn't want to speak to me? Had he found somebody else and got away from me as fast as he could?

So deep in despair was I that I didn't notice the movement at the other side of the street, and it wasn't until the vehicle door slammed that I looked up.

'Oh, Doris I'm sorry,' Jimmy gasped as he ran towards me. 'I was thinking about . . . oh, nothing important, and I was well past you before I looked in my rear view mirror. I couldn't see your face, but I was sure it was you, and I was scared you'd have gone out of sight under the arches and disappeared if I took time to turn round, so I reversed all the way back.'

Thus we stood, saying nothing else for a while, just drinking each other in as if we hadn't seen each other for twenty years – which it felt like, to be honest. Young people of today likely wouldn't understand why we didn't hug and kiss since we'd been apart for a such while, but hugging and kissing in the street was not done in those days, not even if there wasn't a soul in sight and there were high walls on both sides of you.

He did say, 'Why didn't you wait for me after I was called up?'

This question had never come up before. 'You never asked me to,' I hedged.

'I'd nothing to offer you. Not a thing. I was only twenty and . . . we were far too young. Besides, I didn't know what would happen. I might have been killed.'

'Thank heaven you weren't.'

We fell silent again, our emotions too ragged to let loose, but after a while, a clock in the distance struck three. 'I'll have to get back,' he said, 'or they'll be wondering where I am. I was sent to Cordiner's Garage to collect a radiator for a car we're working on, and they're waiting . . .'

'That's funny. I work in Cordiner's. It's my dinner hour, and I wouldn't have seen you if we hadn't . . .'

It turned out that he had been at the main branch in Menzies Road, so he wouldn't have seen me anyway. Then I recollected something I should have told him straight away, but I'd been so taken by surprise. 'Sandy *did* divorce me, after all. I got the notification months ago.'

He took my hand at long last. 'I wish I'd known, but . . .' He broke off with a long sigh, then brightened. 'D'you think we could make a go of it this time?'

Absolutely certain that we could (and we have) I arranged to meet him that evening, and giving my hand a long squeeze, he ran back to his van and roared off, while I took my time about covering the last few hundred yards I still had to go. I couldn't get over it. If I hadn't taken an earlier bus, if I hadn't spent that two or three minutes in the shop putting on a bet, if he hadn't been sent to Menzies Road and come across the Suspension Bridge at that particular time, we might never have seen each other again.

When I went into the office, Irene, the manager and all the garage staff were gathered round the small wireless set, and I was just in time to hear the result. Pinza had come in first. A foregone conclusion, really. Hadn't I known all along that this was my lucky day? My winnings couldn't have been more than a few pounds but, even so, they'd have been as much as my weekly pay.

Mum didn't seem all that surprised to hear my main news at teatime; she must have guessed that it would happen sooner or later. Jimmy was waiting for me on the outside road when I went out, probably a bit timid of coming to the door, and we walked up to the top of the hill, crossed the Ring Road and went along the Lang Stracht. The council had not long begun to build houses there, and what had once been a lovely country road would soon be the division between the vast housing estates of Mastrick – so named because the original owner of the land had traded with Maastricht in Holland – and the smaller Summerhill.

At this particular time, there were still some stretches of the dry-stane dykes enclosing the fields, still some secluded spots to sit and talk. Which we did! We talked and talked, about what had happened to us in the intervening years, of how we had felt when we had to stop seeing each other, of how ashamed we were at what we had done to cause the ban. We also vowed not to repeat it.

To prevent this, we started to plan ahead. What would have to be done? He said that he'd have to make peace with my mother, and prove that he had been serious about me. I said he would have to tell his folk, too; they might not be happy about him marrying a divorced woman with a nine-year-old daughter.

Then we discussed the financial side of things. He said he didn't want his wife to go out to work (this was frowned on, suggesting that the man couldn't earn enough), but I said that was silly. We would be glad of the money until we got on our feet.

When I went home and told Mum we were definitely going to marry, she said, as she had said about Sandy, 'He'll have to come and ask for my permission first.'

I was just a couple of weeks short of my thirty-first birthday, but I didn't want to throw a spanner in the works by denying her that privilege, old-fashioned and uncalled for though it was.

On my first visit to Laurencekirk to meet his father and the aunt who had brought him up – his mother had died giving him birth – I was amazed at how much older they were than my fifty-five year old mother. Auntie Ann, the elder, was over eighty, had once been a tailoress but had given it up to look after her brother's two children. Daniel was almost seventy and had worked in a linoleum factory in Kirkcaldy until his wife died in November 1919. That was when he had given up his job and his house and returned to his childhood home. He was a very quiet man and I never really found out anything about him.

Auntie Ann reminded me of my beloved Granny, the same couthy way about her, the same aversion to hurting people. She welcomed both Sheila and me into her house, and said how pleased she was that Jimmy was getting married at last. It was clear that she had always looked on him as her blue-eyed, blond curly-haired boy, which she did until the day she died. Jimmy could do no wrong in her eyes. He had hated the curls when he was a teenager, brushing his hair flat and plastering it with brilliantine until a slight kink was all that remained of them. His sister, Minnie, had always been jealous of his hair – hers was dead straight.

I'll jump ahead briefly, here. In October of 1955, I stayed in Laurencekirk for a week to nurse Auntie Ann, and even when she was obviously at death's door she lingered on, unconscious. When Jimmy turned up on the Saturday afternoon, it became clear that she had been waiting for him. The moment he spoke to her, she opened her eyes and whispered 'Jamie'. Now she could go.

The house, on the High Street, was an old building, brick-built with harling on top. Kitchen and parlour downstairs, one bedroom and an attic room upstairs. At one time there had been an outside privy and water tap, but by this time, a lean-to scullery had been built on (they called it the back kitchen), with a tiny lavatory off it. Auntie Ann slept in the bed recess in the kitchen and Jimmy's father had a wee room somewhere between the kitchen and the back-kitchen. I never saw inside it.

With no electricity or gas, they were still using oil lamps; small ones for carrying to bed, but a tall brass lamp on the kitchen table. All the cooking was done on the wide, gleaming range. While I was still working, Jimmy and I saved up enough to have electricity installed, but the two old people were never very happy with it.

Our wedding took place in the registry office on fifth December 1953, with a reception in the Bon Accord Hotel in Market Street. I say reception, but it was actually only a meal with enough time to linger over the coffee so that both sides could get acquainted. Sixteen of us sat down at the table and everything went very well. I was wearing a powder-blue, woollen two-piece suit, while Jimmy had bought a new navy suit from the Fifty-Shilling Tailors. The only other suit he had was too easily recognised as demob issue, and he considered it unsuitable for such a special occasion.

The repast over, Jimmy and I took a taxi to the Joint Station – an extravagance since it was just round the corner from the hotel. We were bound for Rosyth, where Jimmy's other aunt lived. Auntie Jess was present at our wedding, and she was spending a holiday with Auntie Ann in order to let us have the use of her house for a week's honeymoon.

We had to leave the train at Kirkcaldy – the first time Jimmy had been there since he was just days old – and take a bus to Rosyth. It was roughly nine o'clock by the time we reached the house where we were to be alone for the next seven days – a marvellous feeling! I made a pot of tea, then we went straight to bed, I too tired and Jimmy too under the weather to do anything other than sleep.

The following morning was Sunday, we made good use of our 'long lie' and after a breakfast of tea and toast, Jimmy went out to buy a newspaper to give me time to organise the lunch. Auntie Jess, a very good cook, had left some pies and tarts for us, and with no fridge available, they had to be eaten quickly. For that first meal, I chose a steak pie and a rhubarb tart – perhaps too much pastry, but Jess's pastry was melt-in-the-mouth quality.

I prepared some of the vegetables she had bought in, and we sat down to a very appetising first course; the steak pie was magnificent and the veggies done to a T. Then I went into her tiny scullery to make some custard for the tart – Jimmy meanwhile washed up the dishes and pans we had used so far. The custard thickened the way I liked it, I poured it into a jug for serving, and we carried tart and jug through to the table in the living room. I allowed my new husband to swamp his helping with the custard and he waited until I helped myself before we began to eat.

If you have never tasted a mince tart swimming in custard, I strongly advise you not to try. My only excuse was that the small amount of gravy that had escaped from the hole in the top looked like rhubarb juice.

We spent many holidays with Auntie Jess in Rosyth, and I was to discover that, often, she wasn't as gracious as she had appeared on first acquaintance. She had been adopted into the Davidson family as an infant, and had turned out to be so clever that, when she was old enough, she had been sent to Mackie Academy in Stonehaven. (This was a bit of a sore point with Auntie Ann and the sister who had died during the war, because they, too, had been clever but finances at the time hadn't allowed them further schooling.) I have no idea where Jess learned her secretarial skills, obviously in a proper college, because she became one of the first typewriters (as they were called in her day) in the Law Courts in Edinburgh. At the age of forty, she met a sergeant of the Leith Police. Anyway, they married as soon as he retired, he was much older than she was, and, sadly, they had less than fifteen years together when he died.

Even having been married, she was still an old maid at heart, and *her* way was the only way possible for everything. She had no patience with children, nor with other people, come to that. On one visit, we were in the middle of breakfast when the postman delivered a letter. She took it in and opened it. 'It's from Mabel.'

Mabel was a great friend of hers and we smiled understandingly. After a few seconds she said, scathingly, 'She's bought a new blue coat. I can't understand why she wanted a new coat, she's got at least three already that I know of.'

Jimmy, Sheila and I exchanged amused glances, then Auntie Jess snapped, 'And another thing . . . she doesn't like blue.'

Her three visitors were sore pressed not to burst out laughing, and Sheila still laughs about it to this day.

On another occasion some years later, we went shopping in Kirkcaldy. She was an avid shopper, and both Sheila and I were quite interested in having a look round although I couldn't afford to buy anything. Jimmy, manlike of course, said he'd rather take Alan (our son, born in 1956) to the carnival he'd noticed as we came in on the bus. We arranged to meet up again at a café for a snack at a certain time.

Sheila and I were exhausted before that time came, but Auntie Jess was still 'knyping' on, as we say in the Doric (pronounced 'k-nyping'). It means striding out doggedly, and I think it's a good description. Alan would only have been about two or three, and he was so tired when we started to walk back to the bus station that Jimmy took him up on his shoulders, so that our progress was slower than it might otherwise have been.

'Stop dawdling!' his aunt ordered him. 'If you don't put a step in we'll miss the bus.'

Sheila consulted the new watch we had given her for her birthday. 'What time *is* the bus?' she asked, innocently.

The elderly woman turned a scornful glare on her. 'I've no idea, but I know we'll miss it if *he* doesn't hurry up.'

She couldn't bring herself to say, '. . . your father.' She never acknowledged my daughter as a Davidson, although we had to adopt her to change her surname. This is another incident that Sheila looks back on with amusement, including the little scenario when we did reach the row of glazed shelters, each with the bus destination on display at the front.

'This is our bus,' Auntie Jess declared loudly, making for the one marked 'Leven' which had quite a queue inside it already. 'The sign's wrong,' she added, even louder still. 'This is the bus for Rosyth, not Leven.'

The line of people looked at each other uncertainly. This woman sounded as if she knew what she was talking about, and some of them actually made a move to shift to another queue. One man, however, stood his ground, fixing Jess with eyes of steel. 'If you're going to Rosyth, you'd better stand somewhere else. I'm going to Leven and I'm staying here.'

The authority in his voice and manner got through to the doubters, who took up their stances again, looking accusingly at the trouble-maker. Jimmy, Sheila and I had already moved along to look for the correct bus stop and, with an 'I-know-you're-wrong', tutting, shake of her head, the old aunt followed us.

On another day out with her, a few years later still, we took the bus to Aberdour. The bus let us off at a shop selling pails, spades and beach balls at ridiculously low prices, so we bought one of each for Alan. We also bought a bottle of lemonade and a packet of biscuits. Our hostess didn't think we would need anything to eat, because she had given us a cooked breakfast before we left. The trouble was, her sparse helpings were never enough for us. (I can remember us having to go out most nights around nine o'clock ostensibly for a breath of fresh air, but really to look for a chip shop.)

Thus provided, we set off on the fairly long walk from the main road to the sea. It was a lovely beach, but Jess padded along for what seemed miles looking for the best spot. Then we holidaymakers stripped down to the bare minimum of clothing, while she sat in a deck chair wearing, working from the top down, a close fitting felt hat, a thick woollen twinset with a shawl round her shoulders, a heavy tweed skirt, thick interlock directoire knickers (she always sat with her legs wide apart, that's how I know) and woollen stockings. Her face was the only part of her uncovered.

The sun beat down on us all afternoon, we finished the lemonade and the biscuits (Jess didn't partake of any), and although we had great fun, playing with the ball, paddling in the sea, making a big sandcastle, we three were glad when she said, around 6 p.m., 'I think it's time we went home.'

We picked up our rubbish and Jimmy deposited it in a nearby litter bin, laying the empty lemonade bottle carefully down the inside. 'What d'you think you're doing?' his aunt demanded. 'You must take that back to the shop.'

'We won't be going near the shop,' he said, though I could see he was itching to tell her to shut up. 'There's another path there, look.'

'But you have to return that empty bottle,' she persisted.

For the sake of peace, we trooped back along the sands to go up the way we'd come down, the bottle was returned to the shop and we finally got a bus after standing for over twenty minutes. By the time we reached Rosyth again, the sun had started to take its toll on us, and I popped into a chemist to buy something to soothe our scarlet, almost raw skins. We ate our salad tea to an accompanying lecture on the stupidity of going around half-naked. She wasn't affected at all, not even her face.

In the morning, Alan came through to our room complaining that he could hardly walk, his legs were so sore. We told him it would soon go away, but when we tried to get up ourselves, we discovered that it wasn't just surface sunburn we were suffering from, it felt as though it had burned deep into our bones.

We made it downstairs by going backwards, but Jess was scathing in her remarks about people with no guts.

She used to spend holidays with us, when we got our house, sometimes staying for three weeks without it crossing her mind that it took me all my time to feed the four of us, never mind an extra, finicky old woman. She did bring half a pound of expensive chocolates with her, handing the bag to Jimmy first, then to me, before taking one herself. When three-year-old Alan said, 'Can I have one, please?' she turned on him angrily.

'These are far too expensive to give to children.'

I tackled Jimmy about this when we went to bed that night: 'She could surely have taken a wee bag of dolly mixtures or something for the kids.'

He shrugged. 'She was the same when I was a kid. Chocolates for the adults, but nothing for Minnie and me.'

I'm afraid my opinion of her at that time was 'Selfish bitch', an opinion that never really changed. I had better qualify that a little. I recently heard about a different side to her. When Jimmy's nephew's wife was learning shorthand and typing (she later became a school secretary), Auntie Jess read out passages from books to help her to gain speed. What is more, Adele says she was very patient and helpful, yet I can't really imagine her having these qualities. They must have been well hidden under her thick layers of clothes.

Although I enjoyed working as cashier at Cordiner's Garage, the Esplanade was rather a long way to travel four times a day, so I kept an eye on the Situations Vacant column in the evening paper. It wasn't long until I saw that the SCWS was advertising for a cashier/book-keeper for McDonald's Garage. It was much nearer home, only one short bus journey, so I applied straight away to the Area Manager, who was pleased that someone who knew the work would be taking over again.

Unfortunately, the manager had also changed, and the new man, who shall remain nameless, was a retired tea planter and knew little of office procedure. This was a mixed blessing, in a way, because I was left to my own devices – good – but I also found myself responsible for making sure that the mechanics' work was being properly recorded, and that any complaints from customers were dealt with sympathetically – not so easy.

Left. Jane Forsyth (the grandmother I never knew because she died in 1920). Apparently she was an extremely elegant lady always dressed to perfection. Note the fur stole and muff and leather gloves. She also had a great variety of stylish hats, but unfortunately the photographs of her wearing them have been stuck down in albums.

Right. Ann Davidson (Jimmy's aunt). Possibly late 1880s or '90s, and included because of her dress style.

Right. Annie Robb, niece of Grandma Forsyth. Possibly early 1900s.

Below left. Annie Robb again. Possibly Edwardian style.

Below right. Annie Forsyth (Dad's sister), who emigrated to Canada in 1920. This may have been taken shortly before she left.

Above. The Brow of the Gallowgate. Dad (L) and brother Jack at door of butcher shop. Note the hygienic aprons and khaki coats. On the extreme right can be seen the opening (close) through to the house above.

Left. Wedding portrait of Billy Forsyth and Georgina Adams (my Uncle Billy and Auntie Ina.) Best man is Hugh Auld, fiancé of Bella Forsyth, the groom's sister, who was bridesmaid. 1920.

Right. Uncle Bob Mackay with his motorcycle combination, possibly 1920.

Below. Mr and Mrs James Paul of Toddlehills, my great grandparents, in 1922. The girl in the middle was their granddaughter Beatrice, my mother's cousin, who died of consumption when she was twelve.

Top. A gathering of Forsyths and their motorcycles at Garlogie, 1922.

Below right. L to R: May Forsyth (Mum), Mr and Mrs James Paul, her father and mother, outside their tenement in Ord Street. Doris is the baby in the pram. 1922.

Below right. My Dad in 1922. I don't know the make of his 'steed'.

Right. A beautifully posed photograph of Bella Forsyth. I don't know if the dress was for a dramatic or musical production, or if she had it for a fancy-dress ball. Most of the Forsyths (including me) were varying degrees of show-offs, but not to any great excess.

Below. Bella and Hugh's wedding. L to R: Nora Forsyth, John Auld and Violet Forsyth. I guess this to be around 1923 or '24.

Above. With great-grandfather and great-grandmother (James Paul Sr, but I don't recall her name.) At Toddlehills, their croft near Peterhead.

Left. Toddlehills. L to R: Mum, Doris, Great Granda, Great Granny and Beatrice. 1923.

Above. Garlogie. Mum is second left, Dad is second right. I don't appear to be there. I think the ca is my Dad's Clyno, with what looks like solid tyres and a running board. 1922/'23.

Left. A wooden erection at Garlogie where the children usually played. Here, the adults have taken over. On left of roof, Vi Forsyth making sure that Douglas Mackay and I do not fa off. Mum is at window directly under Douglas.

Below. Cousins Violet Lawrence and Doris Forsyth (right), wearin the latest children's fashion of droopy drawers to feed the hens. 1924/'25.

Above. The croft at Toddlehills. It seems to be in a state of disrepair, and the photo was likely taken after the Pauls moved out. 1924/25.

Left. Kintore, 1926. Veteran poser, parasol at the ready.

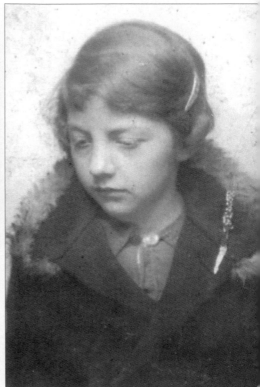

Top left. Doris out for a walk in Sunday best. Judging by the straw hat, it must be summer, but note the woollen stockings and the umbrella tucked under the arm. Typical Aberdeen weather for the time of year.

Top right. With tortoiseshell hair-slide, fur collar and sprig of white heather – what more could a five-year-old want?

Right. Granny and Granda Paul at back door of Ord Street tenement. Possible early 1930s.

Above. London 1928, Regent's Park Zoo, I think. L to R: Auntie Gwen, Bill Gammack (a neighbour from Aberdeen), Mum, Uncle Jim, Mrs Gammack. My hat was lost soon after it was bought.

Left. Doris in front of our house in Hilton Drive (upstairs). Note plaster on knee.

Above. Villa in Mid Stocket Road, late 1933, when we had recently moved in. Garden may just have been sown with grass seed.

Right. Bob Forsyth (Dad) and my sister Bertha in early summer of 1934, at Mid Stocket Road with the shop van.

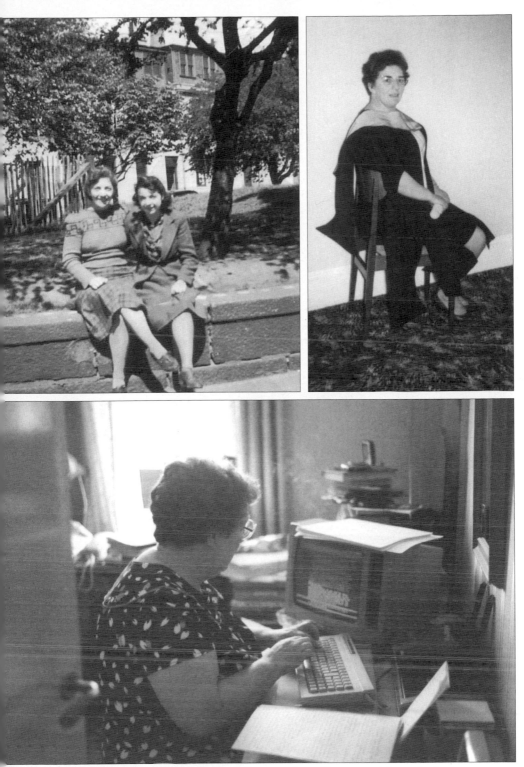

Top left. With Peggy McLeod in Bon Accord Square, after office moved from the harbour area. 1941.

Top right. Graduation. Wearing hired gown. June 1967.

Above. Creating a 'masterpiece' amid utter chaos – my usual method of working.

Above left. Being supervised by Jimmy before I started a signing session for *Time Shall Reap*.

Above right. With Bertha at the tenth anniversary of the Hawkhill Nursing Home.

Right. With sister Bertha, in the north of Scotland somewhere.

Top left. Jimmy with Bill Jamieson, Bertha's husband.

Top right. Daughter Sheila with husband John English (once again, away in the wild north.)

Above left. Alan, in front of the Scottish National Gallery of Modern Art in Edinbugh.

Above right. Matthew taking a bow in Aberdeen.

At eighty-two, I'm looking forward to the future: it's not a policy to look back.

There were no other clerkesses, either – I never discovered why – and it was as it had been when I started there back in 1948. It was just this new man and me, and we got on reasonably well, although I think he did have a problem being taught his job by a much younger person, particularly a woman.

I'll tell you of one day in particular, back in my first stint, and when I was also the only clerkess. Mr T. often came back from lunch in a foul temper, and I used to suspect that he'd had a row with his wife and was taking it out on me as the first one he came in contact with. I forget why he actually chastised me, but it was for something that was not my fault, and I was still seething with righteous indignation when I prepared his coffee – so indignant that something had to give.

When I carried through his cup and saucer, I banged them down on his table and snarled, 'There's your coffee and I hope it chokes you!' I brought my little display of protest to a suitable conclusion by slamming the door as I went out.

There was absolute, deafening silence and I sat down with legs trembling. I'd done it now. I'd get the sack for sure, thrown out on my ear for speaking back. At last, after perhaps ten long minutes of guilty apprehension, I took a sip of my, by now, almost ice-cold coffee, and practically jumped out of my skin when Mr T. burst out of his office. He strode over to the counter and riffled through the taxi order book, not something he often did, before turning to face me. This was it! This was the pay-off! And I'd only myself to blame!

'We'll have to get something straight, Doris,' he said, his face grave, his tone very, very serious. 'There's no room here for two people with tempers, so there's nothing for it but . . . well, we'll have to take it one at a time.' Then he burst out laughing and apologised for his own behaviour.

That put us on a different footing, and it was shortly after that when he took on the second girl, Annie.

Back to the tasks I had to do when Mr X. was my boss. As you have no doubt noticed, wedding cars always have lovely white ribbons on the front, and someone has to keep them in pristine condition. Yes,

I'd to take them home, wash and iron them and put them in a drawer until next time they were needed, which was fairly often. Most weddings took place on Saturdays, and we sometimes had more than one booking for the same day. We kept spare sets of ribbons for the occasions when times overlapped.

The charge at that time for both weddings and funerals was 12/6 an hour (twelve shillings and sixpence, or, in today's funny money as I still consider it, sixty-two and a half pence). A full service to a private car cost fifteen shillings (seventy-five new pence). Of course, a weekly wage was around £4, so on that basis, a service cost about one sixteenth of a man's average income. I'm not sure how that compares with the present time.

Less than six months after I returned to McDonald's, I discovered that I was pregnant. Jimmy, of course, was delighted, and wanted me to stop working, but we needed to save for when we got a house of our own, and this job was perfect for camouflaging my condition. I stood behind a counter when people came in to pay bills or book a taxi, and I was dealing with petrol and oil sales through a hatch, so nobody actually saw the whole me, a whole that steadily grew larger and larger.

I was well into my pregnancy when I got quite a pleasant surprise. As a customer handed me the money for his petrol through the hatch, he said, 'Don't you recognise me, Doris?'

I hadn't looked up, but when I did, he was smiling broadly. It was Bob W., one of the two mechanics who had gone to Australia around 1950. He opened the door from the garage and came into the office to have a chat. 'I see you're in the best of health,' he grinned, looking at the bulge I was trying to hide with a smock.

'You're looking the picture of health yourself,' I grinned back. He had put on a lot of weight in the six years since I'd wished him good luck in his new life.

'Ah, well,' he replied, brown eyes twinkling mischievously, 'you've got me beat there, haven't you? In a month or so you'll have got rid of your excess baggage, but I'll still be stuck with mine.'

We chatted companionably for a short time, learning that we had both married and were easy with each other as a consequence. He told me about his wife and two children and asked me about my husband (also a motor mechanic, remember), but we were constantly interrupted by customers wanting to pay for something. Why did they need to be buying petrol, or oil, or Upper Cylinder Lubricant? (This last had been a source of knowing winks and lewd jokes amongst the men at one time.) The phone was shrilling constantly, making a conversation really difficult to sustain, so Bob eventually took himself off, saying that he hoped everything went well with me. I was glad he'd come to see us, although the only other people he knew were two of the drivers and John Fraser, the garageman, a sort of general dogsbody, who served petrol, repaired punctures and stood in if we were short of a driver.

Tall and upright, John was an enigma, an educated man whose entries in his timesheets included 'To access and egress of cars . . .' I hadn't known that the opposite of access was egress, and I wondered how *he* knew. His manner of speech, quiet and grammatically correct, suggested that he'd held a position of importance at some time, but I never found out if that was so.

He was occasionally ordered to do something that he was reluctant to carry out, but he obeyed without question. I was actually involved in one such incident. My duties included working out how many miles each taxi got from a gallon of petrol (the number of miles done per week divided by the fuel consumed.) Rolls Royces generally averaged about ten to twelve mpg, so I was shocked to find that one car we had got only managed four one week. It was such a drop that I reported it to the manager. Poor John Fraser was instructed to make sure that the driver (let's call him Bruce) was accurately recording the fuel he was putting into the tank of his vehicle.

It was almost six on the second evening, just as John was finishing for the day and Bruce was making his taxi ready for the night shift, that the scam was discovered. He was siphoning petrol out of the Rolls Royce into a large petrol tin, for use in his own car (or perhaps to sell without coupons at an excessive price.) I remember that he was fired there and then, but I can't recall if the theft was reported to the police. I don't think so, yet he was such a nice lad that John and I both felt really bad that we'd been the cause of him losing his job. If I hadn't involved the boss, a warning from the garageman might have been enough. Oh well, I was only doing what I was paid to do, after all.

I worked on until my eighth month. For the last few weeks, I felt like a mother elephant, I was so huge . . . but I knew that living on one wage would mean struggling to survive, and I was putting it off as long as I could.

13

I had applied for a council house not long after we married, only to be told that we did not have enough points. There was a long queue and we were at the very bottom. I pointed out that we had a daughter of nine, and that she had to sleep in the same room as her grandmother, but that, apparently, counted for nothing.

Soon after Alan was born on the sixth of March 1956, I went to the Housing Office in Broad Street again, to update their records. The baby, unfortunately, made no difference, according to the clerk who dealt with me.

'Points are given for each child you have,' he said, heaving a sigh and rolling his eyes heavenwards as if he thought I was trying to jump the queue, 'but your present accommodation is also taken into account, and judging by your address, you are certainly not overcrowded.'

I don't know about the people who deal with housing applications today, but I felt insulted by that man's supercilious manner. How many offspring would I need to produce before I'd have the necessary points? Should I tell a barefaced lie in order to get a house? Pretend that my mother didn't want her granddaughter sleeping in the same room any longer? But no doubt they would ask my mother to verify that.

Actually, we were quite comfortable where we were, but Jimmy and I would have felt freer if we had a place of our own. Not that Mum ever said anything. It was just . . . I couldn't explain it – the aura of disapproval?

Astonishingly, just a matter of weeks later, we got a letter saying that we had been allocated a house in Mastrick, and if we refused it, we would be relegated to the bottom of the queue again. So strongly did I feel about having a place to ourselves that I'd have taken up the offer whatever the state of the house, but Jimmy was more cautious. 'We'd better see what it looks like before we commit ourselves,' he warned.

We could have taken a bus – our route had been extended to include this new housing scheme, its population increasing by leaps and bounds and eventually reaching over 80,000 – but it wasn't too far to walk.

We had been given a small map to guide us, and when we turned off Mastrick Drive into Ness Place, leading to Deveron Road, my spirits sank at the sight of the tenements. I didn't want to live in a tenement, even a brand new tenement, yet if we refused this, it could be years before we got another chance. Fate, thank goodness, was on my side. Deveron Road, a continuation of Ness Place, had no tenements, and 'our' home was fourth in a row of six terraced houses.

We wouldn't get the key until I signed the Missive of Let, so we had to content ourselves by looking through the ground floor windows, going round the end of the block in order to see into the scullery and discovering that the living room had a window at the back as well as the front. Two windows in one room? We would have sun coming in all day, and even if it wasn't sunny, it would still be light and airy. We were quite impressed with what we had seen so far and decided to take it . . . to be perfectly honest, we jumped at it.

I signed for the key the following morning, and in the early evening all five of us (Alan in the pram) went to inspect the inside of our domain. The living room was a fair-sized rectangle with a recess at each side of the fireplace. A water pipe ran up the left hand side, which we discovered was to enable the fire to heat the water. During our entire tenancy, we were to be bothered by irritating gurgling noises from this pipe, especially in the evenings, as the water came to the boil. In the wall opposite the fire was a hatch from the scullery, ideal for serving meals.

The scullery itself was well fitted: a large cabinet that would hold dishes and loads of other items, with a drawer for cutlery. It also had a walk-in larder with a cool space (actually over the coal cellar that entered from outside); a new cooker, with one solid round ring, one rectangular flat plate and a grill; a shallow sink and a deep sink, with a division in the middle for attaching a wringer. I was pleased to see the cooker. At least one appliance that I wouldn't have to buy, but thereby hangs a little tale.

A year or so after we moved in – it may even have been less – the council sent all its tenants a letter saying that they would have to pay £4 for the cooker that had been supplied with the house. £4 for what was practically a new cooker? I paid it before the powers-that-be decided to double the price, but a few of my neighbours thought it was outrageous. I don't know what happened about this, but I would imagine they'd have had to stump up or lose it.

Back to our pre-entry inspection. The stairs were quite steep, but we were young and fit and thought nothing of the bathroom being on the top landing. I'd be in dire straits if I still lived there today. There were two bedrooms, one quite large with two windows to the front, and a large, shelved cupboard. The smaller back bedroom had one window and a cupboard for the hot water tank, fitted with slats for airing clothes. Luxury!

The worry now was how to furnish our house. Thank heaven, Jimmy still had most of his demob gratuity left, but I still couldn't buy what I liked; everything had to be within our finances. An oak dining room suite (table, four chairs and sideboard) cost £32, a bedroom suite (double bed with spring and flock mattress, double wardrobe, dressing table and chest of drawers) roughly the same.

For Sheila's room (Alan's cot would remain in our room until he needed a proper bed), I bought a set of cheaper whitewood furniture – kidney-shaped dressing table, bureau and wardrobe – and a single bed. I made a frill for the dressing table to make it look more feminine, and Mum had given me an old cabinet that had originally belonged to my granny, useful for storing all the odds and ends a twelve-year-old amasses.

My description of this back room will show that it wasn't so very small, only in comparison with the other, which, as I thought when planning ahead, could easily be divided into two separate rooms. Jimmy and I could then move into the back room to let Sheila and Alan have a room each. Things did not work out as planned, of course. They seldom do.

I gradually collected some wooden orange boxes to use as bookcases (I've always been snowed under with books), painted them then made curtains to hide the contents, which were apt to get quite untidy, as even proper bookcases do.

That was the furniture sorted out; now for the other necessary items, things I'd never thought about until I needed them, like a sweeping brush, basin, towels, a scrubbing board and brush, light shades and bulbs, an alarm clock to get us up in the mornings – we had been given a wedding present of a lovely Westminster chiming clock for the mantelpiece. I'd have forgotten to buy a washing line and pegs if Mum hadn't reminded me. She also let us have two huge easy chairs that my father had got specially made when they were married, and which he had also had covered in deep crimson velour at one time. The seats and arms were getting threadbare, but Bill Jamieson, Bertha's fiancé and an apprentice carpet fitter and up-holsterer, recovered them in brown Rexine. Just like new!

We did manage to purchase a bed-settee a year or so later, giving rise to a phrase that we still laugh about today. I had taken a left-over cutting to a furniture store and ordered a settee with the same Rexine. The shop wrote in three weeks to say that it was ready and would be delivered two days later. Then came another note saying that something heavy had fallen on our settee and cut the seat. But not to worry, they would have another one made as soon as possible.

Weeks passed and Auntie Jess had invited herself to stay for a week or two (or three), so Auntie Ina (not the same side of the family) volunteered to speed things up. She had a habit of inventing words and phrases of her own, and these are her famous words to the manager of the shop. 'If you don't replace my niece's settee double quick, she will take her custom some other where.' They did the trick.

The new settee was delivered the day before Auntie Jess was due
. . . and even if it wasn't an exact match, we were obliged to keep it,
otherwise where would Jess have slept. Probably in our bed, while
we'd have had to sleep on the living room floor. But ever since then,
if something is not delivered when it should be, Jimmy and I say to
each other, 'We should take our custom some other where.'

*

I actually had my education finished in Mastrick. The mixture of
tenants amazed me, and the way some of them lived was past belief,
but on the whole, they were good people. Most of them were in the
same financial straits as I was, but instead of doing without something
until they could pay for it, some bought on 'tick'. I once noticed a
van delivering two large mats to one tenant (I'll call her Mrs Y.) on a
Saturday forenoon, and on the Monday morning, I happened to catch
sight of her walking past with the mats slung over her shoulder.

Wondering what she was doing, I was glad when Mrs Sievewright asked
me if I'd seen Mrs Y. taking her two new mats to the pawnshop. I had
never heard of anybody doing this before, and I couldn't understand how
it worked. If she had bought her mats on the never-never, as I was sure
she had, and was pawning them because she needed money, she would
still have to pay the shop where she bought them in the first place.

I didn't have quite so much to do with Mrs D., my neighbour on the
other side, although we shared the same path to our front doors. Her
husband was a trawlerman, so we sometimes got a 'fry' of fish from
him. He once gave us a large enamel pie dish full to the brim with
prawns. It was the first time I had seen these, but he told me they
were a delicacy. Not altogether convinced, Jimmy and I discovered
that they were delicious. It wasn't until I spotted prawns in a high-
class fish-shop that I realised how much of a delicacy they actually
were. We must have eaten a few quids' worth without knowing it.

When we had been in the house for a year, I thought it was safe to decorate. Sheila was in bed with pharyngitis and I decided to do her room first. Perhaps it sounds stupid to decorate a room where someone is ill – my mother thought I was absolutely mad – but it was company for Sheila and saved me running up and down the stairs so much. I went to a shop in Rosemount where the man left me to take my time over choosing my wallpaper, and then gave me a demonstration of how to fold it once it was pasted, so that it wouldn't fall down or trip me up, or get torn. This was an invaluable lesson, for the only decorating I had done before was painting my mother's bathroom and scullery walls *eau de nil*. Papering was a different matter, but I set to with gusto.

I made a presentable enough job of it; there was nothing unusual, just plain, straightforward walls. I left the paintwork as the council painters had done it; it was only a year old and after a good wash, it looked as good as new.

The next job I set my mind to was the scullery, like my mother's, just paint. I think I chose Ice Blue, and was amazed at how much paint I needed. I mentioned this to the man in Rosemount when I went back for another tin, and he asked, 'A new house? Did you size the walls first?'

'Size?' He had lost me.

'I'll sell you a packet. You mix it with water, brush it on and let it dry before you actually paint. It seals new walls, you see. If they're not sealed, they suck in the paint.'

I thanked him for another invaluable tip, and went home to do what he'd said.

I was very pleased with the result, and when Mrs Y. came to the door to ask me something, I took her inside to see my handiwork.

She was deeply impressed. 'And you did it yourself? I'd like to paint mine, but I've never used a paintbrush in my life.'

I showed her how to go in the same direction always, and then added, 'But don't make the same mistake as I did. You need to size the walls first, or they'll just suck in the paint.'

'Size?' Her brows came down in thought, then her eyes cleared. 'I'm sure there's a packet of size in my sideboard drawer. My man took it hame once for something, but he never used it.'

I was almost certain that her husband had not intended to paint anything – he wasn't inclined that way – but I could have been wrong. At any rate, she turned up again in about ten minutes carrying a pail. 'Does that look like size to you?' she asked, holding it up for my inspection.

It appeared to be all right, but I stuck a finger in to make sure that it was sticky enough. The packet could have been lying around for years before it ended up in her sideboard drawer. It was just as well I tested it, for it wasn't in the least bit sticky. It felt just like water with grains of fine oatmeal in it, so I shook my head. 'No, that's not size.'

She gave a sheepish laugh. 'Well, you see, there was two packets kicking aboot in that drawer for ages. I kent one was goldfish food and one was size but the labels had come aff. This must be the goldfish food, then.'

Collapse of would-be decorator instructor.

The living room came next, but this time, Jimmy volunteered to give me a hand. Again, I was leaving the original paintwork and had only bought paper. My friendly mentor had given me another tip, which I imprinted in my memory, because I had a strong feeling that we would need it.

Mum came up on the Sunday morning and took Alan out of our way for the day, and we set to. We started at the left side of the fireside recess where it met the back wall, and intended to go right round to the front wall that day, including the area above the fireplace. We agreed that I would measure and paste and Jimmy would hang the paper. I'm not going to say that this caused our first row – we'd had a spat or two before – but this was the biggest so far. I got annoyed because he was so pernickety, taking so long to place each strip that the paste dried in and I'd to take the brush over the edges again to make them stick down.

At last, after he took about ten minutes to make up his mind how to do the paper behind the water pipe and wouldn't listen to my advice, we both lost our tempers. So we stopped – having taken a whole day to not-quite-finish one small recess.

On Monday morning, Jimmy off to work, Sheila off to school and the baby having his forenoon nap, I started the job by myself. I measured the first strip, cut, pasted and folded, praying that what I was about to do would actually be successful, and worked from the ceiling down to the obstruction. Now, I ripped the paper roughly so that it would go behind the water pipe. As the man in the shop had told me, the torn edges fitted together so that the join wasn't noticeable, and thus I continued until that bit of wall was done. Then I did the fireplace breast and the other recess. When Jimmy came home that night, he had to admit that I'd been right . . . or at least, the man in the shop had known what he was talking about. Naturally, I was quite pleased to do the rest of the walls by myself.

Having papered our room and painted the tiny bathroom, I was faced with the final, mammoth task of decorating the staircase. We got a long ladder from the window-cleaner who lived up the road, a short pair of steps from my mother and Jimmy borrowed what looked like a railway sleeper from Tawse's yard to lay between them. At one point, there was a tremendously long strip needed, so I suggested that we should both start from the middle, he would work up to the ceiling and I'd work down. That way, as far as I could envisage, there would be less likelihood of wrinkles than if he started at the top and I started at the bottom. It didn't work out how I had hoped, though, and let me just say that I finished this myself . . . after another flare-up. My temper matched the colour of my hair . . . as Jimmy can vouch. Poor soul, he has been at the receiving end for fifty years.

*

Mrs D. surprised me occasionally with some of the things she said, and I'd better tell you this little gem from the beginning. Our fourteen houses were built diagonally across from what had once been the estate of the derelict Springhill House. The area was a natural playground for the kids in our community, the young ones staying within sight of their homes, but the older few venturing that bit farther in.

One afternoon, when nine-year-old Margaret D. came home from an hour or so of an exciting game in the dense undergrowth with several others, she said that a man had been displaying himself to them. I don't suppose this was the actual phrase she used, but afraid of what could happen unless he was stopped, her mother went to the nearest police office to report it.

I knew nothing about the incident until Mrs D. came to tell me that Margaret had been examined by the police surgeon in case the worst had already happened. Then she went on, anxiously, 'They said she was still a virgin, but how auld have you to be afore you're a virgin? Do you ken, Mrs Davidson?'

I managed to keep a straight face. 'It's how old a girl is before she's *not* a virgin – that's what mothers have to worry about.' The poor woman clearly had no idea of what the word meant and I had to explain the ins and outs of it (an unfortunate phrase) as basically as I could.

Even after digesting the biological information for some time, however, she still hadn't understood, because she suddenly burst out, 'So, if my man was to die, how long would it be afore I was a virgin again?'

Her husband did die just a few years later, but having had five children to him, I doubt if she ever became a virgin again. By the way, I did get her permission to recount this tale. She hadn't remembered the incident, but considers it hilarious.

Mrs S. also dropped the occasional clanger – life was never dull. At one point, her mother and sister departed these shores and went to live in America – I don't know why – or if I *had* been told at the time, I've forgotten. At any rate, she used to give me titbits of news when she got a letter.

'It's been snowing in Illinoise, Chickargo' was one of her comments. Another was (and this is not a word of a lie), 'They have the same problems ower there as we have here wi' the Catholics and the Prostitutes.'

I have heard that same sentiment expressed as a joke many times since by comedians on the wireless and television, but that was my introduction to it, the difference being that she was deadly serious. It didn't put her off going to join them some years later, and as far as I know she and her family are still there.

But she was a good neighbour, really thoughtful. One local holiday Monday, I had risen with the lark and had a big washing on the line by nine o'clock. My knuckles, naturally, were almost red raw from having to rub the dirt out of Jimmy's working clothes. He had suggested that we should go for a picnic somewhere, so I prepared some sandwiches and other eatables, and two flasks of tea. The sun was shining, and we took the bus to the Bay of Nigg, a favourite spot and one bus went all the way. We were having a heavenly, relaxing time, we adults stretched out on the grass while Alan and his little friend searched in the rock pools for anything that took their interest. At one point, we heard Alan shout, his shrill voice higher with excitement, 'Graham, come here and see this f---ing beastie.'

Jimmy gaped at me, appalled. 'Did he say what I thought he said?'

'Let it be,' I cautioned. 'He doesn't know what it means. I'll have a quiet word with him when I'm putting him to bed.'

We had finished all the food and drinks by just after our normal lunchtime, and I was on the point of asking the two little boys – they couldn't have been more than four at the time – if they wanted to go home, when the heavens opened . . . with no warning whatsoever.

We had no choice but to put all our rubbish into one of the paper bags to take home with us, there were no litter bins then, and trail our tired, sodden bodies along the road past Girdleness Lighthouse to the bus terminus. We had some time to wait, but there was a shelter, so it wasn't as bad as it might have been. On the way home, it occurred to me that my washing – my greenful of sheets, pillowcases and towels as well as lots of clothes – was hanging outside in the downpour. They'd have been dry before the rain came on, and now I would have to wash the lot again.

Not taking time to do anything when I went into the house, I ran straight through and out of the back door – front and back doors were directly opposite each other – stopping in astonishment when I saw the four poles standing forlornly with no ropes, no washing near them.

Guessing that Mrs S. had taken them in, I knocked on her back door. (For as friendly as we were, we never got into the habit of walking into each other's house unannounced.)

She handed me a basket full of beautifully folded clothes, sheets and whatever else had been out. 'I took them in as soon as I saw spots of rain on the window,' she told me. 'There wasna a soul left in the *cul-de-sac* except us, and I was that fed up, I ironed the lot for you, an' all.'

My thanks were heartfelt, and Jimmy could hardly believe me when he saw what she had done. The other families had all taken a day out because it was a local holiday, but her husband, a stone mason, had been sent to Perthshire on a job, and hadn't had the weekend off.

I should explain here that, although Mrs S. and most of the neighbours called it a cul-de-sac, the fourteen houses (blocks of four, six and four again) were actually built around a half circle of grass, with entry and exit from both ends.

This incident, however, also had a sting in the tail. As I had promised, I had told Alan quietly that evening that he mustn't use that word again; it wasn't a nice word, and that was the finish of it, as far as I was concerned. On the Wednesday following this, I took him to visit one of my cousins, who was in Woodend Hospital recuperating from an operation. It was an easy walk from our house, and like all small boys, Alan's tongue never halted as we strolled along. Visiting time was from three o'clock until half past, so he managed to keep reasonably quiet by watching all the comings and goings of staff and visitors in the ward.

We said our goodbyes and emerged into the fresh air again (hospitals always give me a queasy feeling) and set off for home. I had noticed Alan glancing behind a few times, but we were within sight of our house, walking along Ythan Road (the streets in this part of the scheme were all named after Scottish rivers) when he said, 'Mummy, that f - f - f - f . . .'

He broke off, obviously searching for a word to replace the forbidden word he had almost used again, but when I turned to see why he'd kept on looking round, I could see only a small dog, nothing beginning with 'f'.

His furrowed brow cleared suddenly as he smiled, 'That f – feathery dog's been following us all the way from the hospital.'

He had taken note of my little lecture – and nothing of the kind ever happened again. But Jimmy and I had a good laugh about it. Mind you, I'd hadn't known myself what the word actually meant until he explained it to me a year or so earlier, which just shows how sheltered my life had been before we moved to Mastrick. None of the men I'd ever worked with would have dreamt of using bad language in front of the female sex. Yes, they told risque jokes, but swearing was taboo, whereas in our little 'cul-de-sac', even one or two of the women swore like troopers, which is how Alan had picked it up.

Unfortunately, it had to be that word, which was the most vile of all in those days; not like today when it is sprinkled liberally throughout almost every programme on television. I can even see it eventually becoming accepted as just a normal everyday word.

Having done all my washing by hand for a few years, even the bulky, oily boiler-suits, I was delighted when I heard of a man hiring out washing machines at two shillings and sixpence per hour (less than 13p). It was quite expensive at that time, but I didn't hesitate to jump at it, as did most of my neighbours; anything to cut down the hard labour washdays usually meant. The procedure started in much the same way as Mum's old hand-worked monster, but once it was filled, it did the washing by itself – worked by electricity.

There was still the same business of rinsing each load, but I now had a wringer attached to the metal parts between my two sinks. That took the graft out of getting the water out of the clothes. An hour, as you can imagine, was a very short time, but it's amazing how a person can make time fit with her needs. Maybe that should be 'make her needs fit into the time available'. At any rate, I had the machine emptied, cleaned and dried out before the entrepreneur came to take it to his next customer.

After another few years, I managed to buy a spin drier, which was another great invention.

Minnie, Jimmy's sister, and her family had visited us on New Year's

Day one year, complete with their ancient spaniel, so when I detected a nasty smell the following morning, I thought that the dog had done his business somewhere in our living room. No matter where I looked, however, I couldn't see anything, and even after I'd scrubbed every inch of my jaspé linoleum (a step up from our original congoleum) with disinfectant, pulling furniture away from the walls, the stink was still there and getting stronger.

It grew so bad that I had to telephone the clerk of works, who had a sniff around and said, 'I think there must be a dead mouse under your fireplace.'

He sent in the health inspector, who shook his head. 'It smells more like a dead cat to me, and we'll have to take your whole fireplace out.'

Thankfully, before he issued that order, he lifted the trapdoor under the stairs to see if anything else would suggest itself. It did! Instead of a drop of some ten feet to the ground, there was water almost up to the floorboards, dirty, filthy water that I'm not even going to try to describe.

'That's sewage,' he informed me, dolefully. 'Something's blocking the drain. It could be anywhere along this block, but because you're in the middle of the row, it's your pipe that's burst.'

The upshot was that I had to take Alan to Mid Stocket for the day, to let the workmen have free rein with whatever they had to do. When I returned about five o'clock, they had gone, the whole house was reeking of some extremely potent disinfectant, the kind that catches your throat, but at least there was only a slight trace of the awful stench there had been before.

The neighbours told me that the men had connected a hosepipe to drain off the sewage and it had run down the brander in the street outside for hours. When that dried up, dozens of barrow loads of 'hard core', like pebbles, were tipped down to prevent a recurrence of the problem.

It was some time, though, before I stopped getting the occasional whiff of what, until then, had been the worst smell I had ever come across in my life.

This wasn't our only acquaintance with a sickening smell, however, and the second was even more revolting than the first – horrifying in itself and with even more appalling aftereffects. I think it would have been in the spring of 1961 or '62 that a bad outbreak of foot and mouth disease affected cattle in Aberdeenshire. We townsfolk had little idea of the devastation this could cause, and when we learned that all herds open to infection were to be slaughtered and buried, all we felt was a slight pity for the farmers. Pity turned to dismay and then horror when the chosen burial ground was named – the grounds of the ruined Springhill House, an area we could see from the windows of our little crescent of houses.

There were hundreds, perhaps thousands, of carcasses to be put away, and we were deafened for days and days on end by the noise of diggers and the thuds as each cow was tossed into the mass grave. When, at last, it was over, we settled down to enjoy what promised to be a glorious summer.

Some weeks later, I heard a van tooting and on looking out of the window, saw it was the butcher. At that time we had no shops near us, and we depended on vans for most commodities – groceries, butcher meat, bakery, vegetables, fish. They were really handy. I couldn't help wondering why the two women already forming a queue were holding hankies to their noses. I soon found out. When I opened the door, I recoiled at the stench that assaulted my nostrils, and whipped out my own hankie. The summer had indeed turned out to be glorious . . . too glorious for what lay underground just a few hundred yards away.

It took the council, or whichever body was responsible, weeks to come to that conclusion; all sorts of other, ludicrous reasons for the smell were offered first. Meanwhile, we poor residents had just to put up with it. To this day, Sheila says she can still remember what it smelt like, and so can most of the people living there at the time, I'll be bound. At last, it was decided that the mass grave would have to be opened again, and proper lime used instead of the quicklime (probably cheaper) that had originally been tossed over the carcasses to dissolve them.

Even so, the smell hung around for another eternity, but thankfully, no one suffered any other ills.

The mention of the butcher's van has brought back some other memories. Our cuisine at that time, and for all the time we lived in Mastrick, was fairly limited. Good plain fare, but still quite limited. Mince, of course, was a staple dish. At a shilling for three-quarters of a pound, it was cheap as well as nourishing. Another favourite was stovies (stoved potatoes). For the benefit of those who are not acquainted with this delicacy, it consists of potatoes, a little meat of some kind, and a sliced onion or two.

The meat, of course, depended on what was left in my purse. Quite often, it was corned beef – a quarter pound was enough to make a big potful, and only cost a few pennies. A quarter of mince would do, but sometimes I was reduced to using a couple of sausages that had been kept back especially for this purpose. If they were sliced thinly, they gave the impression of more meat than there actually was.

Macaroni and cheese, in fact any dish with cheese, was acceptable, but the mainstay of all households at that time was homemade soup. A piece of boiling beef, plate sometimes, or rib, along with whatever vegetables you had (home grown mostly) would make enough for three or four meals – lentil soup, tattie soup, broth – thick enough to stick to your ribs. A fish-and-chip van parked not far from us every night, but this was a luxury, only to be bought when finances could stretch to it, and enjoyed all the more because of that.

Salads were not very common, in our house, anyway. Jimmy didn't think they were filling enough, and neither were boiled eggs. 'Not enough for a working man,' he'd say, and I suppose he had a point.

There was always a pudding to follow. No fancy desserts, though. Rice baked in the oven, custard with raisins, sago or tapioca with a spoonful of jam, seven-cup-pudding if I was flush, roly-poly, sponge. On someone's birthday, I always made a dumpling. This was fairly expensive, but I couldn't let a birthday go past without a dumpling, with tiny threepenny bits in it, or little metal favours, like a motor car, a top hat, a boat. These were, naturally, wrapped in greaseproof paper in case the consumer choked on them, and the same ones were used every year. The Christmas pudding had no metal additions, but was much, much richer.

These dumplings and puddings were usually cooked in a steamer, but the most delicious of all, a clootie dumpling, was boiled in a cloth for hours and hours. Eaten as it was on its first outing, it might be eaten cold the next day with sugar sprinkled over, sliced and fried the day after . . . a clootie dumpling was the most versatile of all.

When we could afford it, we ate quite a lot of fried food – bacon and eggs, sausages, fish. No one worried about calories or cholesterol – they'd never been heard of. If you were meant to be fat, you were meant to be fat. That's what I told myself, and bearing in mind my three colossal aunts, there was every chance that I would grow like them . . . which I nearly have. I did mention my aunts once to the doctor when he said I should watch my weight. I excused my size by saying that fat ran in our family.

He laughed that off, of course. 'Bad eating habits are what run in your family.'

Maybe he was right.

14

Back to everyday life in Mastrick. Having a continual struggle financially, I became an adept needlewoman, creating new trousers for Alan out of old material (no front openings), making skirts for Sheila with new material bought from the fabric stall in the Castlegate Market. This was sold cheap because it was flawed, but the defect was never so big that it couldn't be avoided. I just had to move the paper patterns around a bit – bought in Woollies for sixpence each or made by myself on newspaper – until they would fit. Some years on, I was confident enough to make myself a coat from blanket material and, although I say it myself, made a pretty good job of it. But that was after I took a part-time job and could afford it.

As with all houses, old and new, the décor didn't take long to fade or get dirty, especially as both Jimmy and I were smokers at that time. Of course, cigarettes were far less expensive than they are now (I can remember how worried I was when they rose to one shilling and fourpence for twenty in a Budget one year), but it didn't cure us of the habit. I bought Player's Weights or another of the smaller brands for myself, and Jimmy preferred Capstan Full Strength, but more often he was reduced to Woodbines, neither of which did his chest any good. There were no warnings then about smoking being bad for your health, so we gloried on, yet I did sometimes shudder to think what we were doing to our lungs when all our wallpaper and paintwork were some degree of brown, depending on what they had been originally.

I changed the colour schemes occasionally to cheer myself up, but this presented something of a poser since money never matched up with ideas. As soon as Alan had the back bedroom to himself, he wanted wallpaper with aeroplanes on it, the colours ranging from the blue of the sky, to the white of the clouds, to the silver-grey of the planes themselves, to the red of the markings. This was ideal for a boy's room and quite cheap; the only fly in the ointment was the bright yellow curtains that I'd made to go with the previous paper. As they say, necessity is the mother of invention, and I got round the problem by using a school paintbox and a sparsely-haired paintbrush to add a touch of yellow to each of the numerous aircraft – hundreds, it seemed like.

On the subject of curtains, I made a proper *faux pas* one day. I was the only one in all the sixteen houses who had a sewing machine – an old Jones box top model inscribed 'by appointment to Her Majesty Queen Alexandra' and inherited from Jimmy's Auntie Ann – and I was often asked to 'run up' some curtains. Not literally, of course; that would have been somewhat beyond my ability, even at eight stone seven. (It's hard even for me to believe that I was ever as lightweight as that, but it's the Gospel truth.)

At first, I didn't mind obliging my neighbours, and I knew they couldn't afford to pay me, but I got a bit miffed when they didn't even supply the reels of thread, sometimes it needed two or three and they weren't exactly cheap when you're on a skin-tight budget. I felt that was a bit thick.

Anyway, that wasn't what I set off to say. A lady who lived round the corner came to my door one day to ask if I'd make an apron for her little boy who was starting school the following week. I took her inside until I drew out a shape on an old newspaper, and then measured that against my table, exactly a yard square, to tell her how much material she would need.

While I was thus engaged, she'd been having a good look around my living room. 'D'you know this, Mrs Davidson?' she said suddenly. 'I thought your house would be like a palace, but you haven't even got a carpet.'

I was rather put out at this slur, because I knew of at least one other woman in the vicinity who was in the same boat as I was – a couple of mats covering the linoleum on the floor. Anyway, Mrs M. asked me to go back with her to see if there would be enough material in an old dress of hers.

I was still a bit piqued as we walked round the corner to her house. After all, mine might not be like a palace, but it was as clean as a whistle and I had never expected anyone to criticise it. As soon as we went into *her* living room, though, I could see why she had. A deep-pile, expensive-looking carpet covered her floor, the furniture was much more impressive than mine and included a flashy cocktail cabinet, as she informed me, proudly – not the flashy, just the cocktail bit. Not only that, but there were fancy ornaments and knick-knacks on all available flat surfaces, and even her table was adorned with a wine chenille cover with long fringes. When I told Jimmy all this later, he said that everything had likely been bought on tick, and at least we didn't have any debts to worry about – which did cheer me a little.

Harking back to the apron, there was enough material in the skirt of the dress to make two, so she produced a large pair of scissors and told me to cut what I needed; she wanted to use what was left for something else. Dusters, I daresay. I smoothed the skirt out and laid the pattern on, using the few pins she could supply to fix it in position. Then I started to cut. Her scissors weren't as sharp as they might have been, but at last I was back where I had started. I laid the scissors down and lifted up what I thought were two embryo pinnies. I was wrong. There were *three*! On inspection, I was mortified to find that two were cotton and . . . one was in gorgeous wine chenille – with fringes!

I apologised as best I could, but Mrs M. didn't seem in the least upset. 'It doesn't matter,' she laughed. 'My mother works in . . .' – I can't remember the name of the factory – '. . . and she keeps me supplied.'

Sometimes, however, I couldn't get round a problem so easily, something that I discovered a man can't understand. Like all the other housewives around us, I was absolutely 'skint' by Thursday, paynight, of each week, but I would have done anything rather than advertise the fact. Instead of waiting like the other wives until my husband came home and handed over the housekeeping cash so I could run to the chip van, I did my best to conjure up something from what I had in the larder.

On one particular Thursday, all I had left was one egg, some bread, a small piece of cheese and half a bottle of milk. After flipping through my old school cookery book – I still have this trusted slim volume, printed by Aberdeen City Council for Rosemount Intermediate School, and now in tatters – I plumped for a cheese pudding, as near as I could manage with the ingredients I had. It rose like a dream, was perfectly browned and I waited hopefully for Jimmy to pay me a compliment on my cooking skills. But he laid his fork into the empty plate when he was finished without saying a word.

Frustrated, I asked him outright, 'What did you thank of that?'

'OK,' he nodded. He's never been one to ladle out praise.

'It wasn't bad for just having thruppence in my purse,' I persisted, putting my foot in it well and truly.

Well, you'd have thought I had committed some terrible crime, squandered the entire week's money on something trivial. He glared at me as if he couldn't believe what I'd said. 'What the devil do you do with all the money I give you?'

As I've already said, we had our ups and downs then . . . we still do. If Jimmy hears a couple boasting, 'We've never had a cross word in all the years we've been married,' he always observes later, 'They're either liars or they've had a helluva boring life.'

I wasn't the only one to be taken for a sucker, of course. Jimmy had come home from work one Saturday lunchtime, scoffed his meal, washed, shaved and changed from his oily working clothes into a pair of flannels (his only other pair of trousers) and a sports jacket . . . because he was heading for Pittodrie. The Aberdeen football team was playing Rangers that afternoon, and he was a staunch supporter of the Dons. He was in the scullery, cleaning his brown shoes, when someone rang the bell.

'Is your man in?' asked the stranger on the step, waiting until Jimmy went to the door before explaining, 'Will you ha'e a look at my car? It'll nae start.'

Jimmy pulled a face. 'Will it no' wait?' (He's from Laurencekirk, remember, and even if he had lived in Aberdeen for twenty-three years at that time, his dialect was still recognisable – still is, another forty odd years on.) 'I'm gaen to the match, but I'll tak' a look as soon as I get back.'

I couldn't hear why the car had to be fixed right away; I only know that Jimmy came in scowling. 'He says it'll no' tak' lang.'

The game started at three o'clock, but there was no sign of Jimmy . . . nor by four o'clock, and I didn't even know where he was. I hadn't recognised the frustrated motorist. The match would have been in injury time before James trailed in.

'Did you manage to fix the car?' I asked, risking having my nose snapped off.

'Aye, but he'd a bloody cheek! "It'll no' tak' lang", he said, 'but the . . .'

Here he reeled off a list of things he'd had to do and the time it had taken him to locate where the fault lay. Moreover, the man had just said, 'Thanks', and driven away.

'Did he not even ask how much he owed you?' I prompted, hoping that he'd just forgotten to tell me, and was about to hand me a couple of pounds . . . even a ten bob note would have been very acceptable.

I don't know how that man knew that Jimmy was a mechanic, but, sadly, there had been no mention of payment. Even so, neither of us ever refused to help if anyone came to us.

We did eventually get a car of our own. It was another Saturday forenoon (most employees worked five and a half days a week, then), and Jimmy didn't stop until noon. I was therefore surprised to have a visit from a man who had married one of girls who had worked in McDonald's Garage with me. He was a driver with Esso, who, I believe, worked a system of shifts.

'I know Jim's aye been wanting a car,' he began (I'll call him Charlie), 'and I thought he might be interested in an old Austin I've been working on.'

When I explained that he wouldn't be home till half past twelve, Charlie lifted his shoulders briefly. 'Well, my brother gave it to me for nothing, but, like I said, I've been working on it for a while. I've got it going a bit better, but there's still a lot to be done on it. Take him down in the afternoon, and he can see what he thinks. I'd let him have it for fifteen quid.'

Excited at the prospect of having a car, never mind what it looked like or how old it was, I said that we'd be there. The next hour and a half dragged past, but at last Jimmy came in, his face and hands absolutely clarted with grease as usual.

'I've bought us a car,' I crowed, expecting him to be as pleased as I was.

'For God's sake!' he exploded. 'What do you know about cars?'

'It's Charlie's,' I explained, 'and he says he'll let you have it for fifteen quid.'

'A pile o' auld rubbish, I bet,' was his scornful answer to that.

'I said we'd go and look at it,' I protested, 'and you've always wanted a car.'

'I want a decent car, no' an auld wreck.'

But I could detect a glimmer of interest in his eyes, and I kept on about it until he agreed to take a look. Walking down the hill, I was whistling softly, a bad habit of mine. My Granny used to say, 'Whistling maidens and crawing hens are nae lucky aboot ony man's hoose,' but it never stopped me.

'And you can stop whistling,' my husband barked, 'cos I'm no' buying it.'

When we reached the house, Charlie came out to discuss business, and I went in to have a fly cup with Pat. We hadn't seen each other for quite a while, and we were so engrossed in catching up with each other's news that I didn't notice the time passing.

It was over an hour before a beaming Charlie and a sheepish James came in. 'I'm taking it. I've had it out for a spin and there's a lot to be done to it yet, but I think it'll be fine.'

Drawing up at our own house, we were pleased to see several net curtains twitching. There was only one other family in the cul-de-sac that possessed a car, and the man was a shopkeeper, not a common blue-collar worker. (They were very nice people, just the same, good friends.)

Jimmy spent eight weeks repairing our fourteen-year-old Austin

Sherbourne, a little angular car that he parked on the verge of the grounds to the old Springhill House – this was before the business with the cattle. At a time when vandalism was just a word in the dictionary, there was no fear of any of the parts, cleaned and spread out around it, being stolen, or tyres removed, or any other damage done. At last, we ventured out on a picnic, our very first in our very own vehicle. Alan would have been about four, Sheila about sixteen, and we had called at the Stocket to pick up my mother – her first run in a car since Uncle Jack paid her £5 for my Dad's Erskine in 1934.

I can't remember exactly where we went that first Sunday, not too far, I know that, but we stopped in a lane at the side of a little wood to partake of our eatables and drinkables. It was a lovely day, and we all enjoyed ourselves . . . until, on our way home, we had a puncture. This wasn't Jimmy's fault; he had checked the tyres carefully. In fact, he had said that the wheel nuts were so loose that they would have come off if he had driven the car for any distance without tightening them. It turned out that the damage had been caused by a rusty nail.

While James did the needful, on his knees on the dirty gravel at the side of the road, Mum, Sheila, Alan and I had a walk up a lovely lane, where Alan and his 'Nanny' played with 'carl doddies' – plantains, in other words – where one person holds out their plant and the other uses his to try to knock the other head off.

When I was putting him to bed that night, I asked my tired little son what bit of our day out he had liked best, and, would you credit it, he said, 'Playing carl doddies with Nanny.'

His first run in a car and no mention of the lovely scenery or even the sheep and cows he'd seen. Just playing carl doddies. The children of today would find that extremely boring.

GGG315 gave us many, many hours of pleasure, and the puncture on that first day was the only real repair that it ever needed for as long as we had it. Jimmy was always pottering about with it, and it carried us over quite a large part of Aberdeenshire and even down to Fife to see Auntie Jess in Rosyth. There were some tiny flaws – Alan cried out one day, 'I can see the road through the floor!' Just a wee gap in the floorboards, that was all.

On another outing, we were going up a hill, not a very steep hill but steep enough for our little jalopy, when Alan shouted, 'We passed another vehicle!' We had . . . a man on an ordinary bike. It was the first thing we had ever passed.

I think we had that black Austin Sherbourne for about a year and a half when Jimmy won £100 on a football competition run by the *Sunday Post*. Having had a few drinks to celebrate, he came home, spread the fivers on the floor and told me, 'You're not getting a penny of this. I'm buying a better car.'

He bought another Austin, a black A40, and for one glorious weekend we had two cars sitting at our gate. Then a neighbour bought the Sherbourne for the £15 he knew we had paid for it, not taking into account the amount of time and money Jimmy, a time-served mechanic, had spent in making it more or less roadworthy. No MOT was needed then. The hundred pounds wasn't enough for the A40 he picked, and for the first time ever, we paid the rest by credit, so much per month.

'It's not tick,' Jimmy excused himself, when I complained that he'd never let me buy anything unless I could pay for it outright. 'Everybody's buying their cars on the never-never.'

'It's still tick,' I persisted, coldly, but hire purchase was used for every car we bought thereafter.

The A40 was followed by a three-year-old, green Ford Anglia, then a two-year-old, wine Ford Cortina and later still a brand new copper brown Ford Escort. This last prompted one wag in William Tawse's yard to fix a label on Jimmy's coat, proclaiming to all and sundry: *This belongs to James Davidson CBE.* When asked why the CBE, he grinned, 'Copper Brown Escort.'

Jimmy had concentrated on Fords because Tawse dealt mainly with this make and all his tools had been bought for it. It was only when Fords became much too expensive that we bought a year-old, silver Datsun Sunny, which we kept for thirteen years. Jimmy, of course, had cared for it religiously, doing all his own repairs and servicing, so that it was almost as good when we traded it in as it had been when it came off the assembly line.

15

Going back to my story, there came a point when my financial situation – non-financial would be nearer the mark – was growing dire. Christmas was looming up and I'd hardly any money for presents. Sheila's was easy enough, buy more material from the Castlegate for next to nothing and make her a dirndl skirt or two. She had started going to the local Youth Club's Saturday dances, and was always asking for something new to wear. A dirndl was simplest of all to make, just a seam up both sides, a hem at the foot and two or three lines of stitching at the waist for two or three rows of elastic. It also used far less material than a circular skirt, which fashion ordained needed a special petticoat, stiffened with sugar and water to make it stick out.

I could just about manage the usual stocking-fillers, an apple, a tangerine, a sugar mouse and some home-made Swiss milk toffee, but what else could I get for Alan? Inspiration came in the guise of an old desk that had once belonged to my sister Bertha and then to Sheila, so Jimmy decided to brighten it a bit. He took home a small amount of green paint from Tawse – a change from Rubislaw grey – and as soon as Alan was in bed on Christmas Eve, he got started.

I, meantime, was engaged in making the Swiss milk toffee – a softer and better version of the 'tablet' now sold in many shops. In fact, it was so good – the recipe, I mean, not my making of it – that my lapsed obsession for condensed milk overpowered me again, and I eventually had to stop buying it, otherwise I'd have been twice the size I am now, and that's saying something.

Our labours over, we both sat down at the fireside to listen to the wireless, no such luxury as a television set for us then. They'd been on sale for a few years, owning one was something to boast about, but they were still far too expensive for folk like us. It would have been about 1960 before we managed to get a secondhand one cheap – a twelve inch, dark green screen in a large mahogany cabinet. It lasted for many years and was only disposed of when the tube went. Unable to pay the £20 a new tube would cost, I resorted to 'tick' to buy a new TV. But that first set was the best we ever had.

Back to business. About ten o'clock on that Christmas Eve, I rose to make a cup of tea before we went up to bed, and as I passed the desk I checked to make sure that the paint was drying. Being industrial paint, not known as quick drying, it was still quite wet, so Jimmy pulled it over to the fire, and we sat down again to drink the tea. You'll have heard the ironic expression, 'As interesting as watching paint dry'? Well, we sat there doing just that for another two hours, then we heard Alan's feet padding down the stairs.

Quick as a flash, we stood up in front of the tacky desk to prevent him seeing Santa's gift before Santa came. Any adult would have twigged what we were doing straight away, but Alan wasn't old enough to suspect his parents of any jiggery-pokery. When we told him that Santa wouldn't come to a little boy who wasn't asleep, he trotted upstairs again and was soon in the Land of Nod. But it was two in the morning before Jimmy and I got to bed, having not quite filled the pillowcases hanging from the mantelpiece and camouflaged the desk with fancy paper tied roughly round it.

*

That summer, Jean Souter, a friend and neighbour and mother of Alan's chum Graham, gave me a little degree of help by asking if I would stand in for her for two weeks. The small West End hotel where she worked had no one to replace her at this, the busiest time of the year, so I agreed somewhat reluctantly. It wasn't that I thought working as a chambermaid would be beneath me, just the opposite. I hadn't a clue as to what would be expected of me, and I didn't want to let the management down . . . or the guests.

On the night before I was due to start, I couldn't sleep a wink for worrying, but it wasn't half as bad as I'd feared; just a case of making beds and keeping the rooms clean and tidy – particularly the bathrooms. Clean towels had to be provided each day, and every inch of the 'smallest rooms' had to be given a thorough going over. Never having stayed in a hotel myself, I prayed that I wasn't missing something vital, but not a soul complained. In fact quite a few showed their appreciation by leaving tips at the end of their stay. Unexpected, but very welcome.

I was quite slow that first morning, probably taking twice as long as Jean did, but once I got into the way of it, I nipped effortlessly through the work. I admit that I was tired at the end of the week, but being handed a pay packet more than made up for that. I was only there for the two weeks, of course, but what I earned, plus the tips, did let me replace some of the clothes the children were outgrowing, and that was one worry off my mind for a while.

Before I knew it, Christmas was just around the corner, and, once again, I couldn't see a way to buy presents for any of my nearest and dearest. Although Jimmy and I agreed not to give each other anything, there were the children to think about. Sheila knew, but I couldn't destroy Alan's belief in Santa Claus.

Then I spotted an item in the Situations Vacant column of the *Evening Express* for a part-time assistant in one of R.S. McColl's shops, evenings only. I applied and started the following week at 5 p.m. I had to leave the house at twenty to five, but Jimmy, who stopped at 4.30 and had to walk home, would be in about ten minutes after I'd gone. Sheila had left Aberdeen Academy (the old Central School) by this time, and was working with a firm of commercial artists. She wasn't home until after six o'clock.

My working 'day' ended at eight, but the three hours I served behind the counter were non-stop; hardly time to draw a breath. Was it just a coincidence that I was back amongst sweeties again? Confectionery, cigarettes and ice cream at our side of the shop, newspapers, cigarettes and fancy goods at the other. I sometimes had to take a turn at the paper side, and two years running I'd to take over for a fortnight to let the usual 'girl' get a holiday.

I enjoyed that, too, although I'd to start at seven in the morning to serve all the workmen with their papers and fags, and didn't finish until two, so it was a long day. More pay, of course, which was not to be sneezed at. Luckily, a neighbour said she would make sure that Alan was ready when her husband was leaving to open his shop. Mr R. had been dropping him off at the Demonstration School since I stopped taking him there myself on the bus. At least I didn't have to worry about Christmas that year.

Christmas Day was not widely recognised as a holiday in Scotland. Tawse's yard didn't stop work until almost 4 p.m., which gave me plenty of time to prepare a festive dinner. Few working class people had turkey, far too expensive, and a hen (we never thought of eating chickens) was a rare treat. We were lucky in having friends whose parents were crofters, so we were occasionally given a hen as a gift – but it had to be plucked and cleaned, a job for James although I did do it once.

As instructed by Jimmy's Auntie Jess, I usually made the Christmas pudding a few weeks earlier, and it only had to be simmered for an hour or so to heat it. Then there were the vegetables to prepare and cook, the custard sauce (no brandy, so no brandy butter) to be made and the mince pies to be baked. As you can imagine, that took me all morning and part of the afternoon, but sad to say, my family scoffed the lot in little over half an hour. They were very appreciative, though, so I didn't mind.

Now came the worst time of the year, for most Scottish women, at any rate. No matter how clean a wife kept her house over the other 364 days, everything had to be absolutely spotless by midnight on Hogmanay. She could not go peacefully into the New Year if she hadn't cleaned and polished everything to within an inch of its existence. Blankets and quilts had to be washed, all cupboards emptied and scrubbed before their contents were replaced. The chimney had to be swept, a chimney sweep was regarded as lucky, but it also meant that the living room walls had to be brushed down, the curtains had to be washed, also every soot-covered ornament.

To be honest, I often didn't get my own face washed and clothes changed until a few minutes to the witching hour, by which time I was too tired to enjoy myself amongst the many neighbours who first-footed us and to whom we usually returned the compliment.

This custom has its drawbacks, depending on where you actually live. In our little group of fourteen homes, if you went to every house, as Jimmy was often determined to do, you would be hard pushed to walk home, plus . . . it took all night to get round them. We didn't start until midnight had struck, of course, not like south of the border where they celebrate during the evening, and I've seen it seven or eight in the morning before we got to bed.

In fact, one earlier year I was pushing Jimmy upstairs at five minutes to nine (he did need some help) when the doorbell went. The doctor had come to see Sheila, who had been suffering for some time with an unexplained illness. He was on his way to see another patient, he explained, and had just popped in. While I took him up to see her, Jimmy went back to the scullery to give the doctor his 'New Year'. He has never been very good at distinguishing whisky glasses (tots in those days) from sherry glasses (the only other drink we could afford for a long time), but I was still mortified when I saw what he had used . . . a thick glass eggcup. For the doctor, of all people.

Mind you, the doc didn't mind. He was very partial to alcohol and was most likely well-oiled before he reached us. By the way, this was not the doctor who ran me home from the garage many years before.

His verdict on Sheila? 'Keep her in bed until I come back.'

He didn't come back, so after a couple of weeks, when she said she felt better and wanted to go back to school, I let her go.

I'll never forget something that Dr C. said when Alan was still an infant. Jimmy and I had been kept awake by his screaming for nights, but we had to go to a wedding on the Saturday afternoon. Sheila had been invited, too, so my mother had offered to stay with the baby. When we got home about 9 p.m., Mum told us she'd had a terrible time with him. 'You'll have to phone the doctor.'

This was a time when very few people had such a thing, and I had to run a good bit to find a phone box. I explained what was wrong and Dr C. asked, 'Have you given him any whisky?'

When, horrified, I said no, he went on, 'Try him with a teaspoonful and if that doesn't work, drink the rest of the bottle yourselves, and you won't hear him.'

It would have been round about this time that my mother's Uncle Alex (Granda's younger brother) died, and Jimmy was given his motor-assisted bicycle. This was a great help to him. He didn't have to leave so early for work in the morning, and he was home a little earlier than before. Now, the peculiar thing about this was that his driving licence didn't allow him to take his 'gift' on the road without L plates. He could drive a motorcycle, a ten-ton lorry, an ordinary motor car, even a tractor, yet it was no to an ordinary two-wheeler with a little engine inside a square box on the rear carrier. I ask you?

It was the year of the Suez crisis, so although he applied for a licence right away, he had to wait many months before he was allowed to have a test. Fifteenth September at 10 a.m., it said on the card, so he had to ask time off work. When he left the house, the big L plates on the front and rear mudguards proclaimed that he was a mere novice, yet he'd been driving since he was seventeen . . . and over five years in the war, on all kinds of vehicles.

'You'd better have got rid of them before you come back,' I warned him, in fun, naturally. He couldn't fail, could he?

Imagine how I felt – and how he must have felt – when I saw the bike coming round the corner into the cul de sac with the white square of celluloid still there, and the red 'L' still to the fore.

'I didn't fail,' he said, shaking his head in disgust. 'They said I was two weeks late, so I'd missed the test.'

I couldn't credit this. The card had said the fifteenth, and this was the fifteenth, so how could he have been two weeks too late? When we studied the card, however, we realised what had happened. Whoever had filled in the date on the printed card had written what we thought was a one and a five with a little squiggly 'th'. What it turned out to be was a one and a big S with a little squiggle for a 't'. Not fifteenth, but first. Fortunately the Licensing Officer got him another test two weeks later, so he didn't have too long to put up with his workmates' jibes.

A SECOND CAREER

16

When Hilda Glennie, née Mathieson, walked into the shop one night in 1963, she was surprised to find me working there. I hadn't seen her for a few years – she was the school friend who had later worked in the Co-op haberdashery department in Loch Street – and remembering what she had once told me, I asked, 'Are you on your way to practise with your opera company?'

She shook her head. 'No, I'm going to evening classes. I want to be a teacher, but I need qualifications to get into the Training College, and here are you, Dux of the school, behind a counter serving sweeties. What a waste of a brain.'

Before I could ask any questions as to how or where or when, a man pushed his way in front her. 'Twenty Benson and Hedges, please.'

Hilda left with a smiling, 'Think about it.'

I was preoccupied for the rest of that evening. As a teacher, I'd have the same holidays as Alan – by this time Sheila was married and living in England – so that would be a bonus to add to the dangling carrot of the salary. When I went home I asked Jimmy what he thought, and as usual he was cautious, 'There's no harm in going to find out about it.'

'You wouldn't mind?'

'I wouldn't mind, if that's what you want.'

After a sleepless night, I waited until my little brood had left for work and school, then dressed carefully to go to the College of Education, better known as the Training College or more familiarly T.C., to enquire how to gain entrance. I was told that I'd need three Highers (the Scottish equivalent to 'A' levels) and two Lowers ('O' levels) and the entrance date was the first week in October, also that I should attend classes at the Commercial College to gain these qualifications. 'There is no grant for your first year of study,' the man continued. 'You have to prove yourself capable of carrying on, but a grant will be paid for your second year, provided, of course, that you have passed the first exams you sat.'

I went home somewhat bewildered. If I wanted to be a teacher and earn a decent salary, I'd have to attend evening classes. That would mean I'd have to give up my part-time job and there was no grant for a first year of study. I explained the position to Jimmy that night, and he was more optimistic than I was. 'You'll definitely get a grant in your second year.'

'Only if I pass what I sit in the first year,' I almost wailed. 'I'll be forty-one in June, and it's nearly twenty-six years since I left school. How do I know I'll cope with lessons again? My brain likely won't take things in.'

He was exasperated with me now, I could see that. 'Don't be stupid. There's nothing wrong with your brain.'

I left it at that, and the next day saw me applying to the Commercial College for more information. Imagine my surprise to learn that the entrance exams were taking place that very evening. The clerk noted my name and address before saying, 'You won't be thinking of trying tonight's exams, though?'

When I nodded, he said, 'There are only two. English for the first hour, then Maths, just enough to let us see if you stand any chance of passing.'

I thanked him and walked out into the lovely May sunshine. He obviously didn't think much of my chances. He had likely been wondering how an old hag like me could hope to pass one, never mind two. I sat down when I went home, trying to think what I could do. I could pass English, I'd no doubt about that, but Maths was a different matter. I'd never been exactly happy with numbers, and I had forgotten most of what I'd learnt.

On my way home, I went in to R. S. McColl's to tell the manageress that I wouldn't be in that night, and then agonised all afternoon over the ordeal in front of me. I had quite enjoyed using algebra at school to solve problems, but I wouldn't know where to start now. Neither could I recall what the formula was for finding the area of a circle. A square was simple, length times breadth, and the same for a rectangle, but that was as far as I could go . . . and as for solids and cubic measurements, that was a blank page. I'd never been able to master logarithms, but surely – oh, surely – there wouldn't be a question on that in the exam?

As soon as he came home, Jimmy could see how upset I was, and bless him; he did his best to cheer me. 'You'll easily manage, don't worry. Look, I'll give you a run down to Holburn Street so you won't have to scutter about taking two buses. And never mind about the dishes, I'll soon clear everything up.'

About three quarters of an hour later, I stepped out of the car, the A40 I think, and tried to pull myself together as I trembled up the stairs. There were about thirty boys and girls already seated at the desks, and they all looked as if they had just newly left school. I stood out like a sore thumb, but I told myself that there was no point in coming this far and copping out now. As soon as the invigilator told us to turn over our papers and begin, I bent my head to concentrate on the English paper.

There were questions on grammar, on punctuation, on changing sentences from past to present tense and singular nouns to plural, that sort of thing. Kids' stuff! Then we came to the business of writing an essay, something I'd always loved. There were about five choices of theme, and I chose: 'Describe a regular ritual or event peculiar to your own town or village.' That may not have been the exact wording, but it's as near as I can remember, and as soon as I read it, I could visualise Aberdeen's 'Timmer Market'.

This was held yearly on the last Thursday of August, and had been a milestone in my life for as long as I could remember. It was held in the Castlegate, a marketplace which, every Friday and Saturday, held stalls selling secondhand furniture, books, clothes, plus my favourite, the fabric stall. There were also the glib quick-sell men with their dishes and gadgets for the house.

The Timmer Market of the twenties to the fifties and sixties mostly sold items made of wood (timmer being the Doric for timber). There were many stalls selling wooden toys, some selling candy, plums, monkey nuts, locust beans or other eatables that children liked. During the morning and afternoon, therefore, it was mainly mothers and children who wandered around, and the kids were soon clutching a monkey climbing a stick, or an acrobat doing somersaults between two sticks, or a handful of balloons. I don't think helium was on the go then, just ordinary blow-them-up-yourself types.

In the evening, though, there was only a scattering of older children, and the rest of the throng consisted mostly of men buying wooden guns or large lorries for their sons, dolls for their daughters or little trinkets for their wives. Because it was pay night, most had already paid a visit to one of the drinking establishments nearby and were in a generous mood, so the stallholders had found business pretty brisk. This was the most impressive time. The stalls were illuminated by naphtha flares, the smell of which – mingled with the sweet aroma of candy and the stink of the rotten plums that littered the ground and made you watch your step – was something I have never forgotten. As soon as you came round the corner from Union Terrace into Union Street, whether in a bus, a tramcar or on foot, your nose could pick up the smell, your eyes were haunted by the flickering flares. It always excited me, even when I was a mother myself and had little to spend.

A Timmer Market is still held every year, but few wooden items are on sale, just the usual type of cheap-John ornaments and tat . . . at least from what I hear. I haven't gone for years.

From what I've written about it, you can perhaps understand why I picked that as a subject for my essay, and I've always believed that what I wrote about the Timmer Market that night won me my pass in English. I was very glad that this came first. If Maths had been first, I'd have panicked, but having successfully handled the English part, I felt more confident. The Arithmetic paper was fairly straightforward, but then came the very things I had dreaded: the formulas that I couldn't remember. Worse, when I let my eye run down to the last section, dotted with a's and b's and x's and y's, I laid down my pencil. There was no point in going any further, so I took my jacket off the back of the chair, handed in my unfinished paper and walked out. Being the very first to go, I could guess that the others were wondering how I had managed to answer all the questions so quickly. Little did they know.

Jimmy tried to console me, but how could I have passed the Maths exam when I'd only answered half of it? But at least I had tried, and as he said, 'That's the main thing.'

We were very busy the following Saturday evening in the shop with the first influx of holidaymakers, and even with five of us working as fast as we could, there were always people waiting to be served. I was giving a woman her change when I noticed that the person behind her was the man who had been invigilating at the examination. My heart plunged until it dawned on me that he wouldn't have known I worked there and he probably wouldn't remember me anyway.

But he'd had time to recognise me – I'd stuck out among the youngsters – and he came forward smiling when I said, 'Next, please?' How could he smile when he must think I was an ignorant middle-aged woman who hadn't a hope of ever setting foot inside a classroom again?

'This is a pleasant surprise, Mrs Davidson, but you will understand that I am not at liberty to tell you your marks.'

'Yes, I know.' I was glad that he couldn't tell me how badly I'd done, especially in front of a shopful of people. I'd never have been able to hold my head up again.

'I'll just say this, in case you are worrying, you came out on top.'

I could hardly believe it, but before I had time to react in any way, he added, 'Half a pound of Chocolate Violets, please. My wife's favourite.'

He handed me the correct money in exchange for the paper bag – closed in the way I'd been taught – and said, 'I'm looking forward to seeing you in August,' before he turned away and was lost in the crowd.

My head was in a whirl. I had passed! I had actually passed. After missing out half the questions, I had come top. That couldn't be right . . . could it?

The official result, letting me know that although I had done well in English, I had passed Maths by the skin of my teeth, came with a letter telling me to report on such-and-such a date to give particulars of which subjects I intended studying in my first year. Higher English was essential, and I chose Higher Geography and Lower Mathematics. That left just one higher and one lower to sit in my second year, giving me scope for resitting anything I failed in the first.

These were duly noted, but I discovered that the Higher subjects were all day classes; only the Lower grades were dealt with in the evenings. This put a different complexion on things. I had hoped to change my part-time job to mornings or afternoons to let me have the evenings free to study, but this meant that daytime hours were out, too.

I did wonder if I could possibly manage on Jimmy's pay when I had textbooks to buy over and above what I'd need for housekeeping. My thoughts went round in a circle – it was only for one year; I'd get a grant for my second year; surely I would manage if I was extra careful?

Sheila had married and flown the coop by this time, so I had already lost the board money she paid me out of her pay as a trainee commercial artist. I told myself that I couldn't give up now, and when Jimmy's niece was accepted at the Hairdressing part of the Commecial College, I agreed to let her lodge with me. Then I was asked to take her friend, who was training as a nurse, and because they got very little in wages, I said I would just charge them ten shillings each, provided they helped me in the house. I knew I'd be pushed to do everything myself, when I would be out so much, plus I'd have to study a lot at home.

I should have known it wouldn't work. They were two sixteen-year-olds, had never been away from home before and, coming to the city from the small town of Laurencekirk, they wanted to make the most of their freedom. I won't go into all the details, but I eventually had to tell them to find somewhere else. This of course didn't please my sister-in-law, and relations between us were practically non-existent for quite a long time.

The year flew past, but I found it exhilarating if hard work. There were only five of us in the Higher Geography class, three young lads and a girl who had left school two years earlier and we all became close friends. Things were made more interesting by having to go to different places for the different classes. For instance, we had to go to Marywell Street School for English, quite a distance from the College although under its supervision. Geography lessons were in St Katherine's Club, even farther away. The 'O' level Arithmetic class was in the College itself . . . in the evenings.

Now, this was 1963 and we had another, rather more upsetting, situation to contend with. An outbreak of typhoid hit the city, and it was virtually cut off from the rest of the country. The gutters in the streets ran with white disinfectant, lavatories in all public places were supplied with cakes of strong carbolic soap for washing hands, and still the numbers of people infected crept up and up. There weren't many deaths, but the illness took a heavy toll, and by the time it reached its peak, over four hundred had succumbed to it.

It gradually tailed off, and Aberdeen was at last pronounced free of the virus or whatever it was, but few holidaymakers turned up that year. This fear of picking something up may have carried on for some time had the Queen herself not paid a visit. This proof of the monarch's belief in our city was enough to make other people see sense. It was a dreadful time, and it started through a tin of infected corned beef in a small supermarket, which was boycotted and finally forced to vacate the premises.

The results of the examinations were sent from Edinburgh by mail during Aberdeen's Trades Fortnight – two weeks in July when the tradesmen went on holiday. All firms, large and small, closed down completely – the same as Glasgow at the Fair – so many of the large manila envelopes had not been delivered. We had gone to Surrey to see Sheila and her husband, and a small card was waiting on the doormat when we came home on the Saturday night. (Jimmy liked to have a Sunday to relax before starting work again.) 'We were unable to deliver a package addressed to you. Please collect from the Parcels Office in Crown Street.'

I left Alan playing with his chums on Monday forenoon and took the bus into town, trembling with anticipation. Fear of failure? I couldn't analyse it myself. The man in the parcels office must have seen hundreds of the envelopes, and said, as he handed mine over, 'This'll be for your daughter?'

'No, it's mine,' I quavered, dying to tear it open, but not wanting to appear too eager.

'Yours?' he said, in amazement. 'Well, open it and tell me if you've passed.'

I had passed all three! If there had not been a counter between us, I believe I'd have thrown my arms round that man and danced him round the small floor. It was a wonderful feeling, but now I had to go to the College of Education in John Street to find out about the grant I would be given for the next year.

Three men interviewed me, and I listened while they discussed my position, though I hardly took in a thing they said. Then one looked at me gravely, and I knew that it wasn't good news, yet I couldn't understand why. Hadn't I passed what I had sat in my first year? What was wrong?

'I'm afraid, Mrs Davidson, that you have been a little too smart for your own good. Since you were here last, the requirements for mature students have been reduced. Two 'O' levels are still needed, but only two 'A' levels are necessary now . . . which you have already obtained.'

'Yes?' I was even more puzzled.

'You have passed one 'O' level, so you only need one more.'

'Yes?' I still couldn't understand what he was getting at.

'This means that you can take an evening class in whatever subject you wish . . . and there is no grant given for attending one evening class. I'm sorry.'

I was devastated as I closed the door behind me. I'd worked so hard and all for nothing. Well, not for nothing, but for no grant, that was sure. I had done myself out of that. Then I heard quick footsteps behind me, and turned round to see the man who had introduced himself as the Deputy Principal hurrying after me.

'Wait, Mrs Davidson. I could see you were disappointed, and I sympathise, but I have a little suggestion to make. You only need one 'O' level, so you should think about trying the equivalent University Preliminary Examination in a subject of your choice. The exams are held late in August or the beginning of September, and results are not given until the end of October, but we would allow you to start with us at the beginning of the month. Should you fail your chosen subject, however, you would be asked to leave us and try again next year. It is entirely up to you.'

He left me scarcely knowing where I was or what I was doing, but I soon gathered my senses together. I'd been given a lifeline, and I wouldn't refuse it.

My next call was to Marischal College, Aberdeen's University, to arrange to sit an exam. This wasn't far, so I hadn't made up my mind about a subject when I reached the magnificent granite building in the Gallowgate, which sadly no longer functions as a university. They intend turning it into flats. Sacrilege!

The lady behind the desk took a note of my name and address, and nodded when I told her what had happened. Then she said, 'Which subject?'

'Botany.' She looked as surprised as I felt. I had no idea where that came from, but I'd always been interested in flowers, so perhaps I'd be OK. All the same, there was one big problem to overcome: where would I find someone to help me through it?

To cut a long story short, I had to resort to taking a large tome on botany from the library and copying it down word for word – the only way I could get some of it into my head. It was actually a textbook for 'A' level students, so I couldn't go wrong . . . if I stuck at it.

17

The College of Education was a different matter, like transferring from primary school to secondary, especially for the first few weeks. I couldn't let myself settle in too comfortably when there was every possibility that I would have to leave in disgrace. I was the only mature student in my section, and the lecturers could always remember my name.

It may not have stemmed from my age, of course. It could have been because of what I said on my first day. In our very first proper class after the registration and welcome from the principal, we went to a lesson marked in our timetables as 'Speech'. This did not involve, as you may think, teaching us how to make a speech, but rather it taught us how to feel at ease in front of an audience, how to sound our vowels and speak clearly. We had to begin by standing up individually and introducing ourselves to the rest of the class, giving name, home area, age and reason for wanting to be a teacher.

I don't know how we were listed, not by age or surname, probably at random, and I came about fifteenth out of twenty-three, so I listened attentively. I wouldn't remember all the names, but at least it would give me an idea of what to say. They came from all over Scotland, short and tall, dark and fair – only two of us had red hair – and the reasons for wanting to be a teacher were very similar.

'I've always wanted to be a teacher, ever since I was very small.'

'I love children and want to teach them.'

'I want to dedicate myself to educating children.'

And so on . . . *ad nauseam*.

I had been so intent on listening that I hadn't planned what I should say, so when my turn came, I stood up sure that I'd make a fool of myself in front of all these self-assured eighteen-year-olds. I was forty-two, old enough to be their mother, and mothers weren't always looked on with admiration. When I gave my name, my voice came out weakly, so I repeated it, louder, and with the effort, I found my feet.

I didn't feel shy now, and gave my home area as Aberdeen, then I looked directly at Mr M. the lecturer, and said, 'I think you've got a nerve expecting a lady to tell you her age.' This was when I got my very first laugh, a marvellous feeling, especially when I hadn't planned it. Ever since then, I've always tried to inject a little humour into the talks I give. This usually makes a bond between the audience and me, even more so if it happens spontaneously.

When the laughter subsided, Mr M., who had laughed loudest and longest, prompted, 'What made you decide to become a teacher?'

Again I answered without thought. 'The long holidays.'

'At least you are honest, Mrs Davidson.'

'Well, I do want to help children to learn the three Rs, but the holidays are just as important for me. I can be at home with my son.' I waited for a rebuke, but none came. In fact, his eyes were twinkling when he asked the others what they thought and thus started a lively discussion.

I was to learn that most of the lecturers liked a bit of controversy, which was good for me. I had never been able to hold my tongue. In our first History Class, the tutor set us a little test to prove that learning dates etc. by rote was a waste of time. 'For a few days before your exam, you had crammed all the dates unto your head but, as soon as the pressure was off, you completely forgot them. I'll give you a small test to prove my point.'

He read out twenty questions – such as what happened in 1066, which battle took place in 1314, when was the Union of the Crowns, which year was the Battle of Waterloo – and we had to write the answers then hand the page to the person next us to check.

I'm not boasting when I say that I had most correct. Eleven out of twenty is nothing to boast about, but it still beat the others, most of whom had scored seven or eight, one or two even less. One of the girls now stood up and said, quite indignantly, 'That wasn't fair. I haven't done History since Third Year.'

She had just left school that summer, and was speaking about two years ago, or three at the most, so I felt strongly enough to say, 'It's twenty-seven years since I left school, so that proves that dates *do* stay in the mind, more or less.'

Mr L. gave a hearty laugh. 'It seems like it, doesn't it?'

But it's not dates that are taught nowadays. We were shown how to teach in patches. The Romans, the Vikings, the Picts and Celts . . . and they didn't have to be in chronological order. The trouble with this method was, as I found out when I was out on teaching practice, the same class could do the Romans with one teacher, move to another the following year and do the Romans again. I'm speaking about the years between 1964 and 1982 here, because I don't know how anything is taught now.

*

We had thirteen subjects to worry about that first year. Apart from English and Maths, we had History (replaced by Geography in our second), Physical Education, Religious Education, Psychology, Biology, Music, Craftwork, Art, Health, Speech and one other which escapes me. I found some of them fairly straightforward – I loved Art and could copy anything that was set in front of me, but I couldn't do anything out of my own head. One Art teacher told me that children couldn't understand or do detailed drawings, and I would have to train myself to do big splotches of colour and work in simple outlines. With that, he tore up the picture I had done, which didn't do much for my confidence.

The PE teacher drew me aside the first day. 'You may sit down whenever you feel tired, Mrs Davidson.'

Awkwardly stubborn as usual, I determined not to give in at anything, so I climbed wall bars, did exercises on the parallel bars, swung myself up on a trapeze and almost broke my arms getting my feet on the floor again, but I didn't sit down. I hadn't felt tired . . . until the lesson was over.

I suffered from my foolhardiness the next morning. Every bone in my body refused to move when I put my feet on the floor, and I had to go downstairs backwards for a few days, at college as well as at home. I was glad to bow to my advancing years after that.

I thoroughly enjoyed Craftwork. Years of making do and mending, and knitting for my own children, bolstered by many things Jimmy's Auntie Jess had taught me – she attended craft classes even when she was over seventy, and every year when we stayed with her on holiday, she showed me her latest skill – how to crochet fancy table centres with delicate rose or pineapple patterns; how to make a poodle toilet roll holder and nail and thread pictures, all sorts of things that came in handy when I was teaching. I was astonished to find that quite a few of the girls in my section couldn't knit or sew, and even when they explained that they weren't taught that in Secondary Schools any longer I couldn't understand it. Hadn't their mothers shown them? Or were they just as handless?

I got on quite well in Music, discovering at one point that I could put any song or piece of music into tonic sol-fa, a result of many years of playing the piano by ear. The lecturer came in one day enthusing about a boy in Primary 7 of the Demonstration School, how he could write tunes down, and recognise notes being played. 'Yes,' he beamed, looking round the class, 'Alan Davidson's full of music.' His voice tailed away as it dawned on him, and he concentrated on me. 'Alan Davidson? He wouldn't be your son, would he?'

Alan was, still is, very musical, but I'll spare his blushes by not giving details of the places he has played, and the musicians he has played alongside.

At the end of October, I had to go to Marischal College (our main university then, but alas no more) to learn the result of the 'O' level Botany that I had tried some months earlier. This made me late for the Music class, first in the afternoon, but Lillias had told the lecturer why.

When I did walk into the classroom, he said, 'Come on, then, Mrs Davidson. Tell us – is it good news or bad?'

'Good news,' I told him, proudly.

'So we won't be losing your company? That *is* good news.'

I had almost forgotten that failure would have meant banishment.

Part of the criteria for passing the three-year music course was to play a piece of music of your choice with both hands. I picked a fairly simple version of Bach-Gounod's *Ave Maria*, and managed to get through without faltering too often. Playing so much by ear has made me lose the ability to read left and right hand notes simultaneously. I can play the right hand with ease, the left hand a little less easily, but putting them together is a nightmare. I was lucky, of course, in having more than a nodding acquaintance with a piano. To quite a few of my classmates, a musical instrument of any kind was a total stranger. I did admire Catherine, though. Starting from absolute scratch, she learned to play by sheer determination.

Psychology, a dry subject, was lightened by the tutor, who had the same sense of humour as I have. He came in quite late one afternoon, explaining that he had seen a man lying in Blackfriars Street (round the corner from the College) and, thinking that he had been taken ill, had asked where he lived.

'Echt,' the man told him.

This small village was some miles from the city, but the 'Good Samaritan' took him there and then asked for the exact address.

By this stage of the story, we were all listening anxiously to hear what had happened to the poor man, but when the tutor gave us the punchline, 'He looked up at me and said, "I bide in echt Blackfriars Street,"' I found myself the only one who laughed. For the benefit of those poor souls without the benefit of the Doric, and for those who haven't seen the joke, echt is Scottish for eight and Blackfriars Street was where the man had been lying . . . the fictitious man . . . with the fictitious illness.

This same lecturer had spent ninety minutes another morning discussing why it wasn't right that the children of wealthy parents should have a better education in their private schools than those who had to go to ordinary schools. It was a lively debate, some (myself among them) holding that private schools were really no better than council-run, but the consensus of opinion, allegedly held by the lecturer himself, was that there shouldn't be any private schools, that all children should have the same chance.

When the bell rang for the lunch break, Mr L. said, 'You'll have to excuse me, ladies, but I promised my wife I'd collect our two girls from St Margaret's today,' and dashed out.

He turned and winked before closing the door behind him. In his position, of course he would send his daughters to a private girls' school, and his stance of being against such establishments had been so much hot air. Again, I was the only one who saw the funny side of this; the rest were angry at being fooled.

Lillias, who had been at Commercial College with me, was also in the same section at TC, and because she had left school two years earlier, she considered the other girls too young for her. I've a feeling that she was afraid that I'd be odd one out – twenty-three won't divide into pairs even if you're a genius at Maths – but we became very close friends, having a little stroll round the shops every day after we had lunch in the canteen, or, if it was bad weather, sitting in the huge common room with whoever else was there. Before I go any further, I must tell you that we are still as close, perhaps even closer, today as we were then. She and her husband, now retired as professor at Cardiff University, come to see us every August at the end of their month's holiday in Cullen.

Getting back to my tale, it happened that Lillias had to go home one lunchtime, and I went window-shopping on my own. I was walking up George Street when I decided to cross to a ladies' dress shop at the other side, and stepped off the pavement without thinking.

I heard nothing behind me, but when I felt an awful thump in my back, I thought I'd been hit by a bus. Fortunately, it was only a boy on a bicycle, but even so, I was knocked to the ground. I must have passed out for a moment or two, because when I realised what was going on, I was surrounded by anxious women clamouring to help me to my feet.

As I am sure many of you have done, I felt so embarrassed, and foolish, that I shrugged off all help and got up, rather shakily, by myself.

The crowd dispersed to go their various ways . . . except one old lady who looked as though she didn't have two ha'pennies to rub together.

She took hold of my arm as I negotiated the kerb and astounded me by saying, 'I've got a bottle o' brandy in my bag. Would you like a wee tootie? You look as if you need it.'

I thanked her very much, but declined. I couldn't have gone back into a lecture room reeking of brandy.

That night, I gave Jimmy my tale of woe, and he was deeply concerned. 'Was the boy hurt?' he asked anxiously. 'Was his bike OK?'

Ah well! I hadn't given one thought to the poor boy, but I was almost sure that he wasn't there when I came to my senses. He must have cycled off. I hope so.

Next day was our very first day of teaching practice, our assignment was every Friday for ten weeks, if I remember correctly . . . perhaps eight. Another girl and I had to go to the Girls' High School, now Harlaw Academy with boys as well as girls. Aileen was scheduled for Primary Fives, and I was down for Primary Ones. I discovered this to be the worst age group for anyone in my delicate condition. I was bruised right down my back, and I ached – really ached – all over, and the little ones couldn't speak to me without grabbing my hand or pulling at some other part of my body.

It was agony, and I had to put up with it for the whole day. I kept hoping that the teacher would let me go home, she must have seen how shaken I was, but she didn't. Worse still, it was January, snowing quite badly and freezing cold, but students were not allowed in the staff room. Aileen and I had to monitor the little ones at playtime, and then rush in to have a cup of coffee when the teachers went back to their own rooms.

We had to go out at lunchtime, so we took the bus back to the College to have something to eat. All the girls commented on how ill I looked and advised me to go home, but I was afraid it would be a black mark against me if I did, so I went back in the bus with Aileen. It was the very last half hour in the afternoon before I was told to give my lesson, by which time I was almost crawling on my hands and knees, my back was so sore.

It took me some weeks to recover but, by my last day at the High, when my tutor came to hear me giving a lesson, I was at least feeling something like normal. I had written a story about wild animals, preparing a strip of paper painted to represent the jungle, with slots to put in a picture of each animal as it came into the tale – stuck to a spill to steady it – all quite technical. I had given a lot of thought to the story, and to the names for the beasts. Some were easy – Leo the lion, Sammy the snake, Mickey the monkey, and so on, but I just couldn't think what to call the hippopotamus. Keeping to my idea of the name beginning with the same letter, I eventually plumped for Hilda, the hippo.

Miss D. seemed satisfied with what I did, and how the little girls reacted to me, although it was difficult to judge what she thought, but I went home quite pleased with my first attempt at teaching on trial.

On the Monday, however, back in college, I was somewhat apprehensive when Miss D. gave us her actual opinion of our efforts – the dreaded criticism. She didn't hold back, praising some and slating some, and I hoped that she wouldn't take too long to put me out of my misery. She was actually taking us in the order of her visits, so I was last. She looked at me balefully, and I wondered what I had done wrong.

'I didn't care much for your choice of names, Doris,' she said – she was the only one of all the lecturers and students to use my Christian name – the words dripping with . . . antagonism?

I couldn't understand, and must have shown my bewilderment, for she went on, 'Why did you call your hippopotamus Hilda?'

'I thought it sounded right,' I ventured. 'Hilda, the hippo.'

'And you honestly didn't know that my name is Hilda?'

I'm sure my chin must have dropped, but unfortunately, it suddenly struck me as very funny and I couldn't help laughing . . . not just ordinary laughter, though. With the release of the tension at having to wait so long for this devastating report, I was almost hysterical – knowing it was the wrong thing to do, but powerless to stop.

It dawned on me that the others were sitting silently, waiting, I suppose, for an explosion, but wonder of wonders, Miss D.'s mouth was lifting in a smile. Not a very big smile, but at least it was no longer down at the edges.

On another teaching practice, I had two 'crits' in the same day. First thing in the morning, the English lecturer came to Victoria Road School to see how I was progressing with my Primary Seven class, and last thing in the afternoon, the Physical Education teacher was coming to watch me taking them for gym.

I had heard that the children knew exactly what was going on in these situations, that the student was on trial, and they generally came out on her (or his) side, but I might not have believed this if I hadn't experienced it myself. My first 'crit' went off quite well, the kids were like little angels, striving to answer the questions I asked, but because I still had the gym lesson to take, I was a bundle of nerves for the rest of the forenoon. This did not escape one girl.

'Dinna worry, Mrs Davidson,' she whispered as she went out at lunchtime. 'You'll be fine.'

I wasn't fine, though. My stomach was churning, I'd a touch of diarrhoea and I wished I could go home. The PE tutor came into the gym at three, shook my hand and then sat down beside a girl who had some problem with her back and couldn't participate. I had planned my lesson carefully; I can't recall anything now except the *faux pas* I made. I had split them into groups and one group had to take a rubber mat out of the cupboard for what they had to do. I could see that they were struggling to get one out of the jumbled pile in the confined space, so I went to help them. Unfortunately, I accidentally stood on the corner of a mat as the two big boys gave it a tug. I wouldn't have minded so much if I had fallen to the floor gracefully, but I staggered a few times with my arms flailing, trying to keep my feet and then collapsed in an ungainly heap.

I was afraid to look at the tutor, and she said nothing as she went to talk to the headmaster later (presumably giving him a laughing account of the stupid mature student he had been harbouring) but when we went back to the classroom, the girl who had also been watching sidled up to me. 'You ken the time you fell? Well, that woman wrote something doon in her book. I couldna see what it was, but will you get a row for it?'

My sense of humour came to my aid. 'Likely,' I giggled, 'but I think everything else went smoothly enough.'

'Aye, but if you'd left the loons to tak' the mat oot theirsel's, you wouldna of fell, would of you?'

And that was exactly what the tutor said back at college, in better English, and I got a long lecture on letting the children do things for themselves. She had nothing else derogatory to say about me, however, and I was given a 'C'.

Then came another kind of test, teaching in pairs, although I don't know what this was meant to prove. Anyway, Lillias and I were placed together in one of the only two Roman Catholic primary schools in Aberdeen. We were told not to go in until half past nine because they had a religious service for the first half-hour. That suited us very well, and we were even more pleased when we saw the class we would be having. We were to be two weeks there alongside the teacher, and two weeks without her, and there were only – would you believe – nine children. Three each for the first two weeks. Not only that, we also got off early in the afternoons, because they had another, shorter, service before they went home.

A little diversion here. Around this time, I decided that I'd like to learn to drive, after all. (You may recall my aborted attempt almost twenty years earlier, when I worked in the garage.) I may say here, categorically, that it's not a good idea to ask your husband to give you driving lessons.

Jimmy had taught my sister to drive, and one day, when he'd jumped down my throat several times for doing stupid things, I said, 'Bertha always said you were really patient with her, so why are you raving at me?'

He heaved a deep sigh. 'She learned in her own car. You're playing merry hell with mine, that's the difference.'

On another occasion, I was driving down a fairly long hill and getting more and more annoyed at the things he was saying, so I eventually slammed on the brakes, shouted, 'Drive the bloody car yourself, then,' and jumped out.

He talked me back in, of course, but I'd had enough. I didn't have far to look for professional tuition. Lillias's father ran a driving school. He was the best person I could have chosen; no mealy-mouthed obeisance, just outright, honest criticism. And I do mean criticism.

I was so nervous that he gave me a slap on the leg one day. Another time, when I asked if he had anybody else as nervous as I was, he snapped, 'There's nobody else in this world as nervous as you.' But his eyes were twinkling and I knew he didn't mean it. Um . . . I think. I was more nervous than ever when he told me to apply for my test, and wonder of wonders, I passed first time.

I had another Primary One class at one point – at Drumgarth School, now no longer. Most of the children were very well behaved, but there was one little monster . . . to put it mildly. He swore (at five years old), he refused to do any work, he wouldn't sit down when he was told and he wouldn't stop shouting if he felt like it, his voice deep and penetrating. This was fairly early in my student days and I was petrified of being left alone with him, even for the half-hour each day I was allowed. At those times, the teacher herself took him with her, to the staffroom or wherever she went. I will call this boy John Wallace, a beautiful, blue-eyed boy with fair curly hair, looking like an angel but actually the devil incarnate. Keep him in mind; he features drastically in my life in a few years.

We had to take a turn at teaching in a rural school, and although I was by then licensed to drive, I wasn't looking forward to an early start in the morning. I could be sent anywhere in Aberdeenshire. As it happened, I had to go to Kingswells School, a matter of ten minutes on the bus (door to door) from where we now lived. We had moved to Hazlehead in 1966, but I'll get round to that in the next chapter.

Rural schools often had two age groups in the same class, and I was delegated to Primaries one and two, to start in the first week of 1967. On Hogmanay, I couldn't breathe properly because of some obstruction in my nose and when the doctor examined me on the second of January, he said I had polyps that would have to be removed. But I would have to wait some time for the operation.

I went to Kingswells, therefore, speaking as if I had a bad head cold. 'I'b sorry, girls ad boys, but there is subthig wrog with by dose.' That was what I said to them, and they were all suitably impressed. I shudder to think what would have happened if I'd been in a school in town, but these dear lambs looked after me like nursemaids.

I think it was into May before I had the operation – a horrible messy business that left me feeling constantly dizzy. Our graduation was in June, and I was nothing like recovered. Then came the day we were interviewed for teaching posts. I hadn't been able to wash my hair for weeks, or let anyone wash it for me, so on my way to the Education Offices in Broad Street, I went into Esslemont and MacIntosh (Aberdeen's most prestigious store, and with a bus stop at its entrance) and bought a hat. It cost over £1 – a lot for me then – and I don't think I ever wore it again.

We were informed by letter which schools would be expecting us at the end of the holidays, and the girls of 3K Section were to be scattered all over Britain, apart from Morag, who was being sent on VSO (Voluntary Service Overseas) to Timbuktu, more a pie-in-the-sky than a real place to most of us. A few years later she was sent to Papua New Guinea, where she met her future husband, an Australian. Catherine, fond of sports, was delighted to be sent to Coylumbridge, with Aviemore a kick-in-the-behind away, where she could ski to her heart's content. She is now in Glasgow teaching English as a second language.

Lillias, my constant companion, was married soon after we graduated. Her husband taught at the London School of Economics, so they lived in the capital for many years, until Ted was given the honour of a chair at Cardiff University. We see them at least once every year, as I've mentioned before. Of the others, I'm not too sure where they are. One, who must have tired of teaching, or perhaps didn't agree with the way the Government was changing education (ruining it?), left to train as a chiropodist, and still works in Aberdeen as far as I know. Another is now a Head Teacher, most probably thinking of retiring now, if she has not already done so.

I was told that I would be at Smithfield Primary School, and had the long school holidays to worry about how I would get on there. I missed the stir of the College, I missed having to study but most of all I missed the twenty-two friends I had made. Life in a school just wouldn't be the same.

18

A little back- and side-tracking here, and perhaps some repetition, to explain. I had been a member of the Church of Scotland at Craigiebuckler since I was fifteen or sixteen, mainly because the old minister had retired and his replacement was a gorgeous bachelor. Betty and I had been too old then for the ordinary Sunday School that went in at the same time as the kirk and meant that the children trooped in to join their parents in the church itself during the service, so we joined the Bible Class. This met in the afternoon, and was taken by the handsome young Reverend himself, not a selection of young and old (mostly old) Sunday school teachers.

The membership had soared from what it used to be – quite a lot of other girls besides us had developed a crush on the unmarried, available, young minister – strangely, although I can picture him still, I can't recall his name. With such a large number of us hanging on to his every word, he must have thought that he was a phenomenal success as a preacher, and when a class was started for the Young Communicants, we, like the rest of them, joined that, too. This resulted in us going to the church morning, afternoon and evening . . . just to see our 'heartthrob'. There were other compensations, of course. Boys as well as girls attended these classes, and two very presentable young lads usually escorted Betty and me back to Ord Street – halfway to our own homes – where my granny gave us something to eat after our mammoth sessions of religion. Our hearts, pining for our hero, were lifted considerably by their attentions. It was good to be young!

Then calamity! The war came, and we lost our film-star mentor to the army. His replacement was much older, not so good-looking or so much fun, therefore attendances dropped. The Young Communicants were sworn into the Church as members and had to force themselves to go to church every Sunday – well, Betty and I had to. For one thing, our parents were there to keep an eye on us, and the boys kept away from them.

Craigiebuckler had originally been a small country kirk, and although some houses had been built a little way off in the twenties and thirties, it still had this aura of 'ruralness', my own word. The huge organ was very impressive with its various-sized pipes behind it, and the beadle (verger in English, I believe) had to pump up the bellows before it would make a sound. This, of course, was made unnecessary when the organ was connected to electricity in the fifties, I think.

Each kirk member had his or her own pew, paid for yearly, with a card at the end of each row detailing the names of the people who had the right to sit there. Some pews had a cushion (ours hadn't) and I suppose this luxury had also to be paid for. Nothing for nothing in those days, either.

There was one rigid rule in Craigiebuckler, though; a reminder of what used to happen in days of yore. The head (doyen) of the family who lived in the largest house in the area was looked on in much the same way as the original laird of the land must have been looked upon, with great reverence and awe. Everyone had to be seated and the kirk doors closed by the beadle and opened again before Mrs F. came in, followed by her sons and daughters. A widow since perhaps the Boer War, she was always dressed in black, and looked neither left nor right as she led her *entourage* slowly up the aisle.

Her pew was practically under the pulpit, and I'm sure every incumbent over the decades had been conscious of her steely eyes on him as he gave his sermon. When the organist played the introduction for each hymn, psalm or paraphrase, there was a rustling of her skirts and some fairly laboured breathing until she got to her feet, always last. At the close of the service, she and her attendants were first to go, a ritual *par excellence*, while we minions waited until they were outside before making any move.

When we were smaller, Betty and I used to watch the performance with great interest, our mouths gaping as the participants swept past, until our mothers tapped our feet with theirs to remind us of our manners.

Alas, Craigiebuckler is now surrounded by so many villas, bungalows and manor-type houses, even a library and, until just a few years ago, an Infant School, so that it can no longer lay claim to being a country kirk, where one family more or less ruled the roost over the commoners who outnumbered them.

After we moved to our new home in Mastrick in 1956, of course, going to Craigiebuckler was out of the question. We'd have had to take two buses, into town and out again (which we couldn't afford) or go by Shanks' pony – a bit too far across country, so to speak. Besides, we had a baby to think of, as well. The best thing for me to do was to join Mastrick Church. It had been planned along with the housing – this was a large estate to start with and expanded over the years – and by the time we arrived in the parish the first year or more of services were held in what had become the church hall at the rear of the building.

Liking the feeling of being welcomed by the congregation, I removed my 'lines' from Craigiebuckler and became a member of Mastrick Parish Church. It had nothing to do with the fact that here was another young, handsome minister. I was married, he was married, so there was no ulterior motive for my attendance there. My mother also changed from Craigiebuckler, because she could get a bus from door to door. Bertha and Jimmy decided to become members as well, but they had to attend a Young Communicants' class first, which, because all the others were in their teens or twenties, made my husband feel conspicuous. He would have stopped going if I had let him.

This was a new church, of course, not quite a five-minute walk from us, and what came as a vast surprise to all concerned was the number of children who wanted to come to Sunday School – over a thousand when I typed out a Cradle Roll. I was the only member who had a typewriter – an old, rattly Olivetti that sometimes missed half a letter, but I managed . . . over a good period of time.

Eventually, it was arranged that two lots of each age group would be catered for, the problem being finding enough volunteer teachers and leaders, plus a superintendent to make sure that everything was being handled properly. I'm pleased to say that our family was well to the fore. Bertha and Bill were roped in as leaders, Bertha for one lot of fives to sevens, Bill for one lot of teenagers. I played the piano for Bertha's classes (there were about seven little groups) and Sheila and another young girl volunteered as teachers, though they were only in their teens themselves, plus a few older girls. In time, Alan became a pupil.

Christmas presented the biggest problem. Each 'Sunday School' had to be given a party, and they all had to be on a Saturday afternoon because most of the teachers had to go to work on the other days. What happened was that there were usually two parties in each of the three venues on the same day, one early in the afternoon and one later on, six altogether. Finding a Santa to give out presents at each party proved almost impossible, but Bertha's Bill (Jamieson) had a motor scooter at the time. Hey presto! Santa was mechanised that year!

We had been in Mastrick for only a year or so when the young minister was called to another church. The committee organised several hopefuls to come and preach, choosing the one they thought would best fit into the parish. As the oldest (in years, for it was a young community), my mother was asked to robe Mr T. when he was ordained, a great honour for her. She, Bertha and I were all in the Women's Guild by this time and I a member of the Drama Group run by the Deaconess. Bill also helped with the Boys' Brigade Company, and when Alan was old enough he joined the Lifeboys, so we were all well involved in church business. Jimmy, of course, was childminder when I was out in the evenings.

Some years on, Bertha and Bill, who had been living with Mum after their wedding in Mastrick Church, bought a new house at the Bridge of Don, at the other side of town and miles from Mastrick. They became part of the congregation of St Machar's Cathedral, but the Bridge of Don community kept growing and growing so much that a new church had to be built, still under the guidance of the Cathedral. The numbers at Sunday school in Mastrick had dropped significantly by that time, and so they didn't feel too badly about giving that up.

It would have been in 1965 some time that I began to consider moving house. I was out all day, studying every evening, cooking was down to a minimum (there were no ready-made meals then, no fridge or freezer) and the cleaning was being neglected for longer and longer periods.

Things became so bad, that I can remember saying to Jimmy at one point, 'If I should die suddenly, get somebody in to clean the house before you tell Mum.'

Visions of moving to a smaller house did sometimes flit through my mind, but it was my son's little friend who gave me the prod I needed. Graham called in for Alan on his way to Sunday school every week and always had to wait a few minutes. I was rushing to clear the breakfast dishes so I could spread out my books, so I left the boy standing at the fireside as usual this particular day, and it wasn't until much later that I noticed how he had been amusing himself.

There, on the lid of the piano, and in huge capital letters, he had painstakingly written his name with his finger . . . in the thick layer of dust. I was mortified and, as I erased it with my sleeve, I prayed that he wouldn't tell anyone. I may have been a slut – I *was* a slut – but I didn't want all and sundry pointing the finger of scorn at me.

I urgently needed that smaller house, or a house that was easier to keep clean, and with this in mind, I scanned the 'Houses for Let and Exchange' column in the newspaper every night. After a while, I gave up and placed an ad myself, stating a preference for a flat in one of the multi-storeyed blocks at Hazlehead, which was a really nice area. To my amazement, I received quite a number of letters, making Jimmy wonder if these 'luxury homes', built just over a year earlier, were all that they were cracked up to be.

By this time, I had passed my driving test, so I drove over one afternoon to carry out some inspections. There were four blocks, Wallace House, Davidson House, Rose House and Bruce House, and I thought that it would be appropriate to go to Davidson House first. I fancied receiving mail addressed to Mr and Mrs Davidson of Davidson House . . . It would make me feel quite important.

Davidson House, however, already had its share of Davidsons, and I could well imagine the postman's dilemma without another one to contend with. I eventually settled on a flat in one of the other buildings because it had a lovely view. We moved in at the beginning of October 1966 and I was soon thankful for my decision to move from a terraced house. When there had been snowstorms at Mastrick, it had been a case of pulling on boots and muffling myself in something warm for the back-breaking job of shovelling snow, not only from the front door to the road, but also along the pavement for the whole width of our garden. I'd also had to clear a path from my back door to the coal cellar and the drying green. None of that at Hazlehead, and most of the ice or mud has disappeared from our footwear before we enter our flat.

Contrary to most people's expectations, living in a multi-storeyed block is not normally noisy. The only sounds that travel are hammering and drilling, very deceptive to the ears. A workman can be doing something on the top (eleventh) floor and it is impossible for other tenants (me, at least) to tell whether the noise is coming from above or below, or even, sometimes, alongside. This is especially irritating when work is being carried out all over the building, and you can't judge whether or not you'll be next to have the door-entry system changed, or your electricity wiring renewed, or whatever, but it's something you learn to live with.

I've never regretted moving here, although my mail does sometimes go to Davidson House; hardly surprising, since one set of Davidsons lives in the same numbered flat as ours. What is surprising is that is doesn't happen more often . . .

One real drawback to living in a tower block is the laundry facility.

When we moved in first, I was given my time as 5 to 6.30 p.m. for the huge washing machine, and 6.30 to 8 p.m. for two of the four hot cupboards. Since one load of washing took the full ninety minutes you were allotted, everything had to be done in one go – towels, sheets, underwear, top clothes, even dark working trousers – so you can imagine the horrible shade of grey all the whites finished up. Not only that, the hot cupboards, although they did dry the clothes, left them as hard as boards; almost as stiff as they'd turned out in frosty weather at Mastrick.

The biggest problem, of course, was that we all had to take our turn. With forty-six tenants in the building, each having one and a half hours to wash and spin, and one and a half hours to dry, we could only do our laundry once a week. There was very little spare time available for emergencies.

I had left my own spinner when we flitted, but eventually managed to buy a new one and a washing machine as well, and then it was plain sailing. I could wash as often as I liked, but I had to find a way of drying. We were not allowed to put up ropes in our balconies, but I can guarantee that almost every balcony had a rope slung somewhere out of sight of the road. As the years went past, I managed to buy an automatic washing machine, and some years later, a tumble dryer. I am completely independent now. The laundry room, of course, was the place to learn all the gossip, so I am kept in the dark about who did what, whose husband walked out, whose wife went off with another man, although perhaps this doesn't happen nowadays.

Some of the original tenants have died, some have moved away, and more than half of the houses are now occupied by single mothers. Not that I have anything against them; I was in the same position once myself. More to the point, we are really lucky with our neighbours. One elderly man whose wife died some months ago, one young girl with an under-schoolage boy, and one girl with a daughter at the Academy and a son who is due to start there after the summer holidays. Both girls have offered their help to me, but Kim, with whom I share a small passage leading to the waste disposal chute and the stairs, is my standby.

I taught her at Hazlehead Primary School and, even then, she was always anxious to help. Nowadays, she occasionally takes in some shopping for me. I mostly order over the telephone and have groceries and frozen food delivered perhaps every six weeks, and both Sheila and Alan ask every week if I need them to get anything for me.

With no chemist anywhere near us, I always tried to order repeat prescriptions so that Alan could bring the necessary items to us on a Saturday, but inevitably there were times when it was not a repeat prescription but a new and urgently-needed medicine. This was quite a worry until I learned that several chemists now offer to deliver. This is a lifesaver, literally.

To go back to what I was saying before, I come to an event that I could scarcely believe could happen to us. When we moved to our present address in 1966, we had much farther to go to church than before, and by that time I was studying a lot, so we only went about once a month or so, at times even less. Along with our Christmas cards one year, I received a letter from a man who had taken over as Treasurer, informing me that if we did not pay in our envelopes regularly, we would be struck off the roll. I had never missed one payment, handing in several envelopes at a time if necessary, so you can imagine how I felt.

My dander well and truly up, I wrote to the minister himself, explaining why I was angry, and reminding him of how much my family had been involved with his church. I even detailed exactly what we had done, and reminded him that my mother had robed him at his ordination, so that he would know exactly who I was. Mum, by this time, was unable to cope with the villa in Mid Stocket and had moved in with Bertha and Bill. She had also transferred her 'lines' to St Machar's Cathedral.

I got no reply to my letter, but a few months after this, I was waiting for a bus at Woolworth's in Union Street, when I saw the Reverend T. walking towards me. He apologised most profusely for the incident, but put his foot in it by claiming that he had no idea at the time of who had written the letter to him.

This whole business made me so angry that I did not join another church, and, although this is no excuse, I'm afraid that the years just drifted past, and I am still not a member of any Kirk. I do feel ashamed to confess that, but I still believe in God, still watch services on TV and croak the hymns. Over eighty now, I am not very mobile, and couldn't go to church anyway, but I hope I can class myself as a silent Christian.

19

There is no comparison between walking into a college for the first time and walking into a school for the first time. At a college, all the people you meet, apart from the tutors, are students, greenhorns like yourself, trying to look confident but only succeeding in emphasising how unconfident they feel.

On the first day in school, I drove into the playground and parked the car beside all the others, glad to see that I had something in common with them, at least. Travelling by bus would have taken me over an hour (into town and out again) but only ten minutes by car. I reported to Mr Robb, the headmaster, who showed me into the staffroom, where an array of smiling faces looked up when he introduced me. I knew I'd be all right. And I wasn't the only newcomer that day; two other replacements turned up, another 'ordinary' teacher and a sewing teacher.

I found that I needn't have worried. All of them, old hands and new, were very friendly, and although I had heard tales of cliques in staffrooms (had even experienced it on my first teaching practice), that wasn't the case here. Of course, the infant teachers did sit together at one side of the room, and the rest of us sat facing them, but there was no sense of 'The Great Divide'. There were, perhaps, a few little hushed secrets told, but in the main, the conversation was general, and mostly regarding the pupils, who were a motley bunch, individuals with their own characteristics.

I must admit – as I'm sure will most teachers – that, even after so many years, I can remember the clever pupils best, those who soaked up everything I taught and yearned for more. They would be closely followed by the bright sparks, full of life and anxious to please, even if they sometimes had difficulty in understanding a specific point. Next, I would say, came the badly behaved, of which there were quite a number; they stick in the memory, and their antics still make me laugh . . . though I didn't find them funny at the time. The middle-of-the-roads, poor souls, who did their work quietly and caused no problems, have slipped into the mists of time. I can recall some names, but not their faces, or faces with no names . . . which is a terrible admission to make.

If any of you in this category are reading this, I apologise. Your type was the mainstay of a class, industrious, pleasant, usually asking shyly for help if something puzzled you but otherwise unwilling to make yourselves noticed. If you should ever meet me, please don't pass by. Speak to me. Tell me your name, if I can't recall it, and the school concerned, and that's all I should need to be able to place you.

On my first day, one of the girls sidled up to me as they were going home at lunchtime. 'I like you better than my last teacher, Mrs Davidson.'

My heart swelled with joy at winning them over so easily, and when they came back in at half past one and another of the girls came up to me, I prepared myself for a second compliment.

'Mrs Davidson,' she said, looking directly at me as if daring me to say a word, 'my sister says you're fat.'

Well, I ask you? What could you say to that?

That first class of seven-year-olds almost drove me up the wall. Out of the thirty-six (classes were much bigger then), I'd say that the nucleus of badly behaved affected most of the others, and by Christmas, I'd had enough. I fully intended to hand in my resignation from teaching altogether, but the headmaster talked me out of it.

'You'll never get another class like that,' he assured me. 'They were the same in the Infants, and we tried to separate the worst of them when they came up to Primary Three, but it seems even that hasn't worked. You should look on this as an initiation, Doris. Do your best to control them and you will see a change in them, I promise. That will give you confidence in yourself, so much so that no other class will upset you.'

Who was he trying to kid?

What he said next astonished me, however. 'Buy yourself a tawse – the belt, you know – and let one of them 'accidentally' see it in your drawer. Knowing it's there can often do the trick, without you actually having to use it. Remember, though, you'll have to carry out a threat if it's necessary. They won't respect you if you don't.'

I learned the hard way as far as that was concerned. I can't for the life of me recall what they were or weren't doing that made me use the threat, 'If you don't do as you're told, I'm going to belt the whole class.' They didn't obey me, so I was forced to carry it out. I knew that most of them had been influenced by the hard core of show-offs, but I lined them all up, girls as well as boys, and gave each of them a slight tap on the hand with the two-tailed tawse, ending just as the lunch bell started to ring.

Imagine my dismay when Mr Robb came into the staffroom at the end of the break. 'I'd like to speak to you for a minute, Doris.'

He waited until the others went to their rooms before going on, 'Rosemary Martin's mother (not her real name) came in to complain about you giving all your class the strap.'

I was shocked. 'Just a wee tap, that's all,' and I explained why. It was on his advice, after all.

'Aye, well,' he said, rubbing his hand over his chin, 'you should have picked out the ringleaders and made a proper example of them; it would have had more effect. I promised Mrs Martin I would repri-mand you, so regard this as a ticking off. Go to your room now, but remember what I've said.'

For the record, Rosemary Martin was the same little girl who had taken great delight in telling me that her sister thought I was fat, so this didn't make me feel any better disposed towards her, but although she was inclined to speak her mind without thinking, she turned out to be an above average scholar and we got on quite well.

I wasn't the only one who learned a lesson from that incident. The offenders had recognised that there was a limit to how far they could push me. The tawse had done the trick . . . more or less. At least, I didn't have to resort to threats again.

I had better explain the system that reigned in Smithfield at that time as far as allocating classes was concerned. There were two Primary One classes and two at Primary Two level. Let's say that Miss A and Miss B taught P. Ones and Miss C and Miss D taught P. Twos. The following year, Miss A and Miss B would take their same pupils into P. Two, while Miss C and Miss D would both have a new intake in P. One.

That takes care of the Infant School. Primary Three was part of the 'big' school, quite a traumatic transition for some of them, so it stood alone. The children were taken by other teachers for Primary Four and Five, and others for Primary Six and Seven.

I was glad to pass my first class on, and my second was far easier, even with its sprinkling of little troublemakers, but my third was a dream come true. It would have been just before the Easter holidays when Mr Robb asked me if I'd like to take them into Primary Four. 'If you feel easy with that,' he smiled, 'you could take over the four and five stage permanently.'

I didn't have to think about it. Primary Three was a difficult stage, both for children and teacher. It was a transition from Infant School to the 'big' school, where they had to learn to concentrate on the work they were given, or whatever they had to do, because it wasn't all straightforward lessons, and there would be little chance of many classes as good as my present one. I'd had them from August 1969 until late May 1970 when the crunch came.

We were coming up to Sports Day, held in the playing fields at Northfield Secondary School, but the practising was done in our own school grounds, where there were several expanses of grass at various points around the school buildings. Smithfield had been built around the late 1950s, I think, a sprawling one-storeyed mass, and we all had our own little patch where we could take our chairs out and work in the summer, or make use of in any way we liked.

Our first practice went off extremely well, the children had learned in the Infants that racing meant that you had to try to beat the rest of the runners, and the sun beamed genially down on their efforts.

On the afternoon before our next practice, Mr Robb told me that I was to have a new pupil next day. 'He has spent some time in the psychiatric ward at the Sick Kids,' he warned me, 'and reacts badly if anyone touches him. The report is that he is fit to be integrated into a normal school again, but be careful, Doris. Let him do whatever he wants . . . within reason. If you have a problem, just send for me.'

I worried all night over how I would deal with this problem child, and finally decided that the first step would be to make him feel welcome. I had another boy with the same surname, a quiet, obedient soul, so if I placed them together, it should make the new boy feel welcome, with at least one friend.

The children had all started on their Maths Workbooks when Mr Robb brought John in. The only introduction he made was to the child. 'This is your teacher, Mrs Davidson,' he announced, then turned and walked out.

I was so intent on not sparking off a tantrum that I ignored the vague niggle in my mind. I couldn't explain it, anyway. I put out my arm to take the boy's hand – as I'd have done to any new pupil – but remembering in time the caution I'd been given the previous day, I merely said, 'This is your seat, John. I've put you next to Colin. He has the same last name as you.'

The new boy gave an outraged roar and started banging into desks and kicking schoolbags out of his way as he rampaged round the room, while the rest of the class, particularly poor Colin, cowered in fear (and that included me, I'm afraid).

Mr Robb had said to let him do what he wanted, so I let him carry on as I did my usual round of the children, asking if they needed any help, or ticking the items they had managed to do. I was explaining something to one of the girls, when I realised that the new boy had quietened and was studying the pictures on the wall. I breathed more freely, assuming that he had got over whatever had triggered him off, but suddenly he roared, 'Hey, you!'

The hum of nearly forty pupils 'working things out in their heads' stopped abruptly, and all eyes were turned to me, wondering what I would say. I couldn't let him speak to me like that; it could incite some of the others. 'Excuse me, John, are you talking to me?'

'Aye.'

'My name is Mrs Davidson.'

'I ken.'

I had never been so glad to hear the interval bell, and I said, 'Colin, would you like to take John as a partner? You can show him where the toilets are, and let him join your games.' It was what I had originally planned, but I should have been more careful.

Colin looked alarmed . . . and no wonder. John was over a year older and much taller, as well as being solidly sturdy, and Colin had been the unwitting cause of his fit of temper. I chose another victim. Philip was the tallest in the class (or had been) though he was still a good bit shorter than John, but he was more able to stand up for himself than Colin. 'Will you take John under your wing?'

Philip didn't look any happier about this than Colin had, but I gave a slight nod and he said, timidly, 'OK. Are you coming, John?'

For a moment, the boy's brows came down, and I held my breath, but in the next instant he came forward and walked out of the room alongside Philip. I don't know what went on in the playground, but everything seemed to be quiet.

In the staffroom, Mr Robb asked me how I had got on, then explained that I had put my foot in it by telling John to sit next to Colin Wallace. 'He has an older brother called Colin,' I was told, 'and they can't stand the sight of each other, apparently.'

'Why was he in the psychiatric ward?' I asked then, just out of curiosity.

'It happened when he was in his second year at Drumgarth Infant School . . .'

'Drumgarth?' Now I knew what had been niggling at me. 'Oh, my God! Of course! I did some teaching practice there. I should have recognised him.'

'The report said that he was knocked down by a car, and when the driver got out to see if he was badly hurt, he jumped up and kicked the man in the shins. The psychiatrist at the hospital said that the knock had affected his brain.'

Something wasn't right about this account, as far as I was concerned. 'But . . . you said he was in Primary Two at the time?'

'That's right. He should really be in Primary Four now, but . . .'

'He was just as badly behaved in Primary One, when I was there. His teacher was nearly demented with him. She took him out of the class when I had the two weeks on my own, but I should have recognised him. It wasn't the accident that made him like this. He must have been born that way.'

Mr Robb pulled a face. 'I don't think I should say anything about that in my weekly report on him, though. It would probably cause trouble, so we'll just keep an eye on him. I see you're down for an hour in the Art Room now, and the report says he reacts badly in big open spaces, so be careful. I'll look in now and then to see how things are going.'

When John learned that we were going to the Art room, he said he loved to draw, and lined up quietly next to Colin after all. This room was big and airy, but he seemed to be quite happy there. I walked amongst the tables, commenting on the pictures that were taking shape, and shrugged to Mr Robb when he poked his head round the door.

Soon after that, came the roar again. 'Hey, you!'

Hands were arrested midway to paints, brushes were left static on the large sheets of paper I had cut from the rolls we used, but I decided to ignore him this time. I did squint at him out of the corner of my eye in a minute or so, and was glad to see that he was looking down at the table as if planning what to do next.

'Hey, teacher!' He had 'thunk'.

This was a fractional improvement, but still not what I wanted to hear. 'I told you before, my name is Mrs Davidson.'

After a moment's hesitation, he growled, 'Hey, Davidson.'

'What do you want, Wallace?' I barked.

Dozens of breaths were held in fear of what this might precipitate, but thank heaven, it did have the effect I'd hoped for. He seemed to shrivel up. 'My name's John Wallace,' he said, timidly accusing.

'And my name is Mrs Davidson. Did you want to ask me something? Do you want me to take a look at your painting?'

'Aye.' A long silence, then, 'Yes, please . . . Mrs Davidson.'

We had got there, by fair means or foul, so I walked round the end of the long table to where he was standing. It transpired that he was really good at drawing, but the subjects he chose were quite weird, to say the least. I had told them a very short story before they began, about different shapes having an argument as to which was most used, and their assignment had been to make a picture using as many shapes as they wanted. Some had been most inventive, with squares and circles, some had used triangles, and, as usual, there were the odd few who hadn't got the idea at all.

Not so with John Wallace. He had understood what I meant, right enough, but he had chosen to draw a cemetery filled with rectangular gravestones. The church in the background consisted of squares and triangles and the whole thing was strangely eerie, because the only paint he had used was black. I suppose the psychiatrists would have made something out of that. In later weeks, he did begin to use other colours, but generally toned them down with a little drop of black mixed in.

The hour we were allotted finished at half past eleven, so, all brushes cleaned and everything tidied away, the children went quietly back up to the top corridor, turned left and along towards Room 8. It was a lovely summer day again, and it was forty-five minutes until dinnertime, so instead of going into the classroom, I took them out to have some further practice for the sports – just straightforward running, not the sack race, egg (potato)-and-spoon, obstacle, skipping and that sort of thing, because the equipment for those was down in the gym . . . or possibly being used by another class. In any case, plain running was the most important.

The children had changed into gym shoes (plimsolls) first thing in the morning, so we just walked past our own room, through the cloakroom, past the girls' toilets (not such a smell emanating as from the boys' area at the opposite end of this corridor) and through the outside doors.

There was one asthmatic boy who couldn't take part, so he went inside to collect two schoolbags as markers, and we started, short races for the girls at first, then the same for the boys, increasing in length until we would reach the stipulated length for Primary Three, which I can't for the life of me recall. Everything was going well, the boys cheering on the girls and vice versa, until we came to the second last boys' race. John had been hanging back, not entering into any that had been run so far, but I was pleased to see him lining up for this one.

How wrong can a person be? I had already made one big mistake with him that day, and this was to be far, far worse. I checked that they were lined up properly, then lifted my whistle to my mouth. As usual, at least two didn't wait for the proper signal, one being John Wallace, and the others shouted out in disgust. I expected a scene, but he trotted back quietly enough.

'Get Ready! Get Set! Go!' I blew the whistle and ran down the grass to see who would win. I was congratulating the winner when a shout got up from the girls behind me. 'The new boy's run away, Mrs Davidson!'

Not only had he run across the grass, he was charging through the small gate on to Provost Fraser Drive, a busy bus route. My only thought was to save him from being knocked down again, so I chased after him, turning left along that street and then left again down Anderson Drive, once a ring road round the city, but now one of the main routes through it.

Unknown to me in my inelegant flight, two of the girls had run inside to tell the headmaster what was happening, and he had jumped into his car and driven out of the front gate and along Kemp Street to find the miscreant . . . and me, at his heels. He didn't have to come far, John had almost reached Kemp Street, but he was yanked into the little Saab screaming and shouting while I was left to limp back to school by myself.

By this time, of course, the dinner bell had gone, and my dear lambs had changed their footwear and were lingering in the cloakrooms to see what was happening. That was the end of my first forenoon with John Wallace.

In case you are wondering, he ran off because he had come last in the race, and his excuse for that was, 'It wisna fair. They'd on their jimmies, and I hadna.'

I had forgotten that he hadn't arrived until the others had changed their footwear, so I suppose he did have a legitimate complaint.

Things were never dull in Primary Three, especially with John Wallace there. I had been trying one day to get the class to give me words beginning with letters going down the alphabet, and had just got as far as B when John's hand shot up. 'I ken, Mrs Davidson. I ken a word beginning wi' B.'

This was something of a breakthrough, so I smiled beatifically at him and he burst out, 'Bugger off!'

I had to keep smiling. 'Very good, John, but I don't think we should use that one again. It's not a very nice word.'

When I related this in the staffroom, the headmaster grinned, 'I'd watch myself going down the alphabet if I were you, Doris, especially the next letter.'

He was right, of course. Smithfield was in what the government would later class as a deprived area, and the language could be very colourful, to say the least. I remember being at a conference once, where the Depute Director of Education was plugging the latest gimmick (whether his own idea or that of the Education Authority, I don't know) but I listened while he went on at length about letting the children use their playground language in the classroom.

'This would give them freedom to speak, and they would be able to say exactly what they think.'

There were murmurs of agreement from all sides of me, but I felt so strongly about this that I got to my feet. 'Excuse me, but this may work in certain schools in certain areas, but not at Smithfield. Every second word that's spoken, or shouted, in the playground, especially from the boys, is a swear word.'

'Ah, yes, Mrs . . .?

'Davidson,' I supplied.

'Yes, Mrs Davidson, but what the children call swear words are usually rather innocuous – like knickers, or . . . What stage do you have?'

'Primary Three, and believe me, Mr Liddell, what they say is far beyond being innocuous. I'm no prude, but I wouldn't think of uttering some of the things they come out with. Four letter words that I never knew existed until I was over thirty, and I wouldn't soil my lips repeating.'

He looked at me in disbelief. 'You must be exaggerating, Mrs Davidson.'

I was wondering if I should let rip and shock him, but, thank goodness, another lady stood up. 'Mrs Davidson's quite right. I teach at Middlefield, and it's the same there. Vile, filthy words from the worst boys sometimes, and they think nothing of it. If what you're advocating comes into being, I for one would have to resign.'

I thanked her for her support as we both sat down. Middlefield School was just a stone's throw from Smithfield, so she knew I spoke the truth. I could see other teachers, however, those in West End Schools or in the better areas, looking at each other as if we were from another planet – which we were, as far as that was concerned.

This little idea was swiftly squashed, to be replaced in a month or so by another controversial plan (to use Mr Liddell's expression). 'We had attempted to preserve the Doric, but I agree that playground language was perhaps a little dangerous . . . in some cases. However, we now ask you to run a competition in your classes for writing a bible story in the Doric. Offer a small prize for the best, and I look forward to reading some of them. We do not want the Doric to die out.'

The Doric, for those who don't know, is a dialect spoken only in the North East corner of Scotland, and remains a foreign language even to the rest of Scotland. To give you a small example: 'Fit div ye dee wi' yer aul' claes?' This means 'What do you do with your old clothes?' The trouble with the Doric, of course, as with dialects in other parts of Britain, is that they change every ten or so miles.

Stonehaven, only about fifteen miles from Aberdeen, has its own accent and words. Laurencekirk, about fifteen miles farther south, is different again. If you recall, my husband comes from Laurencekirk, so I can give you a couple of his choice words (innocuous, of course) as samples. 'Sheenin' means shining, as in 'The sun is sheenin'; a 'thievel' is a spurtle (stick for stirring porridge) as in 'Far dae ye keep the thievel?', which I first heard years ago when he was drying my mother's dishes, and I hadn't the faintest idea what he was speaking about.

The Doric is something I feel quite strongly about. I do not side with those who maintain that we should get programmes on radio and television in the Doric every day, as we do in the Gaelic, because ours is not a national language, but I'd hate it to be lost altogether. The competition Mr Liddell had suggested may have gone down all right in rural schools, and I don't know how other teachers got on, but my children wrote in the only dialect they knew, what I might call 'the Smithfield Doric'. The stories were hilarious; I even let my kitchen sink overflow one evening because I was so engrossed in them. For instance, 'The Prodigal Son didna wint the fatted calf, for he was wintin' a bug o' chips an' a funcy.' In other words, 'He would rather have had a bag of chips and a fancy cake,' which, to most of them, would have been a proper feast.

No more was heard of the idea, thank goodness, but I regret not having kept those gems of Scottish literature.

John Wallace did settle in to a certain extent, his work did improve but . . . I never knew what would light his fuse. I was on heckle-pins all the time, and it must have affected the other children, too. Thankfully, however, one or other of them came to my rescue, voluntarily, by running to fetch the headmaster at the least sign of imminent danger.

To give the boy his due, though, there was one occasion when he was punished for something that wasn't entirely his fault. The regular 'janny' was off for some reason and a temporary man had taken over for a week or two, so what happened wasn't entirely his fault, either. He had been cleaning out the boys' toilets late one afternoon when he was called away to attend to something else – I know not what. Unfortunately, he left the hose pipe connected with the water still running, and the bell rang soon afterwards for 'going home' time. Well, you can guess what happened. A Primary Seven class was nearest the area, and so the big boys appropriated the hose and drenched everyone who came near them. My Primary Three kids were, as I think I have mentioned, next to the girls' toilets, and my boys were last to reach the battleground. When they did, our friend John Wallace took over, punching the boy who was holding the hose and setting the jet of water on anyone who tried to take it away from him.

Then the janitor came back and yelled at him. Instead of dropping the weapon and taking to his heels, a surprised John turned round still holding the hosepipe. The man, as you can imagine, was anything but pleased about this, and let fly at his attacker, who retaliated in like fashion, while dozens of boys stood around yelling, mostly hoping that John Wallace would get his come-uppance.

As usual when John was on the warpath, another of my boys came charging back to tell me what was going on, but by the time I got there, Mr Robb, alerted by the din, had fixed John by the collar and was dragging him down the few steps to his room, the boy's arms and legs flailing as he roared, 'It wasna just me. I wasna the only ane. It was them in Room 17 that started it.'

I followed on, trying to explain that John was right, that it wasn't fair to single him out, but to no avail. I was told, 'He shouldn't have soaked the janitor. He deserves . . .'

'He didn't mean to soak the janitor,' I pleaded, only to have the door closed firmly against me. I lingered for a few moments, hearing the furious shouts from both man and boy, and the first yell of pain as the belt came down. I wondered if I should go in to stop this miscarriage of justice, but . . . let me say I was a coward, and John had done more than enough at other times to deserve what he was getting now. I crept away, into the staffroom two doors up, and it wasn't long before the secretary came through.

'Mr Robb's taking John Wallace home in his car, but God knows what his mother'll think. They're both absolutely soaking.'

I couldn't help laughing as I pictured this, although I suspect that this was due more to relief that it was over than to real mirth.

Neither Mr Robb nor John mentioned it the following day, and I was quite glad to let it remain buried.

In the eighteen months (years?) that I had him, I had many confrontations with John Wallace, but his work did improve. At first if he was doing addition sums, he wrote them round in a circle, but he did come out of that and was coping fairly well, which made his next outburst all the more of a surprise.

We had progressed as far as hundreds, tens and units, and I had written ten sums on the swivelling blackboard on the wall – no easel like we had when I was young. I sat down to mark the spelling homework they had handed in, and told the bright half dozen who had finished first to hand out the marked jotters for me. Then I asked if anyone was still working, and getting a proud 'No', I got various kids to work the answers on the board. All well and good, you may think.

Then I asked if anyone had got all the sums correct, and ignoring the forest of hands that shot up, John bawled out, 'Me, Mrs Davidson. I got them a' right.'

'That's very good, John.' It was, for he'd had quite a struggle understanding.

'Mrs Davidson,' piped another, deeply indignant voice from the next desk, 'he didn't get them right. He copied the answers off me.'

I was so disappointed that I said, 'But that's cheating, John, and I'm sure you wouldn't have been the only one with some wrong.'

Looking back, I suppose I should have known what would happen, but the eruption took us all by surprise, and I was glad that it was directed at me, not the poor soul who 'clyped'. John came charging towards me, picked my fountain pen off my desk and snapped it in two. Then he flung a chair at me while I was still trying to get round my desk to take hold of him, followed by a schoolbag in the face as I was trying to gather my senses together.

Warned against touching him or not, I was seeing red now, and I was damned if I'd let the little monster treat me like that. I grabbed at the neck of his jersey and heard it rip as he struggled free, then the next thing I knew, he punched me in the mouth.

Now, I don't know how many of you have ever been punched in the mouth, but even the pain didn't stop me from pushing him against a wall. The jersey tore a little farther with him struggling so madly, but he was only eight or nine, and I was over five feet and almost eleven stones with it.

While all this was going on, a little messenger had scooted down to tell Mr Robb and he came racing in to take this disruptive little devil in hand. One look at the tableau, blood steaming down my chin, and he yanked the miscreant into the corridor. I will draw a veil over the next five minutes or so, all I can say is that when I opened the door to stop what I was sure would end in murder, I was told to go inside and 'leave him to me'.

I had been fortunate to get off with a punch in the mouth. My scissors, a large pair used for various purposes, had also been lying on my desk, so the murder could have been mine.

But I'd had more than enough, as I tearfully told Mr Robb when I ventured out of the staff toilets, where I had taken refuge until I got over the shock. 'I'm not having him in my class again.'

'I'm not surprised. I'm bloody annoyed with the Sick Kids. I rang them just now to tell them what had happened and they said you could have refused to have him at any time. A pity they didn't think of telling us at the very start.'

I couldn't go to school the following day, Friday, because my face was all puffed up and the pain was agonising, but by Monday, it felt a little bit better. My nerves were still quite fragile, so when my pupils handed me 'Get Well' cards they had made, and asked if I was all right now, I very nearly dissolved into tears.

It would have been about three days later when someone knocked at my classroom door, and when I answered the man said, 'I'm John Wallace's father.'

I could picture him giving me a thrashing, or, at the very least, threatening to report me to the Education Authority for abusing his son, so I was feeling sick as I closed the door behind me – little ears could hear a lot more than they were meant to – and said, 'I'm sorry, Mr Wallace.'

'No, no, you've no need to be sorry, Mrs Davidson. I've just come to thank you for what you managed to do for John. He's a lot better behaved at home now, and he seems to be settling in at Cordyce.'

I hadn't given a thought to where the child was now, but I was glad that he'd been sent to this special school, to be taught by teachers trained specially to deal with disruptive children.

'He liked you, you know,' Mr Wallace continued, 'and he was sorry for punching you.' He hesitated briefly. 'He hasn't told us what happened, so could you tell me why he went off the handle at that particular time?'

I explained the situation, and he nodded his head when I came to the end. 'Aye, I understand now. It was being found out in a lie that did it. His mother used to stick up for him when the teacher at Drumgarth complained about his behaviour. That was the school he was at before we moved up to Northfield. I couldn't get my wife to admit he was just as bad before the accident. She got him referred to the hospital, and they put him in the psychiatric ward, but I've aye said it was a good walloping he needed. She wouldn't let me lift my hand to him, more's the pity.'

So that interlude came to an end, thank goodness. But . . . it wasn't the last I saw of John Wallace.

*

I had been teaching for perhaps three years when Smithfield was hit by a series of tragedies. First, the senior remedial teacher, quite elderly and already crippled with arthritis, had to have a mastectomy, and although Mr Robb assured her that he would collect her every morning (she only lived a few minutes away from school) she hated the idea of being dependent on anyone. Then one morning, the milkman could get no answer when he was collecting the money, and looking through the kitchen window, he saw her lying with her head in the gas oven. It was a terrible shock to all of us, but we couldn't all attend the funeral. Someone had to stay behind to look after the doubled up classes.

Not much more than a fortnight later, the headmaster came into the staffroom with shock stamped all over his face. 'I've just had a phone call from Margaret Lorimer's sister. She . . . was taken out of the Don last night.' (Not her real name, for obvious reasons, but, strangely, she was the junior remedial teacher.)

Another suicide! Another funeral!

Just weeks after that, we learned that a third teacher had died. She had gone off work because of trouble with her legs, so her death was just as unexpected as the other two. This time, however, we *did* all manage to go to the funeral, the secretary and the janitor included, leaving eight poor students to look after the doubled-up classes. On our return, they reported that there had been no problems, everything had gone smoothly, but we had our doubts. On the other hand, as the assistant head pointed out, perhaps the deaths of three teachers in such quick succession had struck home to the pupils as much as it did to us. Who knows?

20

I not only taught while I was at Smithfield, I also was taught . . . or poor Eleanor Hutton, the teacher in the room next door to mine, tried to teach me how to play the guitar. She and her husband sang and played lovely folk songs, and she was very patient with me. I bought myself a cheap guitar and did master the usual, easy chords, but I was too slow in changing from one to the other to be of any use as an accompanist, never mind a soloist.

It was my son who became interested, and although he complained at first that his fingers were too small to stretch to the proper positions, he was stimulated by watching Lillias's husband (who hummed to his own accompaniment). Alan became so serious about it that he now plays classical as well as his own compositions, and makes records and CDs. He has also appeared on stage several times, both amateur and along with professionals, in Britain and in America, although he probably won't be very happy about me boasting about him.

I was seven when my father enrolled me with Bessie Jenkins, well known as an excellent piano teacher. I did quite well under her tuition until, at the age of ten, I began to take an interest in the popular songs on the wireless. I tried them out and was soon tinkling away quite happily with no music.

This didn't please my Dad, who said, 'What's the use of me paying for lessons for you when you're playing by ear?'

When Miss Jenkins was told that I'd be stopping my lessons at the end of the session, she said, 'Oh, what a shame. I was going to enter her for her first grade exams.'

But Dad was adamant, and many years later, I was playing as much without music as with, but not well enough either way to be confident in front of other people.

The next instrument I tried, when I was still around ten, was Dad's Japanese (one-stringed) fiddle, which had a large horn attached to the side. I got as far as picking out the scale, but that was it. I also tried the saw, longing to produce the haunting tunes he coaxed out of it so easily, but I could only make horrible, ear-shattering, teeth-on-edge screeches.

When I was about sixteen, the tuner told my mother that the piano was being ruined by being kept in the lounge where the fire was seldom lit, and advised her to sell it. It was a lovely piece of furniture as well as having a beautiful tone, but this coming at a time when her finances were pretty grim, she sold it for £40 – if I remember correctly. I don't know if it was advertised in the local paper, or if the shop where it had been bought made her an offer, but whoever it was got a bargain. What I do know for sure is that I missed it.

Once I was in my own house in Mastrick, the first thing I wanted, of course, after the bare necessities of furniture, was a piano, but we could definitely not afford that. It wasn't an essential item, and I had to go on living without one, as I had done for more than fifteen years.

Perhaps eighteen months later, we were visiting Mum's cousin Meg and her husband one afternoon, when George happened to say, 'I've bought a new piano for Margaret . . .' (their daughter and Bertha's closest chum), 'so I'm throwing out the old one.'

I was afraid to look at Jimmy then, but as soon as we got home, I broached the subject tentatively. 'Would you mind if I asked George for his old piano?' and was delighted when he said, 'Why not? I know you want it.'

Sadly, George saw how eager I was and decided to cash in. He asked for £15, which I could ill afford and had to take out of the tin in the sideboard drawer where I laid past the rent money every week. I had never seen the instrument, but a piano was a piano, after all. Sadly, I was to find that there *were* differences in them, and this was a real corker – out of the ark. It had fretwork decoration on the front, a candlestick holder at each side – and it would have been a proper honky-tonker, if all the yellowing keys had played, just like Winifred Atwell's 'other piano', although in no way could I compare myself with her.

I was quite disillusioned, but I persevered doggedly, slowly recognising that it was hopeless. It was too far-gone to be tuned into shape even if I could have afforded it, particularly since I hadn't yet replaced all I'd borrowed from the rent money.

But, miracle of miracles, I spotted an advert in the evening paper one night.

'Piano for sale £15.' I'd have to dip into what I had laid past for electricity this time. I later did away with saving to pay the quarterly bill by having a slot meter installed. No coins meant no lights, no heat, no cooking. Anyway, the seller didn't live far from us and we saved the cost of a van by pushing it round on its castors. It was a beauty, a lovely mahogany with a gorgeous tone, and came with a stool filled with sheets of music. I was in heaven for days going through them all, and, of course, I added to the collection by buying many more at sixpence a time (two and a half of today's pence) from Woolworth's in Union Street, when I had any spare cash . . . and sometimes when there was none to spare.

I treasured that piano until we decided to move into a multi-storey flat. There wasn't room for it. The only available space, between the kitchen door and the outside wall, was just not wide enough, so I traded it in for a smaller piano, a little, angular thing with corners, which fitted the space but didn't have the tone or the appearance. Jimmy could see that I wasn't happy with it, and mentioned this to one of his workmates who offered to buy it. I think I let him have it for what I paid for it, which left both of us quite happy about the deal, although I discovered later that the price of pianos had been rising steadily.

At one time, with my son having lessons on the accordion, I gave that a try and did manage to play recognisable tunes, but, again, not for other ears. Then a friend remarked, 'Does your chest not get squeezed sometimes?'

He was obviously joking, but I wasn't so eager to play after that.

I next bought (on credit) an electric organ. I had some fun with the different instrumental tones and rhythms, but I never quite mastered that, either. I exchanged it for a smaller piano – only six octaves, and at the horrendous price of over five hundred pounds. I was teaching by this time, and was just able to make the monthly instalments. The story of its delivery is reminiscent of one of Laurel and Hardy's funniest short films, but it is absolutely true.

I had asked the clerk in Bruce Miller's to have it delivered after four o'clock, but said that I had left a key above the door if they came before I managed to get home. When I went into the living room, I was quite pleased to see that the piano was already there . . . a tasteful walnut, it is the same style as an upright, but not so high. So everything had gone according to plan . . . or so I thought.

It was two days before I saw our caretaker, who gave me the sad tale. It was the era of the electricity cuts, early seventies when various zones had the power shut off for three hours at a time. The van had arrived at a few minutes to three o'clock (an hour early but it wouldn't have made any difference), but by the time they had unloaded it and rolled it inside to the lift, the few minutes had been ticking away, and the lift ground to a halt just after passing the sixth floor. The Hazlehead area was scheduled to be powerless from three until six, but they hadn't known of this.

The alarm bell brought the caretaker, who hand-cranked the lift up almost five floors to the eleventh with great difficulty, then went to his own flat to recover. He had done all that was needed, so the other two men pushed the piano across to the number marked on the delivery note – only to find that they had come to the wrong flat. They took a closer look at the slip, and came to the conclusion that they had misread the number. The alarm bell brought a furious response from the exhausted caretaker.

'I'm not cranking you anywhere else. You'll have to carry the damned piano down the stairs yourselves.'

'But we don't know which floor we've to go to.'

When they told him the name on the docket, they had to wait until he finished swearing before learning that they should have gone to the sixth floor. They could understand his anger – they had only been a short distance away from their target when the lift stopped – so they had no other option but to carry the heavy piece of furniture down the cement stairs, manoeuvring it round the tight corner at each half landing. At last they tottered on to the sixth floor landing, heaving a sigh of relief at seeing the nameplate and wiping the sweat from their brows as they waited for someone to answer the door.

Disillusionment came quickly. This Davidson had not bought a piano, didn't need a piano, didn't want a heavy great thing like that scraping the tiled floor, so would they please watch what they were doing? The door slammed in their faces, they appealed to the caretaker, a sardonic watcher, but no amount of persuasion would make him crank them anywhere else.

After a long exchange of colourful words, however, he said, 'I've been thinking. Have you got the right building? It's easy to mix them up.' He finally agreed to ring their shop to check the address.

It *was* the wrong building. Whoever had written out the delivery ticket had written 'Davidson House' because of our surname – a common mistake, made by doctors, taxi drivers and many other deliverymen.

I don't know what had gone in the shop; I wish I'd been a fly on the wall. Having learned that the two original men were refusing point blank to carry the b— thing any farther, the manager and an assistant 'volunteered' to do the needful. Seething with resentment when they turned up, they bore the weighty burden down the six flights to ground level.

Then came the crunch! Because our building was so near Woodend Hospital, it was connected to the same electricity grid . . . which was NEVER cut off! The piano, once installed in our lift, sailed up as it should have done originally.

By the way, in case anyone is wondering, the tenants of the three other blocks complained bitterly about us not having our electricity cut off, and we were then taken off the hospital grid. Was this the start of neighbourhood watch?

I did have a little flirtation with a more unusual type of musical instrument – which I'm sure my family was glad came to nothing. It started when we visited one of Jimmy's ex-workmates, Sandy, who had found the job of his dreams – a water baillie on Invercauld estate – next to Balmoral. Their house actually looked across the River Dee to the Castle and his wife, Lil, usually landed a part-time job when the Royals were in residence every August. Employees were expected to curtsey when they met any of the family, and because Lil cycled to work, she was forced to come off her bike many times during a summer, even if the rule applied only to the first time of meeting.

I remember her once saying ruefully, 'I feel a right blooming twit.'

Lil and Sandy had two sons, one called Alan, the same as ours. Anyway, their Alan was learning to play the bagpipes, and watching him striding up and down outside their cottage, his cheeks puffed out, I could picture myself moving just as majestically through the heather with my pipes – tucked under my arm in the traditional style – skirling patriotic Scottish tunes.

Sadly, as with the recorder I tried when a music teacher at Smithfield was teaching my class, I found the chanter a thing of mystery. I never got beyond a painfully slow display of the scale on both these instruments.

When my first book was published, I was asked by *Yours,* a magazine for the elderly, to give a telephone interview, and after some expected questions, there came one, which I certainly had not expected. We had established that I had written the book straight on to a word processor; I had written three others, unpublished, by hand before typing them out . . . several times each.

The question was: 'If someone were to come to you and say you could have two hours off from your word processor, how would you occupy the time?'

I answered, off the cuff, 'I'd probably go and play the piano', but when I had time to think about it, I knew that I wouldn't *want* two hours off. I love writing and it's what I would honestly prefer to do. In fact, I have scarcely touched my piano for a long time now. Just sometimes, if I hear a tune on television, an old favourite or a new one that has taken my fancy, I sit down for a few minutes to see if I can still pick out a tune by myself.

To return to the 'tramlines'. I was quite pleased at being 'promoted' to a higher class. At least I knew that I'd mostly have well-behaved pupils for the next two years. There were the odd little hiccoughs, of course, but nothing bad enough to relate, and the time passed quite quickly. The kids were accustomed to my style of working, and I knew exactly what to expect of each of them. Even better, I didn't have to worry about having to go back to Primary Three again. I was to be with Fours and Fives permanently. I said goodbye to this class sadly in the summer of 1972 – it may have been 1971, I'm not too clear on this – after having taught them for three whole years, and sure that I'd never have such a biddable, hardworking crew again.

At this time, the style of education was undergoing many changes, and a new team-teaching in Primary Seven had started; I'll explain this shortly. The Primary Four class I was given now was perhaps not quite as good as my last, but not far off it. They, too, were a lively bunch but they soon got to know how I wanted things done and I quite looked forward to having them for another year.

One of the team teachers, however, had applied for promotion and was to start at her new school as deputy head in the autumn term, but I could scarcely believe it when Mr Robb asked me if I would like to take her place. This new style of teaching was still in its infancy, although some of the rough edges had been rubbed off during that first year, so I was somewhat apprehensive. Still . . . it was a challenge, and challenges should not be ignored.

Now comes the explanation I promised. The team teaching took place in the hall, and the Primary Sevens had been divided into three groups for the three teachers, placed round the large room, but still leaving the stage free. It wasn't a case of one teacher, one class, however. The pupils were shared in three-week cycles, thus for the first lap:

Teacher One took Seven A for English, B for Maths, C for

Environmental Studies. (History, Geography, Biology and anything that isn't included in the other two.)
Teacher Two took B for English, C for Maths, A for Environmental Studies. Teacher Three took C for English, A for Maths, B for Environmental Studies.

After three weeks, it was a case of 'All Change', so that, over the entire nine weeks' cycle, each teacher had a spell with each class for each subject. Clear as mud? It worked!

The good side of it, of course, was that if there was a disruptive pupil who didn't like Maths, for instance, you only had him (or her, for they came in all shapes and sexes), for three weeks and not again for another six weeks for that subject. Of course, you had him/her every day for something, but it wasn't such a grind. Not only that, as far as the pupils were concerned, they had three different teachers explaining things to them, which gave them a far better chance of understanding. It sounds complicated, but it ran quite smoothly.

Astute readers may have spotted that one of these classes consisted of the same children I had taken through Primaries Three, Four and Five, although in Primary Seven I only had them for a third of each day. I have never been able to make up my mind if this was a good thing or not. Having the same pupils for four years means that you get too familiar with them and they with you. Not that any of them ever took advantage, but, apparently, it was noticeable to others.

A student I had once said that she could pick out the pupils I'd had before because they spoke respectfully to me and never argued. We had been on a coach trip to Craigievar Castle, and she added that 'my' kids spoke 'properly' to me . . . in other words, in proper English. Trying to stop children using their 'Smithfield' dialect was quite a stiff job sometimes, but that lot had been well schooled.

To give you an example of what we had to cope with, I had drummed home to one class that people outside Aberdeen wouldn't understand what they were saying unless they spoke in decent English, and I was delighted (not the most appropriate word, but you'll understand what I mean) to see an article in a newspaper about an Aberdeen seaman who'd been having an argument on board a trawler in Hull with a local man. When he started shouting, strange words that seemed as if he were swearing in a foreign language, his adversary gave him a punch that sent him over the side of the boat. Tragically, they did not recover the body for some time. Even that story, however, did not get through to the children, who came up with all sorts of reasons for the attack.

'The other mannie was deef.' 'Maybe he *was* sweiring.' . . . and so on.

What did get through to them came about accidentally. I happened, at one point, to have a student who came from Stornoway. She had great difficulty making herself understood as well as understanding what they were saying to her. One of the stock excuses for not doing homework was, 'I didna hiv a pinnel.' Or, 'I left my pinnel in my desk.' This word flummoxed me at first, too, but it turned out to be just a slovenly version of pencil.

With the poor student having to ask them constantly what they meant, and vice versa, it eventually dawned on them that I had been right. Other people *couldn't* understand them.

I might also mention here something that I should have spoken of before. A trip to London was arranged in 1971, to see the Tutankhamun Exhibition. I was still teaching younger children at the time, but when the headmaster asked for volunteers to accompany the group of Primary Sevens, I was one of the six who said we'd like to go. With only twenty-six children booked, this would have meant each of us having only four or five pupils to look after.

We were expecting the headmaster to pick three or four, but, as he pointed out, it was the first time away from home for most of the children and six teachers wouldn't be too many. As when I went to London as a pupil myself, the rule was that one person was allowed free for every ten paying pupils, so only two teachers would qualify for this and four would have to pay the full amount of travel and hotel charges. To make things fair, however, Mr Robb divided the cost of four between the six of us so that we all paid the same.

We had a most enjoyable week in London, but having to queue from 9 a.m. until 4 p.m. to see the Exhibition did take the gilt off the gingerbread. The amazing thing was that not one child complained at the wait, but they were really too tired to take in what they had come to see. When we came to the souvenir shop, they all wanted to buy something for 'my ma'.

Everything, naturally, was very expensive, but one of the boys was studying the paper carrier bags emblazoned with the young king's head and various ancient Egyptian symbols, costing one shilling each. Very politely, he said to the elegant assistant behind the counter, 'Twa o' them bugs, please.'

She looked at me in bewilderment. 'What does he want?'

'Two of the carrier bags, please.'

Those pupils also learned by experience.

I thoroughly enjoyed the team teaching, and it was into the New Year before I had the fright that made me apply for a transfer. I did mention earlier that it took ten minutes by car to get from Hazlehead to Smithfield, and over an hour to go by buses, so I tried to avoid taking public transport for as long as I could in the winter. There always came a time, of course, when the roads weren't safe, when the council advised people to leave their cars at home. On one such day, I thought I would try walking to school. It was across town, but not too far, I thought. The trouble was that the shortest route I could go – through the grounds of Woodend Hospital then wading through drifts on side streets the snowploughs hadn't cleared – took me exactly one hour and ten minutes. Not only had it taken longer than going by bus, but I was covered in icy snow and absolutely worn out by the time I reached the school.

On the following morning, therefore, I decided to go by public transport and save myself the hassle. Unfortunately, the storm hadn't stopped, and as the outlying districts of Aberdeen are all very much higher than the centre of the town, dozens of buses had got stuck on the hills in various routes, including the bus I took. I had still a good bit to go, so I'd no choice but to get off and walk – in a blinding blizzard – and arrived for the second day running cold, bedraggled and exhausted.

By the next morning, the skies were clearer, the storm had abated but the roads were still packed with ice. Telling myself that it would be OK, I took the car and drove very, very slowly, turning into any skids and correcting the car's direction, and was congratulating myself on my dexterity as I reached the highest point on Anderson Drive, with the school in sight and just a short run down to get there.

Then I saw that three cars and a small van were sitting broadside across the road, and panic made me hit the brake hard so that I wouldn't crash into them. A big mistake! This skid took the car to within a hairsbreadth of the van, and as I sat thanking my lucky stars I'd missed it, trying to steady my racing heart and praying that I'd be able to get myself out of the pile of snow I'd landed in, I noticed that the janitor had arrived, complete with a large bucket of sand. One of the children on his way to school had seen the original four vehicles stuck there, so he hadn't come for my sole benefit, but at least I did get out eventually.

I had such a fright that I applied for a transfer, explaining the circumstances and asking for a school nearer my home. I didn't hold out too much hope of having my request answered, so you can imagine my delight at being told that I would be starting at Hazlehead Primary – practically on my doorstop – at the beginning of the next school year (mid August 1975.)

Before I end the Smithfield saga, I must tell you another little story. One of the girls amongst the 'team-taught' classes was called Amanda Wallace. Yes, you've guessed. She was John Wallace's sister, a quiet, well-behaved girl who was quite like him facially, but she, at least, upheld their angelic looks. Only a week or so before the summer holidays, when I would be leaving Smithfield for good, Mandy waited behind one afternoon when all the others had gone out.

'Did you want to ask me something, Mandy?' I asked her.

'Yes, Mrs Davidson, and I hope you won't be angry.'

Wondering what she was going to say, I assured her that I wouldn't be angry, so she gave a nervous sigh. 'John wants to see you.'

This did take me aback, but it wasn't the poor girl's fault. Knowing her brother, I guessed that he had threatened to do something to her if she didn't do as he told her. 'All right, Mandy. Tell him to come tomorrow afternoon. Will he manage that?'

'Yes, he gets taken home in a Rolls, so he's always home before me.'

Coward that I was, I dreaded seeing him again. His sister had likely told her family that I was going to another school, but what could he have to say to me? Had he been harbouring resentment at me for ripping his jumper? But that was a few years ago. Surely he wouldn't even remember it?

He came through the glass doors smiling benevolently, but monsters could do that, couldn't they? Smile one minute, pounce the next, 'Hello, John,' I said, as normally as I could, 'it's nice to see you. How are you getting on at Cordyce?'

His smile widened to a grin. 'It's great, Mrs Davidson. I get to draw as often as I like, and I don't have to do anything I don't want to.'

'But, John, if you don't listen to the lessons and don't do what you're told, how will you ever learn?' I had to say it, whatever the consequences.

The grin faded, but just a little. 'I came to say I was sorry for what I did to you when I was in your class, Mrs Davidson. I didna hate you, you ken.'

'Well, I'm glad of that.'

I don't know what became of him, but I must just say here that although another two of my ex-pupils are now serving time for murder, he is the one I'd have backed as a killer. I have to admit that one of the other two was a little hooligan sometimes, but he was a likeable rogue, really. The other one, I just can't understand. He was never any bother, in fact, just the opposite. If anyone in the class wet the floor (in Primary Three) or was sick, it was this lad who offered to clean it up. He was a poor scholar, but very anxious to please. As I write, it is only a matter of weeks since he was tried and sentenced for killing an older man and I haven't got over it yet. His photograph was in the newspaper, and although he must be over forty, he hadn't changed much. I still recognised him.

I had been told to report to the Hazlehead headmaster before the schools broke up, so I was allowed off half an hour early one afternoon to make myself known.

I was later to learn that Mr Robb had learned much from Mr Robertson when he was an assistant under him, and their methods were very similar, but their natures were completely different. I sat down when I was told to sit, and watched my new boss reading the information he'd been sent about me.

'Oh, my God!' he exclaimed, suddenly. 'Not another Davidson?'

'Yes,' I trembled. 'Is that a problem?'

'Not really, but we've a Mrs Davidson in Room 10,' (I might be well out in this), 'the sewing teacher's a Mrs Davidson and the janitor's Jimmy Davidson.'

'My husband's called Jimmy,' I volunteered, then wished I'd held my tongue.

'Oh, well, it'll maybe be all right. We're putting on a concert tonight, so if you like to come along, you'll meet the rest of the staff.'

With that he picked up another piece of paper and I knew that the meeting was over. I did go to the concert that night, and was glad that it was every bit as good as the concerts we had staged at Smithfield. I had seen other school concerts that were pretty poor, and I'd heard of some that were awful, but both these schools were fortunate in having teachers who were very musical.

After the concert, of course, there was a cheese and wine party, a time for the teachers to relax after weeks and weeks of rehearsals and one evening of utter bedlam although it usually kept to the saying, 'It'll be all right on the night'. I was made very welcome by all, and went home in a very 'merry' mood. To put it succinctly, I'd to make more than one attempt before I managed to get through the school gates on my way home . . . and I was on my feet not in a car!

Then it was time to say goodbye to Smithfield. By this time, Mr Robb had been transferred to what was classed a 'better' school (it was in a less rundown area) and the deputy head had been promoted to fill the post. I was sorry to leave such a friendly staff, and just as sorry to leave the children. Hazlehead's pupils were an unknown quantity to me, although I lived a mere five minutes away from the school, and there were three who actually lived in the same building as I did.

I had been eight years in Smithfield, happy years on the whole, and goodness knows what was to come.

21

My first class at Hazlehead School was as bad as my first at Smithfield; worse, in a way, because it was a Primary Five and the children were two years older. Both sets could be very likeable if they wanted to be, but very hard to control if they didn't. There was one big difference – I didn't have to slave at trying to get the Hazlehead pupils to speak proper English. They already did.

I hadn't been there long when I came across another difference. I was marking the homework jotters while they were doing an exercise from a textbook, when one of the girls – let's call her Annette – said, 'Mrs Davidson, Malcolm's swearing.'

Bearing in mind the kind of bad language that had been exchanged at Smithfield, I thought it best not to ask what he had said. Instead, I assumed my sternest face as I looked at the boy. 'Surely not, Malcolm.'

There was five minutes' silence, then, 'Mrs Davidson, he swore again.'

After the third announcement, I said, 'Malcolm, stay behind after the bell. I want you to take a letter home to your mother.'

The threat was enough to nip it in the bud, but, remembering what had happened once before when I didn't carry out a threat, I wrote the letter, telling his mother that I'd had to reprimand him several times for swearing, and that perhaps a few words from her would stop it.

When Malcolm went home, sulkily clutching the envelope, Annette came sneaking back into the classroom, 'He did swear, Mrs Davidson.'

That's when I made another mistake. 'Can you tell me what he said?'

She drew her mouth in for a moment, as if debating whether or not to sully her lips by repeating the word, but then she muttered, 'Hell!'

My heart sank. That wasn't really what I'd have called a swear word, but the letter was probably being handed over right now, because he lived only a stone's throw from the school. Sure enough, Annette had just gone out when the Head walked in. 'There's a lady on the phone asking for you, Mrs Davidson.'

It was Malcolm's mother, in a filthy mood because I had addressed the letter to her, when she and her husband brought up their son together. 'Most mothers prefer not to let their husbands know about this sort of thing,' I excused myself.

She ignored that, and asked what I had dreaded her asking. 'And what was this awful swear word that he is supposed to have used?'

Ice was dripping from each syllable she uttered, but I could only say, 'I didn't find out until after Malcolm went home. He had said "Hell", that was all, but . . .'

She didn't let me explain about my last school. 'Oh, dear! Hell? Now that *is* a dreadful swear word!' This was sarcasm to the *nth* degree. 'My goodness, your delicate ears must have been truly assaulted by that!'

She slammed the receiver down, and I turned apprehensively to Mr Robertson, who had heard only what I'd been saying, and gave him the whole story. His reaction, thank goodness, was completely different. 'Silly bitch!' he grinned. 'Never mind her.'

At Hazlehead, Primary Five classes went to Stirling for a day in two coaches, and although I was to have my student and one of the parents to help, I wasn't looking forward to it. As it happened, it wasn't bad behaviour of any kind that upset the apple cart. The trip was at the end of May, and I'd been instructed by the mother of a girl called June on my first afternoon that she was a diabetic, and that she always carried two sugar lumps, which I had to give her if she started acting peculiarly. There had been no sign of anything so far, and I had almost forgotten the warning.

The day of the trip eventually arrived, the bags containing the children's packed lunches were stowed into the boot of our coach, and off we set. This wasn't like Smithfield, where an afternoon's outing to the beach had revealed that it was the first time most of them had seen the sea. This bunch, or most of them, were accustomed to being driven around in cars, and were quite blasé about the scenery. The second coach, Mrs McLean's class, was to visit the Robert the Bruce Memorial first and then the Wallace Monument, while we were to go to the Wallace Monument first and then the Bruce Memorial. The two coaches were to meet up eventually at the Castle, where they could accommodate larger numbers.

Arriving in Stirling, our bus went to the Wallace Monument as scheduled. It's a long, very steep walk up from the car park to the monument, and when I saw the toilet block at the foot of the hill, I said, 'If any of you want to go to the toilet, you'd better go now.'

My student went in with the girls who opted for it, while Mr Smith, the parent helper, went in with the boys and I took the remainder very slowly up the hill. Everything was going well; we all enjoyed what we saw inside the tall building, the boys, especially, being impressed by the armour and weaponry – in particular the huge double-handled sword hanging outside, said to be the actual one William Wallace had used.

Before we attempted the descent, I warned my class, 'Please keep behind me, all of you. If you start running, you won't be able to stop, the path's so steep.' I set off, slowly and steadily downwards, and we were almost at the foot when I became aware of heavy feet overtaking me. When I looked round, I saw June plodding purposefully, one foot after the other landing with a thump on the gravelly surface. 'June!' I warned, trying to grab hold of her, but she appeared not to have heard and carried on.

I couldn't run after her, it was too dangerous, but she had only a few yards to go to reach level ground, so I let her go. At the toilet area, of course, those who hadn't paid a call before we went up, were now desperate to go, myself included.

I was washing my hands when I heard the racing footsteps. 'Mrs Davidson! Mrs Davidson!' and in burst about half a dozen girls. 'June's gone all stiff, and she doesn't know what the student's saying to her . . . or anybody. She's on a seat and you'd better come quick.'

All of us ran as quickly as we could to where June was sitting on a bench with her legs straight out in front of her like a dummy. The other girls were hovering anxiously around her. It was only then that I remembered that she was a diabetic, and searched her blazer pocket – no sugar lumps. I asked if anyone would recognise her lunch bag, but all I got was a mass of negative headshakes.

By means of getting each child to take out his or her own bag, I was left with the one I needed, but even after going through it with a fine toothcomb, I found no sugar lumps. Mr Smith ran to ask the nearby hotel to phone for an ambulance, but the receptionist went one better than that. She offered to take the girl to the hospital in her car.

As a matter of interest, if you have never tried to stuff a board-stiff ten-year-old girl inside a Mini, you have missed one of life's most frustrating experiences. We did pack her in eventually, and Mr Smith accompanied her to hospital. The rest of the class had still to see the Bruce Memorial, and I couldn't leave them in the hands of one poor student.

Sadly, because of the long delay, we had missed our time slot at the Memorial, and pupils from another school had already gone in. We did see the statue, the warrior King Robert sitting proudly astride his mighty steed on the grass outside, but that was all. On, then, to our last port of call – the Castle and there was June, running around amongst Mrs McLean's pupils, an ice cream cone in her hand. It seems that the insulin injection the hospital gave her had been all that she needed.

In Primary Six, I went to Edinburgh with the same pupils for five days. The boys were most impressed in the Science Museum, while the girls loved the story of Greyfriars Bobby and took photos of the dog's statue sitting outside the cemetery where his master lies buried. They all seemed to be fascinated by the Waxworks, even if some of the girls

– and one or two boys – were wary of going down to the Chamber of Horrors.

What did surprise me was their lack of interest in the Museum of Childhood. They raced through all three floors within ten minutes, while I was still on the first floor recognising toys I'd had as a child but which had been thrown out years before. My nostalgia was brought to an end by the pounding of feet on the stairs and the cries of, 'Can we go to the Pancake Shop now?'

The Castle got a mixed reception, but the Zoo was more to their liking, and taken all in all, our visit to Edinburgh was quite worthwhile. As a last treat, we took them to St James' shopping centre to buy something for their mums.

I had the same class in Primary Seven, and the trip was more adventurous – seven whole days in Belgium. This time, Mr Robertson came with us, taking a final responsibility before retiring. Our hotel was a tramride out of Ostend, thoroughly equipped for parties of children. There were two buildings, one old and one new, round a covered quadrangle lined with slot machines. This was ideal for wet spells, but we spent most evenings on the beach. We also had a two-hour bus run into Holland one day to a theme park, which was a great success – before such pleasures were made more available by Disney. On the very last forenoon, we went shopping in Ostend, the headmaster gave both children and teachers free rein to go where they liked as long as we all met up at a certain time.

There were fifteen boys and fourteen girls on that trip. Mr Robertson split them up thus: five boys each to the three men (himself and two fathers) and the fourteen girls to me. Most of the party was in the new building, but I was in the old part with only two of the quiet girls next door, so my nights were undisturbed. The men, however, didn't get off so easily. By this stage, with most of the kids eleven or twelve years old, the boys (and some of the girls) were up to all kinds of tricks. As one of the fathers said to me one morning, 'Some of the little blighters are like dogs after bitches on heat. We hardly got a wink of sleep for making sure there were no shenanigans.'

Even with unbroken nights, it took me all my time to keep watch over the fourteen girls during the days. There was a small nucleus of them who flirted with every boy who passed, and the Belgian youths would have been delighted to make merry with them . . . if I hadn't intervened.

The next three years followed the same pattern – Stirling in Five, Edinburgh in Six and Belgium in Seven, and there were upsets of some kind during each trip. I've heard people saying that teachers are lucky being paid for going abroad with pupils, but they have no idea of the stress involved. These trips are no picnic, and take that from one who knows. I also heard, while standing in a queue at a baker's van, two mothers talking to each other during the first week of summer holidays.

One said, 'My two kids are driving me mad already.'

The other agreed. 'My two are the same. I wish it was time for them to go back to school.'

If they found their own two children too much of a handful, how did they think teachers coped with well over twenty of other people's?

In spite of all that I've said, I look back on my days in both Smithfield and Hazlehead Primaries very fondly. For every troublesome child, there were usually ten or more who posed no behaviour problems. On the other hand, as far as learning was concerned, quite a few in every class had difficulties with one aspect or another, and it was a wonderful feeling when, after struggling for weeks, even months, to get a child to understand something, he or she suddenly saw the light. That, I would say, is why teachers teach. That is their reward.

Because of the amount of preparation for lessons that needed to be done, I had given up all thought of writing, but promised myself that I'd give it another go once I retired. My sixtieth birthday, 30 June 1982, meant I could stop working, but I spent the next twenty-one months helping my sister to care for Mum, who had suffered a stroke in 1981.

Sadly, she died in March of 1984, something I took many, many months to get over. I often thought back to the stroppy youngster I'd been, spoilt rotten until Bertha came on the scene and put my nose out of joint. I had given my mother much stress in my time, though we became very close as she grew older. Bertha and I have also grown closer, time has narrowed the gap between us. A woman of thirty-one had more in common with a woman of twenty-one than a woman of twenty-one had with a girl of eleven, for instance. At one time, I resented being saddled with a little sister when I wanted to be speaking to boys, but, since our own children grew up, we've had many lovely weekends away together with our husbands, in Edinburgh, Cardiff, Coylumbridge and so on, staying in hotels that would have seemed like palaces to me when I was younger and having to count every brass farthing. Some of them still did, even when we were seasoned travellers.

Even now, when Jimmy and I are not fit enough to be going far from home, we have many days out with Bertha and Bill, and also with Sheila and John, who moved from Surrey to Cruden Bay a few years ago. Alan doesn't like driving and has never bought a car, but he has been roped in over the past two or three years, to drive his dad around a bit if the weather is good. I am quite content to enjoy the peace at home, to get on with some writing while I know Jimmy is being well looked after.

It was 1986 or into 1987 before I felt the urge to write again, but this time, my sights were set much higher than short stories.

I wanted to write a novel.

22

The interwoven initials on the pendulum of our grandfather clock had always fascinated me. JT and WD. The story goes that William Davidson, Jimmy's great-great-grandfather, had the magnificent Spanish mahogany clock made as a gift for his bride, Jean Tawse, on their wedding day. It has been passed to the eldest son down through the generations and Jimmy, an only son, fell heir to it when his father died. The weights, unfortunately, had become entangled during the transportation from Laurencekirk to Aberdeen, and we thought it best to have it thoroughly checked and overhauled. We chose Jamieson and Carry, one of the city's finest jewellers, and it cost us £9 10 shillings (in 1957) to have the innards made like new again – fully three weeks of the average weekly wage.

'It's over 150 years old,' said the man who brought it back, 'and the new plates we put in should keep it going for as long again.'

I have no hope of living long enough to learn the truth of that prediction, but it was made almost fifty years ago and our 'old friend' is still sending its comforting 'tick tock' along the hallway. Sadly, we had to stop it marking the hours when we moved into the flat, because we didn't want it to annoy the neighbours. Not that any of them had complained, but it sits very close to the door to the landing, and its chime, despite being elegantly sweet, was also fairly loud.

Mind you, it used to sit in the living room at Mastrick, next to the fire, and I can remember times when I sat down of an afternoon for half an hour's rest before getting ready to go to my evening job, sure that I'd hear the clock striking four. My chair was practically rubbing against the long-case, so how could I fail to hear it? Believe me, I could and often did! You can get used to anything . . . as the auld wife said when her bosom got caught in the mangle. Oops, sorry!

I regarded the pendulum's duogram – if that's the correct word for two sets of initials – as the absolute epitome of romance and often wished that I knew the whole story of that long-ago love affair. With more time for thought after I retired, it eventually dawned on me that I could invent a story, and that is how I came to write *Time Shall Reap* – my very first attempt.

In the late sixties, I had attended a Creative Writing class in the evenings; following this, I became a member of a Writers' Circle. The highlight of each year for me was the Writers' Conference held in Pitlochry, which most of our group attended. There were competitions for short stories in the different genres: love, children's, mysteries, etc., and although there were almost 100 people from all over Scotland in the same hotel, we could talk comfortably with anyone we met in the corridors. They were all, like we were, aspiring to be *published* writers. There's a great difference between saying, 'I'm a writer', and being able to say, 'I'm a published writer.'

One of the carrots dangled in front of us was that whoever wrote the winning first chapter of a novel would have the finished book accepted by a well known publishing house. At that time, of course, I wasn't interested in writing a novel and entered only the short story competitions . . . with no luck, let me add.

Over the course of perhaps four or five years, however, I did have a couple of short stories published – one in the *Sunday Mail,* one in *Women's World*. The latter, a weekly magazine, folded up shortly afterwards, but I don't think that my story was the cause of its demise. I hope not!

I also had a couple of articles accepted: one by *Woman's Own* about choosing the quickest-moving till queue in a supermarket, and the other by *Education in the North,* produced by Aberdeen City Education Authority. I had been asked to write about my experiences with John Wallace, concentrating on how hard he had worked. The final showdown hadn't then occurred, worse luck, for it would have made for much more interesting reading.

But this was a time when dozens of hopefuls were starting to write, anything from short shorts of 1,000 words, to 4,000 magazine length shorts, to novellas of around 50,000, to full-blown novels of 120,000 and upwards, and I collected so many rejections that I wondered whether to paper the toilet with them or give up writing completely. I gave up . . . for many years.

I wrote *Time Shall Reap* in exercise books in pencil and revising in blue biro and then red biro. More or less satisfied with it, I typed it out on a portable Smith Corona typewriter, giving each chapter to my friend Doreen Cruickshank on the floor above me for approval or otherwise. She was with me on this book from the very beginning and is still my No.1 fan. I selected some chapters of the completed manuscript to show how I dealt with love, tragedy, humour, jealousy (as we'd been advised in the Writers' Circle) and sent them to one publisher after another. They homed back faithfully after every outing.

Then I remembered something else that we had been taught in the Writers' Circle – if a manuscript is sent to a publisher without being addressed to a specific person, it is liable to be thrown on the 'Slush Pile' and returned unread. So I looked in the current version of the *Writers' and Artists' Year Book* for a name to put on the packet.

From the names under the heading 'Collins (William) PLC, 1819', I chose Kenneth Murdoch – he had a good Scottish name, I was a Scot and the story was set in the northeast of Scotland. How could it fail?

By return of post, I received a letter informing me that Mr *Rupert* Murdoch was meantime in America, and, in any case, he took no part in the publishing side of the business. Would you believe it? I'd bypassed all the Indians and gone straight to the chief. Redemption was at hand, though. The letter ended by saying that my manuscript had been passed to the proper department. I was still in with a chance.

It turned out that the proper department wanted nothing to do with it, so, having had enough disappointments to last for a long time,

I finally put the entire story into a box and laid it to rest under the bed.

I started a whodunit next, as I'm quite partial to a good murder story myself – I've got all Agatha Christie's. I decided to send the whole manuscript out this time, not just a few sample chapters as I had done before, as I had been taught to do at the evening class and the writers' circle. How could anybody judge a whole novel from only a few unrelated chapters – especially a whodunit? I posted the compact parcel to Collins' Crime Club but had it returned as too long – almost twice as long as was needed. Before I did anything to cut it, I thought I'd better phone to ask if it was worth my while to spend time on such a task. I was told that it was, and so I went ahead, chopping out as much as I could, but the new version was returned to me, too.

'While we enjoyed your humour and thought that your detectives were well handled, the story lost its impact in the shortening.'

Jam and Jeopardy, therefore, also disappeared under the bed.

I wrote a third book but considered it a bit too autobiographical and never sent it out at all. (I've reached an age now when I'm not nearly so easily embarrassed, which is why I agreed to write a proper account of my life.) This third novel also languished under the bed for years. I'm not sure where the last two are now, kicking around somewhere no doubt, because I never throw anything out. My family will vouch for that. I could start a secondhand goods stall anywhere at the drop of a hat – if I could bring myself to part with any of my old rubbish . . . correction, any of my old treasures.

It was around this time that I came across a photograph of my father and his brother in front of their butcher's shop at the top of the Gallowgate. This made me recall many happy hours spent in the house above the shop, with aunties and uncles . . . and cousins galore. So this was where I set most of my next attempt. People have asked me if it's a true story, and I have to say no. The setting is as near as I could describe the actual house, but my grandfather would turn in his grave if he knew the kind of things I've made some of the characters do.

By an odd coincidence, I had just finished printing this out on the word processor I'd bought some time before when an editor from one of the large London publishers appeared on Grampian television. My spirits rose when she announced that she was looking for Scottish family sagas written by Scotswomen. This was a really good omen; I had exactly what she wanted, hadn't I?

I packed the whole 700-plus pages into a box and despatched it with high hopes, and waited . . . and waited . . . and waited! It was six months before she sent it back – with a short note. 'While I enjoyed your book, it is not really the type of story we publish. Good luck.'

I'm not exaggerating when I say that I was utterly devastated. After waiting all that time, with expectation increasing by the day, it was as though I'd been cut off in my prime. I phoned Sheila to tell her the bad news, and ended, 'That's it! I'm finished! I'm going to tear up everything I've ever written.'

She told me not to be silly, to persevere. One swallow didn't make a summer. One rejection didn't mean that it was no good. 'Send it to Collins,' she ordered. 'They did say something nice about your whodunit.'

I telephoned Collins this time and asked who dealt with family sagas. I was given two names, and one being so obviously Scottish, I settled on him. Without changing one word, I enclosed a new covering letter and sent off the box again, with little expectations, I must admit.

Only a week later, I got a phone call saying that they would accept *The Brow of the Gallowgate* if I shortened it by twenty per cent. To give you an idea of exactly what this involved, I was being asked to cut out what almost amounted to the length of an Agatha Christie novel, but if this was the only way to get my book published . . . I was on top of the world, dancing my own height, or however else you care to describe that feeling of absolute heaven.

I set to with gusto, chopping bits out here and there, whole sentences, whole paragraphs, even in one or two instances, whole chapters . . . as long as it didn't interfere with the plot. I got a letter asking if I needed help, that Collins would supply someone to do the hatchet job for me (not in those words), but I held firm. It was my baby and I didn't want anyone else spoiling it . . . or to be more specific, it was my pie and I didn't want anybody else's finger in it.

Then, of course, there were the long months to wait until my manuscript went through all the various stages, although, apart from the shortening they didn't want any further changes made. First to come were the proofs, the sign that it was truly, definitely, happening. I took my red biro out of retirement and set to work to mark any printers' errors with the signs indicated in the instruction sheets I got. I said 'work', and I really mean work! I couldn't believe the amount of misprints there were . . . and not of my doing. I may be haphazard as far as housework and so on is concerned, but I'm a perfectionist with my scripts. An odd few errors might slip past me unnoticed, but very, very few – then, at least. I'm more fallible now.

The time of publication drew nearer and nearer, and at last, one morning in late March 1990, the postman delivered *my* copy of *my* very first book. I showed it to Jimmy as soon as I unwrapped it, and revelled in his congratulations – he was almost as excited as I was. But that wasn't enough for me, so I ran upstairs to let Doreen see it. My heart was beating sixty to the dozen with excitement and pride, but I also wanted her to allay my fears that it may not be a success. After all, she had read it in its infancy and at almost every revision, and I wanted her to praise it once again.

I waited, my heart nearly bursting out of my rib cage with impatience to show off the most important piece of literature ever printed, but I finally had to admit it – SHE WASN'T IN!

What an anticlimax! I stood there with my beautiful hardback in my hand contemplating whom else I could boast to, but the decision was settled for me. The door from the stairs opened at that point, and out came the postman – the deliverer of this most precious article in the first place. When I flung myself at him in relieved delight, he must have wondered where the avalanche had come from, but give him his due, he spent some time inspecting the tome, admiring the cover and asking all kinds of pertinent questions. What is more, he and his wife came to more than one of the talks I gave in the Central Library on later occasions.

I was taken aback (but thrilled) by the attention given to my book. Collins had arranged for it to be launched in the Main Library, where I was expected to give a talk, too. I was petrified. Standing up every day in front of a class of ten- to eleven-year-olds does not prepare you to face around seventeen adults ranging in age from early twenties to the seventies, male and female. I had, of course, written out what I intended to say and had to keep referring to that, but it seemed to go down quite well, and during the refreshments break, most of my audience came up to ask me something. It was heady stuff!

Then I signed books in a few shops in Aberdeen – one giving it a second launching with wine and savoury bites – and in places as far away as Inverness. One of the local newspapers sent a reporter to interview me, and my book and I had quite a write up. Also in the local *Leopard*, as I've already mentioned.

One little anecdote (as true as I'm sitting at this computer) before I leave this topic. At that time, a mobile library van came every Tuesday for the benefit of the elderly residents and young mothers of our community. (This service has long since ceased, but that is by the by.) Doreen attended it regularly, bringing books for me as well as for herself, and came back one afternoon desperate to tell me what had happened while she was there. Hearing my name mentioned by one of the two ladies in front of her, she had pricked up her ears. Their dialogue went something like this:

Mrs A: Do you ken far this woman bides that wrote the book aboot the Gallowgate? It's in Hazleheid some place, I ken that.
Mrs B: I dinna ken, and you'd better nae buy it. They say it's real dirty.
Mrs A: Well, I canna help that. I've bocht it already, to gi'e my lassie along wi' a pair o' bloomers for her birthday.

I have no idea whether or not her 'lassie' enjoyed *The Brow of the Gallowgate*, but it couldn't have been in more basic company, could it? Bloomers, huh?

In the interval between the revision of the novel and its publication, I had begun another, *The Road to Rowanbrae*, also suggested by a photograph – of the croft belonging to my mother's grandparents. I naturally gave this the title *Toddlehills*, and forwarded it to Collins as soon as it was completed. I was horrified when it was returned with the comment, 'We are not keen on the idea of jumping from the early 1900s to the 1980s with alternate chapters.'

I had begun, as the book stands now, with the discovery of a skull, and then gone on to have the young man trying to place whose it was by finding out the names of the people who had lived in the croft that had stood there originally. One chapter followed what he thought had happened and the next told what had actually happened those eighty or so years earlier, and time about until the final denouement. The editor said that she wanted me to leave the first chapter as it was, but to follow the old story to just before the end.

This meant a tremendous amount of work, and I found myself with far too many words. It was at the editor's behest that forty years were cut out, the tale jumping from 1942 to 1982. I've always felt that this must annoy readers, but the people I've asked have said that, although they did notice the gap, it didn't detract from the plot. Thank goodness!

Even with the revision over, they were not happy with the title, and dozens of my suggestions were turned down, even *The Bargain Wife*, which I thought was quite clever since it turned out that she wasn't a bargain to him at all, but which the editor considered too ironic. Jimmy and I then went down to Surrey to spend a holiday with Sheila. On the one and only rainy afternoon we had, my daughter and I sat down to think of a suitable title to give my second book, inventing some hilarious names by joining the first part of a place name with the second part of another, and eventually came up with *The Road to*

Rowanbrae. This originated from Gowanhill (remember my childhood holidays there?). Thank goodness, this pleased the editor.

When I first sent off *Rowanbrae*, I had decided to revise *Time Shall Reap* and try it again. In only a few weeks, it had to be set aside again until the editor was satisfied with *Rowanbrae,* but then I knuckled down to it. Collins, if you remember, had already rejected it a year or two before, but the revision must have done the trick, and *Time Shall Reap,* although first to be written, was third to be published. Doreen, naturally, was delighted about this. She'd played a large part in its life.

*

In September 1993, Collins made a change in their publishing system. Previous to this, hardback books had been sold under the name of Collins, and paperbacks under various names, Fontana and Grafton to name two; now they were to take all their books out under HarperCollins Publishers Limited.

The launch was held as a buffet/dinner in the Cholmondoley Room, House of Lords, to which grand 'do' Jimmy and I were invited. He didn't want to go. He couldn't mix with people like that. He'd just feel like a fish out of water. He was only a common working man and he would likely put his foot in it – or both feet – as soon as he opened his mouth. He'd just let me down. He wouldn't change his mind for me, but Sheila eventually persuaded him that he would be letting me down by *not* going.

The invitation specified '7.00 p.m. for 7.30 p.m., Carriages 10.45, Black Tie', so the problem now was what to wear. Neither of us had clothes suitable for such a grand occasion, and Jimmy hated the idea of having to wear a 'monkey suit', but Bill took him in hand, and Bertha came with me to make sure that I'd choose something appropriate. In my mind, I could picture myself in something floaty, and as soon as the lady in the very exclusive shop took out this beaded, sequinned two piece, I knew it was the one for me. It sounds tacky, but it really was lovely – colourful, yet not gaudy, with the background mostly navy. The floor-length skirt was scalloped round the hem, as was the loose top, which came to below my fingertips.

The price horrified me, but I'd set my heart on it. There were, of course, all the accessories to buy, a small evening bag, dainty navy shoes, a navy stole (I couldn't spoil the effect by wearing a coat). Jimmy got his 'monkey suit', a bow tie, decent black shoes.

We had now booked a room in a hotel not too far from Westminster, being told that we didn't need to confirm by letter, but on the day before we were due to fly down, I thought I'd better make sure that everything was in order. Thank heaven I checked. Our booking had been missed. There was no room at the inn!

Panic-stricken, I phoned several London hotels, but all were fully booked. At last, I chanced upon one between Buckingham Palace and Scotland Yard. The reservation clerk said that they would require confirmation by fax, so, not having this facility, I'd to ask my nephew to do this for me. Off we went next morning. I knew that the hotel would be satisfactory, the price guaranteed that, but I really wasn't expecting the opulence, the almost suite-like proportions of our room – with an L-shaped dining and sitting area. We didn't dine there, of course. We had the buffet/dinner on the Wednesday evening, and on the Thursday, we ate in the hotel's vast dining room. In for a penny, in for a pound – that was us, and Sheila, working in London at the time, got Thursday afternoon off to come and hear how we had fared the evening before.

We took a rest after we arrived there on the Wednesday, to refresh us for the evening meal. We had also been offered a tour of the Parliament buildings if we turned up at 6 p.m. instead of 7 p.m., and we jumped at the chance. It was most interesting but very exhausting, and although we enjoyed every fact-filled minute, we were glad when it was time to go to the Cholmondeley Room. We were welcomed by the Earl of Buckingham and two of HarperCollins' executives, and given a glass of champagne. Then we had time to mingle a bit – glasses being topped up every now and then most discreetly by the waiters – and met several well-known authors, plus a few, like me, not so well known.

Jimmy surprised me – and himself, I think – by chatting quite easily to other husbands, probably in much the same boat as he was, rather uncomfortable at first. Quite a few of us were standing out on the balconies admiring the Thames in the lights from other buildings, when the thunderstorm began, and we were quickly taken inside and the windows closed against the rain. The display of lightning, reflected in the water, went on for about twenty minutes, a rare and unexpected addition to our items to talk about when we got home.

Then we had to consult the seating arrangements and the first course was served. There was a lovely camellia in a plastic container for each lady and a huge golf umbrella for each gentleman, with the HarperCollins logo on it. There were only two authors from Scotland, so Jimmy and I were alongside Christine Marion Fraser and her husband, both extremely friendly people.

Having disposed of the melon and port, we were asked to help ourselves from the long tables set up in a smaller room off the main area. They were absolutely groaning with meat and fish dishes, and every kind of accompaniment the most fastidious eaters could have wished for.

The selection of desserts was not so large, but large enough, including an array of different kinds of cheese. This repast was rounded off with coffee and mints, and it goes without saying that during the entire meal, all glasses were replenished with wine as soon as the level dropped even a fraction of an inch.

The evening ended around 10.40 p.m., when the carriages arrived. We didn't qualify for a carriage of course, but we did need a taxi because we didn't know how to get back to the hotel. With so much alcohol on offer, some of the men were standing at the side of the street waving their colourful umbrellas to attract a cab, so Jimmy followed suit. We were only charged £2 – in London, mind you, at 11 p.m. – so you can understand how far we had to go. Just round the corner, really.

After breakfast the following morning, we had a walk to the Palace and along Birdcage Walk a little, returning through St James' Park. It was a lovely crisp, autumn day, and we sat for a while watching the world go by. Sheila was joining us at 12.30 p.m. for a drink before lunch, and after that was over, we went up to our little 'sitting-room' to tell her about our experiences of the night before.

She left around four in order to avoid the rush hour on the underground – she had to go to Waterloo for her train home – so we walked a little bit with her, past Scotland Yard. We were afraid to go much farther than that, in case we got lost, and in any case, we were beginning to feel quite tired. We spent the next two hours in the lounge, then went back to our room. After our tuck-in at lunchtime, we didn't need anything much to eat, so we ordered sandwiches and watched television before having an early night.

We left for Victoria Station the next morning, on our way to Heathrow to get the plane to Edinburgh. Bertha and Bill met us at Turnhouse at 1 p.m. They'd been to an exhibition of some kind in Harrogate, I think, so this was a midway stop (almost) for all of us.

We had a very enjoyable few days with them, as we have always done, visiting all the old favourites and also finding new places to explore. We left Edinburgh on the Monday, and had an easy journey home in Bill's Jaguar, following the coast to a large extent.

And so ended a week that will remain forever in my memory.

It has just occurred to me that, although I have touched on some of our holidays, I haven't included the times we went abroad. I started teaching in 1967, and by the spring of 1968, I decided that we could afford to splurge out a little . . . if we were careful.

I booked a trip to Linz on the Rhine, costing £32 for twelve days (half price for twelve-year-old Alan) but a few weeks before we were due to leave, we were notified that, because there were not enough bookings for that particular place, we had been transferred to another. Our destination now was Boppard.

The coach left from Victoria Station, but when we turned up, the courier had no note of us. I, of course, panicked, but he assured me that it would be all right. He would book us in separately at each hotel we were to use. In actual fact, we came off far better than any of our fellow passengers. The cheaper rooms given to package tours were completely full, so we were given far better accommodation.

We were based for a week in a small hotel, awakened each morning by the ringing of the church bells at the crack of dawn. Apparently, a rich merchant had once been lost in the forest in a snowstorm, and only found his way when the bells at Boppard had started to ring. He left money for this to be done every day, as that might help other poor travellers. They didn't help us, however. We tourists could have seen them far enough.

We spent a night in Amsterdam going there, and on the way home we stayed in Luxembourg for one night and Brussels for our last night. It was here that we had the best accommodation ever. Instead of being on the top floor with the other Overland passengers, we were given a huge *en suite* room on the first floor, usually reserved for VIPs. It was 1968, remember, and very few rooms with bathrooms were available.

All this for £32 each – coach fares, full board everywhere we went, and entry paid to each place of interest. The place that interested Jimmy most, of course, was the Asbach Uralt Brandy distillery.

It was a few years before we could afford to go abroad again. We spent the intervening holidays with Sheila and her husband in Aldershot. This, although the home of the British Army, lies in lovely countryside, and having travelled there by train, we had to use public transport to get around. However, we saw quite a lot of the area, going to Windsor, Reading, Portsmouth, and so on. Eventually, with a decent car, we were able to get there under our own steam, and go farther afield while we were there.

Our second continental holiday was in Austria, flying this time, and at a much higher cost, which for the life of me I can't recall. I can't remember the year, either, but it was the time of a go-slow strike by the pilots, and our flight was four hours late in taking off from Edinburgh. This meant that we landed in Munich after midnight, and we saw not one single soul as we went through the airport to board the coach that was to take us to Innsbruck. The café we were meant to stop at for something to eat was closed by the time we reached it, and when we arrived at our hotel, we were shown to our room . . . and that was that. It was two or three in the morning, of course, but it didn't make our hunger any the less.

We had one week there, and than we were transported to just outside Salzburg. This time we were in a much more upmarket hotel, all rooms having *en suite* bathrooms. One whole week of this made us decide that it was the only way to travel. We have kept to this rule ever since, wherever we go. Salzburg, of course, was the home of *The Sound of Music,* and we were taken round the various spots where it was filmed. I was quite disappointed to learn that things weren't exactly as they had appeared, but it was still a lovely holiday.

Another few years on, both Jimmy and I had been quite ill for some time, and it was into July before we began to feel better – to feel we deserved a real break. As his holidays were fixed in the Trades fortnight, I didn't have much time to look for somewhere. To be honest, most destinations were fully booked up. The only place I was offered was the Costa del Sol, and Jimmy had always said he didn't fancy Spain. The lady in the travel agency advised me that waiting would mean losing it, so I booked it there and then. As you will imagine, I wasn't flavour of the month when I told my husband what I had done, but it turned out to be a wonderful holiday.

Spain was followed, at various intervals, by Majorca and then Ibiza. In both cases, we chose venues that were not yet popular with the public – they are now – and Santa Ponsa was delightful, as was Ibiza town itself, although we were staying in a large hotel at the other side of the water. We had to take a ferry across every day (it cost the equivalent of eight pence) but that was all part of the attraction of the place. We used to sit by the quay in the town itself to watch the cruise ships leaving. There were all sorts of people, and all sorts of yachts in the marina, with celebrities and suntanned beauties (male and female) sallying around with very little clothes on.

Ho, hum! If only we could have enjoyed ourselves like that when we were young.

We booked for a Greek island (Aegina) at the beginning of 1981. I can remember this because my mother suffered a stroke about two months before we were due to go. I wanted to cancel, but Bertha said it would be a shame to lose so much money; there were no refunds paid at that stage. I promised to phone every day, but I could never get through to Britain. It was a lovely holiday, lazy and relaxing, but I could never rid my mind of the worry of what was going on in Aberdeen. As it happened, Mum lived for another three years, paralysed down her right side and confined to a wheelchair, but her mind was still as clear as ever it was.

We were both pensioners when we decided to have one last holiday overseas, but it would have to be reasonably priced. The travel agent checked fares for me, and came up with a wonderful bargain – £129 each for two weeks in the Algarve . . . if we could be ready to leave in a few days' time. We were ready to leave at any time, nothing to keep us back, but I had never fancied self-catering. I'd always looked forward to being looked after, that was the best part of holidays, and I'd heard horrendous stories of the squalor of some of the apartments offered.

We had to make up our minds there and then, though, and fortunately, it wasn't like that at all. The chalets were in the grounds of a large impressive hotel, and we could use all the facilities. Not only that, a girl came in every morning to clean for us. It was great. The only meal I cooked each day was breakfast, and we ate out the rest of the time. Cafés and restaurants were really cheap, and the hotel itself only charged us £15 for the one evening meal we had there – which, sad to say, wasn't particularly exciting.

In between these forays onto the continent, we spent our holidays with Sheila and John, in the bungalow in Ash Vale they had bought. This small village is on the edge of the Army Training Grounds, with lovely paths through the Surrey woods, and we explored much of the surrounding area, too . . . when we went by car. In later years, when driving so far became too much for Jimmy, we flew there, being collected at Heathrow by Sheila and John and driven around while we were there.

We found dozens of superb eating places, although one especially stands out in my memory because of its position. The village was called Friday Street and the original building, named the Stephen Langton was extremely old (another part had been added far more recently).

Langton had been born in Friday Street, but after suspecting that he'd been let down by his childhood sweetheart, he left his birthplace and became a priest. Many years later, when he returned to his roots with the burning desire to marry the girl whatever she had done, he learned that she had died . . . of a broken heart, by all accounts. He had devoted himself to the church again, and eventually rose to Archbishop – an instance of local boy really making good. The tale was sad, but the cuisine and the service in the inn could not have been bettered.

On another holiday, we passed through another village with an intriguing name – Christmas Pie. I did wonder what its origin was, and was delighted to read in a local weekly some weeks after we came home, that some time in the eighteenth or nineteenth centuries the land had belonged to a farmer called Christmas, and had originally been known as 'Christmas's Piece'. It's easy to understand how the contraction had been made. I think that whoever had written that article must have come across the village and been as fascinated by the name as we were. He, however, had probably had the time and, being a journalist, the expertise to make enquiries about it.

Since Sheila and her husband moved to Aberdeenshire, John has been amused at many of the names here. Maggieknocketer is one of his favourites, and the villages where the pronunciation bears no resemblance to the spelling – Finzean being Fingin, Strachan becoming Strawn. An old local 'chestnut' goes something like this.

After hearing of several places in this category, a Yorkshireman on holiday in Scotland's northeast came across Aberchirder, and was stunned to be told it was pronounced Foggieloan. It's not, really. It's actually pronounced Aber-hirder, but it has the nickname Foggieloan – goodness knows why.

Enough! Enough!

23

I gave in to the many requests I'd received for a sequel to *The Brow of the Gallowgate,* and brought Albert Ogilvie's children and grand-children through the Second World War. As always, as soon as it was finished, I gave it to Doreen to read. Not only does she spot misprints and errors (a real boon to me), she gives me her honest opinion of my stories, and she thought that this was every bit as good as the original. Unfortunately, my editor (Ruth is as good a name as any) deemed otherwise. She gave me no explanation for the rejection, so I phoned the agent she had recommended when my third book was accepted, to ask if he could tell me why. As he had instructed when I went to meet him in London months earlier, I sent him the manuscript of *Cousins At War* so that he could suggest any alterations he thought it needed, but he said it was perfect and passed it straight over to Ruth. If he thought it was good enough then, what did he think had gone wrong when she got her hands on it?

She had already been in touch with him, however, and I got no satisfaction from him either, so I asked to have my manuscript returned. He advised me to change the names of the characters, in other words to create an entirely new family, and try it again, but it was meant as a sequel and I found it impossible to change the names. I couldn't banish the feel of the Ogilvies; they kept coming into my mind and no other names seemed to fit them. I gave up. This box, too, has languished in some forgotten corner of my home ever since, but perhaps I will resurrect it some day – enough time has surely passed since I wrote the first tale.

*

I come now to *Waters of the Heart* and Louise (another fictional name), a new editor, who suggested as many alterations for this book as Ruth had done for the second and third. This book had just been published when I was asked to give a talk to the children in Catterline School, just south of Stonehaven. Aberdeen was celebrating 200 years since the making of Union Street, our main thoroughfare, and I was supposed to talk about the history of the two centuries.

I didn't feel competent enough to tackle this subject and pressure of work wouldn't allow me to spend time in researching it, but I offered to give the pupils some tips on how to make their own stories more interesting. It was a glorious summer afternoon when Jimmy drove me there and, because I feel nervous when he's there, I don't know why, he went down to the shore to pass the time.

The children were really good and listened eagerly. I had begun by asking them if they knew what describing words were called, and got them thinking by giving them examples of wrongly-placed descriptions. For example, two advertisements in a newspaper column.

> *For Sale, as good as new, one green lady's bicycle.*
> For Sale, go-car for twins with waterproof flaps.

I wish I had taken a note of the hilarious adverts the boys and girls produced. Then I asked them to write a story, remembering to put in some description, but not too much. The end results that the headmistress posted on to me were extremely good, and I still regret not having time to comment on each one individually. At the time, I was deeply involved in wrestling with an ending for my next novel, at a stage when even a small diversion made me lose the thread of what I had intended to do.

Jimmy collected me in an hour and a half, and took me to see where he had been sitting after having a walk along the shore. We were on the bench, looking down on the sea, when two men walked up the stony path from the rocks. One, let's call him Fred, asked Jimmy if he'd been taking photographs – this part of the coast is a favourite with photographers and artists – and Jimmy said that I'd been giving a talk at the school.

'Oh,' said Fred, turning to me, 'what was your talk about?'

Hearing that it was about writing stories, he said, 'Are you a writer yourself?' Hardly waiting for confirmation, he went on, 'What sort of stuff do you write?'

'Family sagas,' I answered. 'My first book was *The Brow of the Gallowgate.*'

His eyes widened. '*The Brow of* . . . Are you Doris Davidson? You're my wife's favourite author.'

With that he stepped back and shouted to his wife, who was sitting in a car a little way off. 'Mary! Come here a minute.'

She looked puzzled as she walked towards us, and before she reached us, her husband could no longer contain himself. 'Who's your favourite author?'

Her brows came down in thought for a few moments, and then, looking up triumphantly, she pronounced, 'Emma Blair!'

My head, swollen with pride, deflated like a pricked balloon, and Fred, his face a picture of outraged exasperation, clicked his tongue. 'Not her! Who else?'

I didn't attempt to correct them on Emma Blair's sex (Ian Blair had recently confessed his pseudonym), and waited while Mary pondered some more. At last, with a nervous giggle, she ventured, 'Doris Davidson. Is that right, Fred?'

'Aye, that's right.' Satisfied now, he took a snap of his wife standing beside her almost favourite author and let her talk to me for a few minutes before they all walked away, the other man having stood silently impassive during the whole interlude.

That happened a good few years ago now, yet Jimmy and I still laugh at the memory of the stupefied expression on Fred's face at his wife's first answer.

My fifth book came about as a result of a leaflet about Cullen given to me by Ted and Lillias – remember my friend from college? They had moved from London when he was offered a chair at Cardiff University, but spent a month in the Moray coastal town every summer, mainly so that Ted could make use of the beautiful golf course. The publicity pamphlet mentioned the Three Kings, huge rocks on the shore that have been one of the local attractions since tourists first discovered Cullen.

As I read, I recalled the times my dad had driven his car off the road so that Mum and I could walk across the sands and inspect them at close quarters. I remembered them as very impressive (which they still are) and was drawn to make them a sort of background to my next story. I consulted some of the many books I had about Scottish fishing – I had been in the habit of buying anything I saw about the north east in bookshops – and Jimmy took me to Cullen several times to soak up the atmosphere.

After my manuscript had been accepted, there was the business of the cover to consider. My editor wanted a photograph of the Three Kings, but there was one insurmountable problem. I had set my tale in the 1930s, but since that time, a golf pavilion had been erected in such a position as to obscure one of the stones from the south side, a travesty, if ever there was one.

However, when we told him our problem, Bill, my brother-in-law, whom nothing ever fazes, said we could surely manage something. Accordingly, the four of us went up and spent a night in the Cullen Bay Hotel, with a beautiful view over the water. While we were in the dining room – windows along one entire long wall – we actually saw a school of dolphins gambolling around a small fishing boat as dusk was falling. We were only a five-minute walk away from our objective, so Jimmy and Bill both snapped away merrily the following morning from every available angle. Yes, we did manage to get a view of the three stones with the unwanted pavilion positioned where it could be airbrushed out by the artist preparing the cover.

When the book was published, I was asked to give a talk in the Buckie Drifter, a modern museum with a wonderful mock-up of a fishing vessel inside. We were in what was actually a conference room with a coffee bar at the back, and there were seventy people present. Jimmy hadn't come with us, so I was accompanied by a representative from the firm that supplies libraries with their books.

When I had finished speaking, refreshments were served, and the books my escort had brought with him were laid out for sale. Time was also allowed for me to sign them, and to have a chat with those who wanted to speak to me. I was lapping up all the compliments when I was brought sharply back to earth. Two ladies were standing in front of me, each with a copy of the book in her hand.

'We've come to tell you about the mistake you've made in your latest book,' said the one who had obviously chosen to be spokeswoman. She pointed her finger at the cluster of houses in the distance (on the cover). 'See they two white houses? Well, I bide in there, and she . . .', nudging her companion, 'bides next door, and they werena built at the time you've written about.'

I apologised for my stupidity, but she went on, 'It doesna matter. Nae many folk'll ken the difference. Only them that bides there.'

So we parted on very good terms.

I had mixed feelings when Louise (the fictional name of my new editor) phoned up one day. 'I love Lizanne,' she told me, 'and I'd like you to write a book about her.'

Lizanne had a very minor part in *The Three Kings* and I had said that she came from the Yardie in Buckie, a place I knew little about. Once again, Bertha and Bill, Jimmy and I set off northwards. Cullen Bay Hotel was fully booked (it was an Aberdeen Spring Holiday weekend) but we managed to get into Banff Springs Hotel, a few miles off and again having lovely views of the Moray Firth.

We toured the area for a couple of days, and left Buckie until the Monday. Lillias and Ted had told me about a small cottage museum, which I thought would be my best bet for research; the Buckie Drifter was still quite new and the Fishing Heritage Cottage had far more to offer at that time. It was very well hidden, though, and we couldn't find it, no matter which street we took, so we made for the Square, where we had noticed an Information Kiosk. The lady there was very helpful, and phoned to one of the volunteers who manned the place.

Isobel Harrison was a gem. The cottage didn't usually open on a Monday, but she came and opened it for us – it snuggled behind the library, which is why we hadn't found it. It was, and is, a marvellous place where all four of us would have been quite happy to stay for hours and hours, but we didn't like to take advantage of our guide. Isobel could not have been more helpful, and the friendship that she forged with me that day has lasted ever since. We still keep in touch and talk on the phone for an hour or more at a time, and it seems as if we have known each other since we were girls.

I did manage to get through *The Girl with the Creel*, which I look on as my next favourite after the *Gallowgate* and *Time Shall Reap*. After it was accepted, Louise said she wanted to know more about the houses in the Yardie, so I phoned Isobel, who lives just along Main Street from the quaint, tightly packed little cluster of houses, to ask if she could give me some details. Because the inhabitants keep themselves more or less isolated in their niche, she couldn't tell me much, so I decided I'd have to go there myself.

I press-ganged Jimmy into taking me up to Buckie again, and he drove round to the sea side of the houses in the Yardie. I had always imagined, from passing them in a car or a bus, that there were less than a dozen, but I learned otherwise. I had meant to knock on one of the doors – any door – and ask my questions, but there, in front of us, was a lady hanging out her washing.

To explain the situation, there is the main road to Elgin and Inverness, then the rows of houses then, running parallel to Main Street, the road where we had parked, then a strip of grass with sets of posts (it may have been an umbrella-type) and clothes ropes. Beyond that, there was only . . . the sea. Nothing in between.

I watched for a few moments as the poor woman struggled to peg her sheets up in the howling wind – I could imagine them taking off and eventually draping themselves round some poor unsuspecting soul in Norway – before she turned round and spotted me. I apologised for bothering her and asked if I could speak to her for a few minutes.

She seemed pleased to have a short respite and stood with arms akimbo as I asked my questions. I was very lucky in finding her. She had been born and brought up in the Yardie, and had moved to another of the houses when she was married. She had followed the herring fleet when she was young, and gave me much information on being a fisher girl and all I wanted to know about the inside of the dwellings. While she was speaking to me, her husband came out and had a long chat with Jimmy – they got on straight away – and then I thought I'd better leave her to her sheets.

Before we went back to the car, however, we walked through this minuscule village, and were amazed at what we saw. We had learned that the name Yardie came from the fact that the houses were no more than a yard apart, so there was street after street, all quite short and amounting to around fifty houses in all, facing each other or back to back. It's difficult to describe the set up, with the end of each street having the gables facing the sea, while at the top, the gables face the main road north – or south, depending on the way you're facing.

They were alleys more than streets and I'm not sure how many there are. We were fascinated, and I couldn't wait to get home to start writing about it, but naturally, we paid Isobel a brief visit first.

The number of words I could add to a manuscript already a few thousands more than I was allowed was limited, so I didn't succeed in writing as much as I'd have liked about the Yardie.

For the cover, I was asked to supply photographs of Pennan, where some of Lizanne's misfortunes take place, and this time, Sheila and John were up on holiday, so we took them with us and had dozens of photographs for the artist to choose from. However, after providing a very attractive rough draft, the man who had supplied all the previous covers died while playing squash, so it was another artist who did *The Girl with the Creel* cover. At first, I didn't care for it so much, none of the photos had been used, but it does give an eerie feel to it, fitting in with the plot, and I must admit I've come to like it after all.

During the week of publication, I gave a talk in Buckie Library. The local bookshop had closed some time before, so the books on sale had been supplied by a shop in Elgin. Isobel was there, of course, and two men from HarperCollins, but I can't remember anything much about that afternoon except the old man sitting reading in a corner; most ungracious, I thought, and not even one of my books. At first, I wondered why he was keeping so far from the other people, and the afternoon was well on before it dawned on me that he hadn't moved as much as a muscle since I began speaking. It was then that I realised the truth. He was a full-sized wax model! Most realistic.

My seventh and eighth books, *The House of Lyall* (2000) and *The Back of Beyond* (2002), were mixtures of snippets of incidents I'd heard over the years, plus a very small part (fictionalised) of a relative's early life in London.

By then, my book signings for these were confined to Aberdeen City, and were most successful. In the space of a week – three sessions of two hours in different stores – I signed hundreds of books, chatted a little to as many as I could, and went home each time happily exhausted, but as high as a kite.

I feel so flattered by all the compliments I'm paid, I have to remind myself that I'm only a best seller in the northeast of Scotland, although I keep being told of shops and airports all over the world that stock my novels nowadays. I think their attraction lies in the fact that they are easily read, a relaxation when on holiday, an introduction to readers from other parts to my home area.

The warmest reception I have ever had was in 2003, when I was asked to talk to St Machar Academy Parents' Reading Group, who were trying to brush up their own reading skills. Apparently they had made hard weather of the books they had originally been given, and then a bookshop had advised the dedicated gentleman who runs this facility to try them with something local, something with which they could identify. My name was among the writers suggested, and it seems that my book (I can't remember which one – it may have been *The Three Kings*, most of the others had gone out of print) did the trick.

They were proud of knowing the real places where incidents in the story were supposed to have taken place; they had discussed where the fictional places might be; and they were all anxious to read more. They made it so obvious that they were delighted to meet me, had dozens of questions ready to ask, and all in all, it was the most rewarding afternoon I had ever spent – that I ever *will* spend, more than likely.

Thus I carried on, launching into a ninth story, bringing in sycamore trees because Sheila's garden has two rows of beautiful old sycamores round which her husband, John, has designed a truly professional garden.

I was intrigued when I heard of a family who were shocked to learn of a grandmother's death in a Mental Institution when they'd been led to believe she had died almost seventy years before. No mention had ever been made of the place where she had been incarcerated since she was a young woman. Not only that, there was evidence that her actual marriage certificate, when it was eventually run to earth, had been altered, very amateurishly. There was, of course, much more to the true tale than this, but I used it as a starting point for my main mystery. What follows is entirely my own invention, and has nothing to do with the facts.

It would have been almost the end of 2002 and I was slightly more than halfway through the first draft of *The Shadow of the Sycamores* when I was asked by Birlinn if I would write my autobiography for them. The trouble was that my contract with HarperCollins stated that they had to have first offer of any book I wrote, so I said I'd have to ask if I was allowed to do this. I called Louise and she said it was all right for me to write for another publisher as long as it was non-fiction. All fiction had to go to them.

I explained to Birlinn that I'd have to finish *Sycamores* before I could make a start, but they wanted my memoirs to come out around Christmas of 2004. To the uninitiated, this may sound like plenty of time, but by then it was well into January and nothing had really been discussed. I flew on with the novel, making dozens of mistakes because I was in such a hurry, and then, during February, I had a visit from my new 'boss'.

He explained that not only did they want my own little ups and downs, but also a background of what life was like as I progressed through the years. He gave me Christmas 2003 as a deadline, but I had to make him give a little on that. The next date mentioned was the end of March, which only allowed eight months for revisions, also for copy editors and proof-readers to do their bits.

My priorities lie with HarperCollins, so I set myself a strict routine of novel in the mornings and autobiography in the afternoons. I should have known, of course, that I wasn't up to spending a full day on the computer, and I was forced to concentrate on my novel and stop working at lunchtime. Having gone over and over it and corrected it as much as I could, I gave it to John to post for me. That was on 18 August 2003.

With this off my mind, I was free to concentrate on . . . I called it *The Gift of the Gab*, which was what my granny called me, but this title was not acceptable. I am still trying to come up with another.

On 1 September, I still hadn't heard if Louise had got the manuscript, so I called and asked. She said she had, and would be in touch with me later. This was the normal procedure. She had to have time to read the story, and pick faults or otherwise with it. I was usually sent several pages of comments – bits she liked and wanted to know more about, or bits she didn't like and wanted to be taken out; characters she liked and those she didn't, and so on. A whole lot of extra work, but she knew what would sell.

I had no premonition of what was about to happen.

CATASTROPHE

24

It was into October before I got the telephone call, and I was shocked to hear the fateful words, 'I'm sorry, Doris, it's bad news, I'm afraid.'

I swallowed hard. 'You're rejecting it?'.

'It's not that exactly. We . . . don't want any more of your books.'

The second swallow was hampered by the huge construction in my throat. 'You don't want any . . . what's wrong with my books?'

'There's nothing wrong with them, it's just . . . it's just that reading styles have changed. People don't want to read about the late nineteenth and early twentieth centuries. They want up-to-date novels, set in the twenty-first century.'

Although I knew that Louise was speaking for only the younger generations, I couldn't find the words to argue with her. My stalwart fans, men as well as women, were in all age groups and told me constantly how much they enjoyed reading about the olden times.

'You're taking it very calmly,' my now ex-editor observed. 'Remember, Doris, you're not the only one. There are quite a lot of writers being told the same thing. And you'll easily find another publisher.'

I found the strength to say, 'Please return my manuscript.'

And that was that. I was in deep shock. I felt indignant, resentful, hurt, mortified. The anger came later. HarperCollins must have known for months that the change was on the cards, yet they'd let me carry on with this last novel to the bitter end. I had even phoned at one point to ask if there was a deadline for the manuscript and was told, 'It doesn't matter. There's no hurry.'

I suppose that should have told me something, warned me. Instead, being so sure of myself, I thought that they were allowing me extra time because of my advanced age. How wrong can a person be? I was devastated.

Worse, however, was to come. I had taken longer than usual to write *The Sycamores* because of a very nasty accident I had in July. I missed my footing going up two steps and went down on my knees – my usual landing position – but hit my head on the corner of the building. Next day, and for two weeks afterwards, I was sporting two lovely black eyes and feeling decidedly unwell. In fact, the force of the impact on my left temple affected my concentration to the extent that I was unable to write for some time.

Just before this mishap, I had been asked by Birlinn to provide a black-and-white photograph of myself for their records. This had to wait, of course, until I was back to something resembling normal, but Alan took some snaps of my shiners as long as they were in full bloom, so to speak. As a joke, I had sent one in an envelope along with the manuscript to Louise on 18 August, to explain the lengthy wait.

When the manuscript duly arrived back, what did I find? The covering letter was still nestling under the elastic bands keeping the loose pages together. Not only that, the envelope containing my mug-shot was still there, too.

This proved that the story had never even been read! How could they do this to me? In a rush of humiliated fury, I dashed off a letter to Louise on the computer giving vent to all the venom I could dredge up. I often take this step if something annoys me, but once I've got it off my chest I usually tear up the vitriolic letter and write another, more tactfully. This time, however, I sent the original.

Some years earlier, I'd been asked to write for another publisher, but refused because I felt it would be disloyal to HarperCollins. I had also asked them for permission to write this autobiography, but they obviously did not feel the same loyalty towards me – after I had written eight novels for them. I'll be perfectly honest. This business really sickened me, and I still haven't got over it.

I do have some good news, however. *The Shadow of the Sycamores* should be published in June of this year, if all goes well. The publisher who had 'headhunted' me before, and whom I had sort of depended on to take it, has now stopped publishing, but handed the manuscript to Black and White, also an Edinburgh firm, as is Birlinn.

I'm on the home stretch now. After my very first talk in the main library in 1990, a lady came up to me in great excitement. 'How does it feel to be an author?'

At that time, I hadn't had time to feel anything other than excitement myself, and even after almost fourteen years, I don't feel any different. I try not to let the compliments I get turn my head. After all, only those who like what I write would take the trouble to come to meet me.

My one regret is that I didn't start writing sooner, but on the other hand, a woman gets more experience of life as she grows older. I count myself very lucky to have the ability to write books other people enjoy reading, also that I enjoy writing them. As for retiring from this career . . .? I'll just say that I prefer writing to any other occupation I've had, and I'll keep on unless it becomes a burden to me.

Thinking over what I've achieved, I feel quite proud of myself. Not only have eight of my books been published, nine counting this latest, but they have also been taken out in large print for the sight impaired and audio for the completely blind. I was more than impressed when I was sent my first audio book – fourteen double-sided cassettes in a very lovely case that opens twice, and lasting for at least fourteen hours. Not only that – if you'll excuse my boasting – *The Three Kings* has been published in Greek.

While I've been compiling this rather garbled account of my life, my problem has been deciding what to include and what to leave out; in which year a particular incident took place; should I tell what people did or said if it may be to the detriment of the persons concerned? I've got round this last at times by giving false names or initials, but if anyone does recognises her- or himself, let me say here that it was an oversight, and I am sorry if they are offended.

I must mention how grateful I am for the support given to me by my family. They have all contributed something – providing photographs for covers, checking facts, suggesting titles, driving me around in the pursuit of information. I'd have been lost without them. I have, however, spared my children's blushes by playing down what they have achieved. I did mention earlier a little of what Alan is doing with regard to his music, but Sheila studied for many years, achieving qualifications to further her career. She has also reached her fourth year of the Open University, although she is due to retire this year. I have one grandson, who is in his fifth year at the Grammar School, and is just coming up to his 'A' levels. I won't embarrass him by saying more, but I am proud of them all.

Finally, I'd like to thank all the readers who have given me as much pleasure with their compliments as I have given them. This last stage of my life has actually been more rewarding, emotionally than any of the others.

That's it, then. I didn't mean to get sloppy, but I've run out of witticisms at the moment. Maybe I'd better finish with a toast:

> Here's tae us,
> Fa's like us?
> Damn few
> And they're a' deid.